FROM ONE CENTURY
TO ANOTHER

THE WRITER

SPINNING WOOL, HOME-GROWN AND HOME-CARDED, 1895

FROM ONE CENTURY TO ANOTHER

The Reminiscences of

ELIZABETH S. HALDANE

WITH 28 ILLUSTRATIONS

LONDON

ALEXANDER MACLEHOSE & CO.

58 Bloomsbury Street

1937

PRINTED IN GREAT BRITAIN BY ROBERT MACLEHOSE AND CO. LTD.
THE UNIVERSITY PRESS, GLASGOW

INTRODUCTION

To look back is the privilege of the old who cannot look forward ; but the young sometimes deign to be interested in the past.

Almost everyone at some time or other keeps a diary. It is often curiously intermittent and sporadic. In my case it was so, but I began to write things down on scraps of paper very early. At seven I had visited a factory and was impressed by the strange fact, stated in half-text handwriting, that children worked and went to school alternately, little thinking that this half-time work was so soon to be under hot discussion by the legislators of the land. Then at nine came the question of women's professions, on which I recorded my views, and soon after that came a long pause because one met other people who didn't write things down and one became conventional. Then there was a time when religious questions influenced one—a long time and a difficult time, beginning with certainty and going on to doubt and finally to a new orientation of one's beliefs.

In grown-up days the diary became yet more objective, and was mainly concerned with any interesting persons I met. Again there were great gaps, but finally a fair consistency.

This part of it, dealing roughly with half a century of life, has had to be rewritten in more or less narrative form ; it is in some parts historic, and of course like all diaries bowdlerized. One cannot say that it will interest anyone unless indeed it shows from one special view-point how the world goes on and how a woman passed from the restrictions of one century to the interests of another. It may also show she may have a perfectly happy and full life, though devoid of some of the ameliorations that novelists and psychologists tell us make life worth living. Things changed—changed on the surface almost incredibly —during the half-century of which I write. Yet men and women have remained the same, with trivial interests as well as serious, and occasionally the trivial things say as much to us as the more important.

I must express my indebtedness to various friends who have helped me, and more especially to Sir Edward Marsh who very kindly read the proofs. The cartoons of ' The Curling Match ' and ' Balfour and Chamberlain ' are by my friend of former years Edith Munro-Ferguson, and bring to my recollection many amusing talks ; the cartoons are reproduced here by kind permission of her brother Major Munro-Ferguson. The picture of the Territorial nurses came from a Hospital Christmas card early in the War, and will be criticized by the modern wearers of the uniform as sadly out of date.

Messrs. T. & R. Annan & Sons kindly supplied the fine photograph of Mr. Cunninghame Graham as also that of the ' Relief ' minister, the Rev. George Jacque.

As in former years my publisher, Mr. Alexander MacLehose, has been most kind and helpful.

E. S. H.

CLOAN,
   October 1937.

CONTENTS

PAGE

THE FIRST DECADE : 1862-1872 - - - - 1

Opening Years

Real Lives in the Nursery : Trade Unions : Second Sight : The Tawse in Schools : The Franco-Prussian War : Walking Round a Clergyman : The 'Must Nots' of Propriety : Rudderless Children : School Examinations : What Girls Looked Like : From Boots to Shoes : Sports : Sunday Reading : Life of the Workers : Country Shops : Tea-Shops : Country Tradesmen : Change in Manners : Driving to Church : Mrs. Oliphant of Gask : Church in the Country : The Country Minister : Preserving the Fiddle : Rest at Last.

THE SECOND DECADE : 1872-1882 - - - - 50

Growing Up

Education Act of 1870 : Tutors and Governesses : Fair Play for Women : Women as Citizens : Religious Revival : Victorian Childhood : Sunday Observance : Calvinist Teaching : The Temperance Movement : A Visit to Paris : Sarah Bernhardt : The Early Eighties : Liberal Government : Country House Visits: The Agricultural Depression : Joseph Arch : Railway Travel : London Cabs.

THE THIRD DECADE : 1882-1892 - - - - 91

Young Womanhood

Grosvenor Gallery : A London Hospital : The Lady Cyclist : Health Lectures : Asquith's Oratory : Electric Light : John Morley : Green and Toynbee : Rise of Socialism : Liberal Ideals : The Social Union : National Trust Movement : George Eliot : Home Reading Union : Translating Hegel : Change among Lairds : Menace of Unemployment : Women and Social Questions : The People's Palaces : Taking Silk : Grey and His Wife : The Baccarat Set : Demand for Better Conditions : Remarkable Women : The Co-operative Movement : Scientific Experiments : The Safety Bicycle : The Early Nineties.

PAGE

THE FOURTH DECADE : 1892-1902 - - - - 148
The End of the Century
*Gladstone : The Franchise Bill : The Parnell Commission :
The 1892 Election : Parnell : Chamberlain and Ireland : Tim
Healy : Meredith : Lady Dorothy Nevill : The ' Souls ' :
Death Duties : The 1895 Election : A Visit to Germany : Jour-
ney to California : Rosebery : Milner : The Diamond Jubilee :
Death of Gladstone : Changes in Social Custom : Curling at
Carsebreck : Lecture on Explosives : Death of Queen Victoria :
A Nurse's Life : Cycling Expeditions : Cecil Rhodes.*

THE FIFTH DECADE : 1902-1912 - - - - 202
The Liberal Revival
*Ignorance of World Changes : Political Meetings : Gifford Lec-
tures : Improvements at Cloan : Freewill and Predestination :
Minister for War : Campbell-Bannerman : Carnegie United
Kingdom Trust : The Old War Office : Territorial Nursing
Service : Voluntary Aid Detachments : Territorial Manoeuvres :
Cigars for Generals : Poor Law Administration : Gertrude Bell :
A Visit to Essen : The King's Speech : Aviation Meeting at Lan-
ark : Death of Edward VII : The Kaiser in London : King
Edward's Coronation : The Insurance Bill : Commission on
Civil Service : The Women's Movement : Sir Edward Grey :
The Great Seal : Randall Davidson.*

THE LAST TWO YEARS : 1912-1914 - - - 263
Before the Crisis
*' Direct Action ' : Militant Suffragists : The Government De-
feated : The Franchise Bill : Life in Dublin : Privy Council
Tribunal : Rabindranath Tagore : General Baden-Powell : The
Asquith Family : The Titanic Enquiry : Respect for Contracts :
Christmas at Cloan : Separation of Ulster Discussed : Edmund
Gosse : Colonel Seely Resigns : Bitter Speeches in the House :
Music at Funerals : Sir Roger Casement : Party at Downing
Street : The Invasion of Belgium : Outbreak of the War.*

LOOKING BACKWARDS - - - - - - 308
*A Sense of Repression : Loss of Religious Belief : Scientific In-
ventions : Emancipation of Women.*

ILLUSTRATIONS

PAGE

The Writer spinning wool, home-grown and home-carded, 1895 - - - - - *Frontispiece*

Cloan in 1869 - - - - - - - - 8

London Schoolboys in 1894 - - - - - 32

Schoolboys in same district forty years later - - 32

George, William, Richard, John, and Elizabeth from a sketch by their mother in 1870 - - - 40

Rev. George Jacque, the 'Relief' minister; and Mrs. Graeme Oliphant of Gask - - - - 40

Tennis in the Eighties - - - - - - 74

A City Omnibus in the Rain - - - - - 89

Asquith, 1885 - - - - - - - - 100

Matthew Arnold, about 1870; and John Morley, about 1880 - - - - - - - 104

Cunninghame Graham, 1905 - - - - - 124

Joseph Chamberlain speaking at Inverness on the Highland Land Question - - - - - 149

Mr. and Mrs. Gladstone, about 1897 - - - 152

Parnell, about 1886; and Balfour, about 1885 - - 160

Lady Dorothy Nevill - - - - - - 168

Curling Match in the Liberal Party; Rosebery and Harcourt looking on, Asquith and Campbell-Bannerman as skips - - - - - - 192

Balfour and Chamberlain - - - - - 204

Mrs. Haldane in her eightieth year, 1905 - - 208

Lord and Lady Roberts at Cloan, 1906 - - - 220

xi

PAGE

Manoeuvres at Cloan, 1907 - - - - - 224

Territorial Artillery crossing the Ochils, 1907 - - 224

Mr. Haldane and Gen. Sir Ian Hamilton and Kaiser,
the St. Bernard dog, 1907 - - - - - 228

Lord Haldane with V.A.D. Nurses at Cloan during
Territorial Manoeuvres, 1913 - - - - 228

Territorial Nurses - - - - - - - 259

Sketch of a Territorial by Lord Baden-Powell - - 281

THE FIRST DECADE
1862-1872

OPENING YEARS

My earliest memories are of a big nursery in a beautiful Edinburgh square whose window looked out on the studio of a sculptor famous in his time, working at an enormous Bucephalus afterwards to adorn one of the streets. Our joy was with hand mirrors to shine lights on the artist and on pedestrians who made their way through a side lane. The nursery was lit by two unshaded gas lights, one over the table in the middle of the room, the other, only lighted if necessary, at the fireplace. At the fire on a low nursing chair sat the most splendid of nurses reading the news, spectacles on eyes and with a black velvet and lace cap on head : a silk apron protected her full skirt. She was probably reading the report of the Tichborne case—a case that gave reading for months—giving utterance to her thoughts about it from time to time ; or else she was exploring the new Education Bill and expressing fears, despite her deep value for education, that no longer would young servants be found. With that she would carry her eyes to the under-nurse who seemed to be living a blameless life carrying hot water and dinners up three or four flights of stairs, always carefully avoiding the gentry in so doing, and otherwise behaving as young servants should. That is to say they must wear cotton 'prints' in the morning which cost 7s. 11d. to make up and were bought out of their £12 of wages; black dresses and black bonnets in the afternoon. No hats nor feathers. How they paid for dress, shoes and everything I cannot think, but they did, and saved for their parents. Our nurse had £25 a year, and each half-year (for wages were paid half-yearly in those days) she made a solemn expedition to the savings bank and another to the post office in order to put money in the bank and send home a money order. Nurses, once they had embarked on their career, had to make up their minds to see no more of their relatives, for holidays there were none. Our nurse always carried the babies in her own arms; she would have disdained a perambulator or any mechanical aid. In my wildest fancy I could not imagine my mother bathing or dressing me, and she never thought of such a thing. To my mind she was always as she appeared in the nursery near bedtime, a lovely figure in a beautiful moiré silk gown so widely spread out that when the boys' tutor came into the room unexpectedly she simply floated her frock over bath and child together, forming for the latter a delightful tent.

Were we five children happy? I think we were, though there were few excitements in our lives. We lived part of the year in town and part—the wonderful part—in the country. We had few if any parties :

our food was good if plain : porridge and bread and butter for breakfast, mutton and plain puddings for dinner, and toast and butter for tea—no supper and therefore no cuddling up in warm dressing gowns and bedroom slippers for the evening meal as happens nowadays. But when in Edinburgh, the younger children were dressed and sent down to dessert, a ceremony which brought little pleasure, though we were given part of an orange or apple and were allowed to look at pictures afterwards in the drawing-room. We loved our parents, but the love was mingled with awe till the time came when we knew them better. The view then often expressed was that children, while children, should be kept out of sight and in nursery or schoolroom. The result was that we were shy and self-conscious when brought to the front and simply longed to get back to freedom upstairs, where we lived our real lives. Children were at least left free within limits, and were not planned for or made accountable for every hour of the day.

What was the country thinking about during the first decade of my life ? Mainly in my dim recollection, the Fenians. To us, the Fenians were mysterious beings who might come by night dressed in black, with sacks over their heads like the weary coal-heavers who wended their way laden with the bags of coal up the innumerable steps which led to the nursery floor and deposited them with a fearful rattle, which I remember still, in the coal bunker on the top landing. They were a terror to us always. The Fenians were

not only in Ireland—far from it. There had been the
daring rescue of two Fenian prisoners in Manchester
and the subsequent execution of the rescuers, and the
Clerkenwell conspiracy followed upon it. Hence
even far-away Edinburgh became alarmed, and
relatives of the children in the safe nursery in Char-
lotte Square were sworn in as special constables. I
wonder whether there was a curious *zeitgeist* that made
us children feel a sort of sympathy with John Bright,
who looked at the causes of the unrest and not just
the results. Quite unknown to these children, he
made a marvellously eloquent speech in the House of
Commons in which he declared his conviction that
' if the majority of the people of Ireland, fairly counted
out, had their will, and had the power, they would
unmoor the island from its fastenings in the deep, and
move it at least two thousand miles to the west '.
Bright was always esteemed, though there were no
subversive influences in our orthodox and mildly
Whig home, and that was because he was a ' good '
man—a man who understood what religion really
meant—the religion which had made our forebears
give up lands and money for the cause of God's service.

Those last were the traditions that made us as a
family care about public events. It was perhaps a lop-
sided view of things that measured them thus and
caused us to dwell on the deeds and lives of our ancestors ;
and when those deeds of days gone by did not fit in
with the events of everyday politics, conclusions were
left to those who were responsible. It was a time

when there were violent discussions over the new attitude of the worker and especially over Trade Unions. The employing and comfortable classes such as the one to which we belonged were violently opposed to such bodies and believed that respectable working men were the same and hated the Unions also. They believed the workers to be led by selfish demagogues playing for their own hands. Strikes were wicked as well as unsocial, and the men were urged never to commit such a sin as to waste time and money alike. No reference was made to what was done in the way of Unions in the higher professions! It was not till 1875 that the fair claims of the Unions were recognized. Till then the feeling about Trade Unions made a disagreeable division between employer and employed which was not obliterated by so-called Liberal principles which approved of Co-operation (if kept in its place) and Friendly Societies, but hated this more advanced organization.

We were indeed told about working people and their struggles by our nurse, and urged to benefit from, and be grateful for, our advantages in having plenty of food and clothing. In those days the credit was always given to ' your Papa, who is doing all those good things for you.' Personally I felt that it was a case of marvellous beneficence on his part to clothe and feed us, and therefore that we must absolutely act on his smallest wishes, and I suppose all children felt the same. Our mother was somehow on a higher and more spiritual level, in which material things did not count in the same way. She no doubt ordered the dinner, but ' the books' were examined and paid by our father, who also paid wages. And yet she had money of her own, though she never received it except through her husband. The Married Woman's Property Act was not passed for many years after this, but that did not concern her, though it made it hard for her when she was left a widow and we were still young. I remember how one of the servants who had been with us many years told me that she would never have thought of asking for a 'rise', but that she rather wistfully hoped when the six months came round and wages were paid that perhaps something might be added. There was an unlimited choice supposing a new servant was wanted, for an older servant was always ready to recommend a friend's daughter. Our nurse occasionally walked twelve miles to see her mother for the day, as she could not be spared longer, and none of the servants had regular holidays : possibly they sometimes got away when there was a chance, but I can't remember this. After my mother's death I found curious letters about servants' characters which read amusingly now and explain many later difficulties. One was to the effect that a young woman was satisfactory excepting in that she had not ' joined the church ' though eighteen. She was a Highland girl, and this ceremony is or was delayed in Highland communities from fear of being ' unworthy '; but that was not understood.

We were very fond of our servants and they were

our loyal and faithful friends, and indeed all through my life I have been indebted to them more than I can tell. I have always wondered at their selfless devotion, sacrificing as they did their private lives for those of their employers. There might have been some out-side men in our country home who had rough ways and words, though I saw none of this. But I did hear wonderful tales in the country of second sight : of hares in which there were evil spirits, to be shot only by a silver bullet, which meant a threepenny bit : of cases where the corpse was thought to have been the victim of murder, and at whose wakes there was a black dog that ' luck, luckit at the bluid ' sup-posed to be there, and other queer tales of ghosts or apparitions. These made little or no impression on a matter-of-fact, religiously brought-up family, though they gave zest to passing certain spots in the darkness. Indeed they could not have had any real effect, for I remember one autumn evening when my youngest brother and I were very small and sent down to the dining-room dressed for dessert, that our father hap-pened to say he had left his bathing drawers in a hut about a mile off through a wood, and that he would give a lad sixpence if he would fetch them. Sixpence was sixpence to children who only got pennies, so without a word we went off in evening frock and kilt and retrieved the goods, though on our return jour-ney we found a regular hue and cry from frenzied nurses.

Though we were not given much money we were

taught in a vicarious way to be charitable, for every month each of us was given a pound to 'put in the plate' by our father, who believed in giving tithes. I don't say that we never thought how wonderful it would be if we had the money to spend instead of giving it, as we imagined, to the 'poor of the congregation' typified by one old woman who though afflicted with a distressing ailment in that her tongue protruded from her mouth must, we believed, at least be wealthy; though of course we never grudged her this wealth for her affliction was great.

On one occasion again my two little brothers went down to the kitchen in Edinburgh and found no one there. They proceeded to heat the big kitchen poker in the fire—that is in the great range which worked the smoke-jack for roasting meat (no meat was ever allowed to be baked in an oven in those days). Presently in an area on which the window gave, they saw a white figure : nothing daunted they seized the red-hot poker and rushed out to deal with the ghost which with great agility leapt over the high wall which shut in the area. The ghost proved to be a harum-scarum medical student of great athletic powers who terrified Edinburgh for a long time under the name of 'Spring-Heeled Jack'. He had intended to scare the maids but was met by the formidable youngsters instead. It was said that he was converted at the time of the Moody and Sankey revival, so that he probably became in the end a respected medical practitioner and cast aside all his juvenile propensities.

CLOAN IN 1869

He never allowed himself to be caught by the police, but the police that I recollect in my young days were stout comfortable-looking men with beards who never seemed to change their beat and did not look like catching anybody.

I wonder whether the people of that time were much more brutal than nowadays. Public executions were only abolished in 1868, and there were many other terrible things taking place of which we in our sheltered existence knew little. Certain it was that there was much cruelty to children. Before the Children's Charter had been thought of cruelty must indeed have been great. But recognized punishments at school were at least to modern minds cruel. In schools of these days the tawse was always in requisition, and even when during the Great War we had a little school for baby children at Cloan, an immense tawse was part of the equipment provided by the Education Department. I have preserved it as a memento. As for ourselves we did not suffer unduly from punishments. Our tutor believed firmly in corporal chastisement, it is true, but this took the form of ' palmies ' for the most part for me, and tawse for the boys. Three mistakes in spelling meant a palmy, followed by more if that number was exceeded, and the result was that I learnt to spell. But they must have hurt and were often followed by ' poenas ', i.e. lessons written out. We bore no resentment excepting when through grown-up interference undeserved punishment was given. I enjoyed my lessons up to the time when I was sent to certain

classes and could not in the least understand what
the teachers meant. This applied mostly to arith-
metic and mathematics, which I quite enjoyed when
a kind brother explained the problems to me, whereas otherwise I had no glimmering of what was spoken
about excepting that Euclid's methods were all wrong.
As far as I remember punishments were of no real use
and our parents and nurse fortunately treated us as
reasonable beings and never punished us. It would
have seemed to us silly to tell a lie, and our nurse had
high ideals of what we should be as gentlemen and
lady, and never dreamt that we should seriously
deviate from them.

I don't think kindness to animals was understood
even by kind people. I used to like to get off with the
boys to a rat hunt when the rat had no chance of
escape ; and though we were devoted to our pets, we
did not sufficiently realize that dogs must not be kept
on the chain perpetually, and some of our young
coachmen were not too kindly disposed, or at least
considerate, to their charges. In the streets one saw
constant cruelty long after this and when one inter-
vened one was met by a storm of oaths which I could
truthfully assure the speaker meant nothing to me as
I did not understand them ! The advent of mechanical transport has changed things more than anything.
Bus horses which had to stop on slippery roads whenever hailed had a terribly hard time : people are more
considerate to mechanized modes of transport which
stop only at stated intervals.

To return to politics which really bore very specially on our lives, Mr. Gladstone's Government of 1868 came in with tremendous tasks before it, for it had in the first place to deal with Ireland, its Church, land tenure and education, to abolish the purchase of commissions in the army, to introduce the system of voting by ballot and then above all to grapple with the great question of national education. Then there was not only the settlement of the claims arising out of the damage done by the *Alabama* which had been built in English ports—a question which I well remember being debated in the schoolroom—but the other questions brought up by the breaking out of war between France and Prussia. This last was of course of infinite interest and excitement to children of school age. Everyone ' took sides '—most of us for Prussia, till overcome by the sufferings of France and the siege of Paris. I remember how we were told by the maids that the wonderful red sunsets so remarkable in 1870-1 were produced by the reflections of the blood-red battlefields. To me the year was associated with nearer events—a terrible murder committed in a toll-house a few miles off, and the dramatic suicide of a well-known judge, by cutting his throat; he fell from a branch of a tree overhanging a pool.

The Liberal Government which was taking its place with Gladstone as its leader, though it had great tasks before it, had no very obvious characteristics to distinguish it from its predecessors. Rich men were as before in the preponderance and the great families were still represented. No one of extreme views obtained a seat, though John Bright was, rather unwillingly on his part, brought into the Cabinet. John Stuart Mill, who refused on principle to pay his election expenses, lost his seat in Westminster, and the workingmen's candidates were all rejected, although this was the first general election with household suffrage in boroughs and a lowered franchise in counties.

Liberalism meant Whiggism still, and that was the atmosphere in which we were brought up. There was no idea of abolishing class distinctions or bringing about equality economically, far less doing away with capitalism. That is to say, socialism was far removed from liberalism and remained so for the next twenty years. There were indeed ideals and very real ones, inspiring to those who held them. Old grievances were to be removed such as that of a state Church that was the Church of a minority, land laws that belonged to distant ages, abuses in the administration of the law generally. But when the relation between employer and employed involved radical changes they were set down as inopportune. The established order had to be maintained. For us, as for other religious people, there was the sense that all men were equal in the sight of God, and intermittently an effort was made to treat them as equals in the sight of man. But the practical difficulties in an order so firmly entrenched were so evident that nothing really eventuated. When an attempt was made to carry out any such scheme it ended in chaos, more especially when the question of marriage came into view.

As regards ecclesiastical affairs, the so-called Pusey-ite movement was in those days much in evidence, as the pages of *Punch* show. We were greatly exercised as to what it meant, and could only gauge it by the strange garb of those who professed this uncanny doctrine, for, in Scotland at least, round collars and deep buttonless waistcoats were unknown. I remember our walking round a clergyman relative to see if we could make out how his collar could possibly fasten, and I confided to my brother John that I had heard of an ' M.B. waistcoat ' and couldn't think what it meant. The boy correctly replied ' I believe it means " Mark of the Beast " but don't on any account say this for I'm not sure ' ! It would have been serious to have made a mistake. There used to be a beggar who tried to ingratiate himself with those who might be sympathetic by calling himself a Puseyite : and with a certain section of the community he had success. We of course, as a family, had no sympathy with the movement or the beggar.

There were many beggars in those days, and no wonder. In pre-State-pension days in Edinburgh a certain number of women called regularly for their allowances in money. Others came incidentally and usually had special names, like the man with a wooden leg, who was called ' the tree-legged man ' ; in the country came the ' dafties ', who were not thrust into poorhouses but wandered about with little boxes on their backs. The regular packmen who came round were welcomed at the back door, and we children loved to see whether we could get a china dog as our exchange for the cook's rabbit skins. The Colporteur was another welcome guest, for as his books were supposed to be unimpeachable, we were allowed to buy of his literature while he had dinner. ' Postie ' or ' Jimmie the Post ' was another welcome visitor at twelve o'clock. The postman was always given a bottle of beer, and the pop of the cork told one that he was there. We children liked to lay hold of the bag and tell him that we had got ' Her Majesty's Mail '. He was often useful, being a joiner, in doing small repairs during his midday rest.

Our nurse, Betsey Ferguson, guided our thoughts and deeds much more than did others of our seniors. She was one in a thousand, and even our tutor trembled at her word. The child of a widow left through accident with a large family to bring up, she was, though without much schooling, an educated woman. She used to get out her spectacles and ' lines ' and write slowly and painfully on thin paper, through which the lines could be seen, long letters to our mother when she was abroad ; or else she would discuss with us how the National Debt—such a poor debt in those days—could be paid off. Above all we were to give our lives to helping other people, though what I could do did not seem to me very clear beyond possibly serving as a prop to those doing more important work.

When about ten or twelve years old I was sent to attend certain classes of girls, for, as I discovered through letters from elderly relations, I was thought to be much too boyish in my upbringing and not to have learned the technique of young ladyhood. Boys had a freedom which I enjoyed in great measure till this time when one was caught up in the meshes of the young lady. They were free to go where they pleased, plan their future lives as they pleased, within limits. The 'must nots' of propriety soon cast their net over the girl and she was directed to find her happiness where it did not exist. To tell the truth we children used to listen to the conversation of the ladies and gentlemen who so mysteriously descended two and two to dinner like the animals in the ark, as we gazed at them from the top landing of the big Edinburgh house, probably engaged in talking a mysterious sort of gibberish which if we 'went into the good society' of which our nurse used to speak, we should have to learn. This produced no desire on my part to join the select throng, any more than did the statement that if I did not eat rice pudding (a constant food which I hated) I should not be able to enter the sacred portals ! I broke my dolls to see what was inside, played cricket and climbed trees, and altogether was conscious of the impossibility of ever attaining to any social success. I wanted to do for myself and not just to be the helper of others who were doing—a quite unbiblical ideal for any woman to have.

The first part of my education was carried on in

the country. I remember being dragged to the school-room to have lessons with the tutor, in tears because the boys had teased me about the horrors of the ' lessons ' that were in prospect. I was consoled, however, by bread and butter sprinkled with sugar given us as luncheon. In those days tea and sugar were given out weekly to the servants as well as beer or beer money, and they were very kind in giving some of the former to the children. But there was also a luncheon for the scholars at eleven o'clock. In the end I loved my lessons, whether given by our own tutor or in his absence by the village schoolmaster, who rewarded us with jujubes from his pocket. He had tea given to him and we a little resented a long grace, seeing that we were not to partake of the fare.

At the classes I met strange girls who had a different sort of outlook. I got forthwith into a terrible scrape by accidentally upsetting an ink-pot. I can remember the scolding I received from the mistress to this day, and the conviction that I had committed some crime the stain of which never in this world could be washed away. What rankled with me however was the fact that another girl, rather unpopular with the mistress, was scolded with me and she had only put the ink-stand on the table. I felt that I ought to defend her, for she was a timid child who cried ; but I could not see how in the world this could be done ; I would certainly not cry and hated her doing so, but I did nothing. Scoldings were formidable things such as I had never before experienced. They lasted for about ten minutes and were administered both to long-suffering servants and pupils. I used to wonder how words were found for them—or indeed time. The other drawback to any pleasure I had in meeting other girls (and I don't think that this was great) was that I was given a glass of milk in the middle of the morning and that the milk, which was put in a dusty place to wait for me, was covered with a black scum which had to be taken off. It is curious that children accept what is provided for them without remark. As a small child I had an hour's music lesson and used to feel faint with exhaustion at the end of the exercises and scales, but one never suggested a rest. Also I had for years a music teacher whose frowning looks on my entering the room so scared me that all power of performance was taken away. I used to lie awake on Sunday nights in order to prolong the time till the hateful Monday morning which brought the lesson should arrive. Yet by nature I loved music and had a fairly good ear. No scrap of pleasure came to me from piano or singing till I grew up into my teens and came to realize what music might mean. Nothing of this was ever breathed to us : we simply had to play the prescribed notes or try to produce throat sounds in some odd way that I never understood. One hopes that the outspoken children of the present day may be able to express themselves about their surroundings and their drawbacks, but I am not sure that they will, though we elders think them outspoken. Children are oddly inarticulate, even the most forth-

B

coming of them, and as they have not got their
standards properly established they are like ships
without a rudder. Then we older people put such
arbitrary rudders on their little ships and bring them
into our own queer conventional world, and the
course we prescribe for them is often so dull. So it
seemed even to the child of the seventies. I used to
ask my tutor if he couldn't give me a subject I really
cared about to write on, instead of something like
' Procrastination ' which interested me not at all.
But he thought I had queer fads and gave me lists of
capes and peninsulas to learn without even showing
them clearly on a map, much less describing the
countries in which they existed, and marvelled when
I asked for longer lessons because I liked them.

Mixing with other girls in later years made me, however, conform more or less to their standards. The
medical missionary tutor left us when I was about
nine and then I had a succession of delightful young
aspirants for the ministry as instructors, all of whom
were desperately shy, and all of whom let me learn
just what I wanted and leave the rest. One of them
confided to me that he thought it nonsense to teach girls
Latin, as my mother directed, when they should be
learning to bake ; so I made him an enormous cake
and presented it to him, to his great embarrassment,
since he did not know how most conveniently to get rid
of it. I expect it went into the nearest area.

Still I did learn from these amateur teachers, whereas when I went to a class for English I found it taught

by an old gentleman of enormous proportions who addressed each of us in solemn tones as ' Lady ' but taught us nothing at all. He was, we considered with some truth, in his dotage. His strong point was elocution, and I can hear his rolling sentence still, beginning, ' Conversation is a most difficult thing'; hence we were to make talk in society with the help of a little dog ! It was not till much later on that we had a real student as a teacher and learned something of what literature and history really mean. Years of one's life were simply a blank, excepting that one read books at home and on one's own. Very early I started on Dickens, for curiously enough, though novels were disapproved of by my parents, Dickens had a special exemption owing to the good work he had done for the poor, and for ill-treated children. I read him from cover to cover and learned a great deal which I never forgot.

If we had known it, we were just passing from one stage in education to another. The school board meant inspection, and inspection meant examinations, and all the poor little mites of the next decade were going to have individual ' passes ', and the school-teachers were to tremble when the inspector came round and pray for fine weather so that he might be in a good temper. It is just possible that Her Majesty's Inspector might himself have had a faint heart, though he dared not show it ! For girls the process was beginning through the exertions of women like Miss Buss and Miss Beale and their modern ' collegiate ' schools. There the standards were to be high and constantly tested by examinations that culminated in an examination recognized in some way or other by the University. In my case, later on, when it was quite evident to any outsider that we were learning practically nothing, it was suggested by one bold mother that we should enter for a ' local examination '. The idea was most exciting, and we, who had never even had an examination of any sort but just learned our day's lesson as it came, regardless of what preceded or succeeded, were delighted at the idea. A tutor was brought in to prepare us for this great ordeal and he did his work admirably, since he knew just the sort of questions we were likely to be asked. But then came a snag, for it was discovered that we could not have an examination in our own class-room but should have to go to the University of Edinburgh. Such a wild step could not be thought of for ' young ladies ', though the original mother who desired examination kept to it for her daughter. We were examined by I forget whom, but by someone who did not know anything of our preparation, and consequently, while the brave candidate produced her parchment triumphantly, we had done none too well and had nothing to show. The head of the school presented us with silver medallions, it is true, but it was not the same thing. Examinations are often enough a curse, but they do have their uses.

Now I should like to say something of what girls looked like, for the clothing of the present day differs from that of our youth as much in quantity as quality. The top of the head seems to disdain being protected either from sun or rain, while in old days protection was absolutely required from both : sunstroke and, for girls, sunburn (almost as bad) would result from one and colds from the other. Fringes and other curls 'went' in damp weather, since electric devices for preserving them were unknown. It would have been difficult for us to imagine that the electro-magnets that came into our lessons could play such freakish tricks on people's heads. Nowadays necks are bare and clothing scanty, whereas in old days ' dressing' was a long process beginning with ' woollen next the skin' as a desideratum. It was a real affliction to those who hated the feeling of wool either on body or legs ! For the limbs (legs were hardly mentioned in polite society) had to be so covered, though men liked to get a glimpse of a ' trim pair of ankles', perhaps because it was forbidden. The overclad babes, with their often lovely embroidered frocks above the multitude of string-confined undergarments, probably suffered most. Thick woollen stockings tied up with garters were worn both by boys and girls, and the girls had, in addition, to wear many petticoats of flannel and even of eiderdown in winter. Everyone who suffered in those days recollects the clothing that tightly compressed the neck, the frills, the ' comforters' that were no comfort, or the ' clouds' that were far from being the airy nothings that they pretended to be. It was no use saying that all this induced colds and even phthisis, for no one would believe it. It was Dame Custom that gradually made rational what was irrational—Dame Fashion one perhaps should say, but after all custom and fashion are things induced by manner of life ; and the manner of life has changed profoundly. Men and women live more healthy lives because they play games and like out-of-door sports and airy rooms, and the doctors soon discovered that these were best and healthiest for the nation, and old age was deprived of many of its fears and limitations. One wonders how far this development may go. Sun-bathing suggests that it may be farther than we anticipate.

Both sexes wore stays, though boys discarded them about the age of seven, while the girls were sentenced for life, and each year they became stronger and more bony.

There is, however, an important factor to be remembered. Materials available altered, for first cotton, then silk—real or artificial—came into vogue and largely displaced wool. White woollen stockings were followed by black stockings of cotton or lisle thread, then came silken stockings such as women love : these became so cheap that most people could have them, especially if content with ' artificials '. Gloves had a similar career. Children used to be given woollen gloves in winter, the fingers too long and very uncomfortable ; boys had ' muffatees ' leaving their fingers and part of their thumbs free, which was not so bad. Kid gloves must have come into general use early in

the seventies. The early gloves had but one button
and were fairly expensive, but they gave one the sense
of being really well set out, so were worth the money.

In the sixties and seventies long buttoned boots
were always worn by women, though they might be
laced for country wear. How these buttons used to
be tugged off at inconvenient moments ! I think
elastic-sided boots then went out of fashion, but our
nurses still wore them with ' prunella ' slippers for the
house. These slippers were soft and yielding, devoid
of heels, and very useful as instruments of mild correc-
tion. When shoes began to be worn out of doors, they
were much looked down upon. I think, however, that
the transformation from boots to shoes happened in
the eighties, and their convenience soon made them
popular. Shoes appeared to become less and less
solid till they ended in the court shoe now in vogue
which looks so elegant but which appears to be better
adapted for a car-using generation than for sturdy
walkers. Probably the stronger shoes came into
fashion to correspond with the coats and skirts of the
eighties which, with the neat blouses, shirts or what
not, make our English girls look their best and give
them the power to bicycle, play games or walk at will.
But there we come to the beginning of the emancipation of women, which not only swept away unnecessary clothing, allowing them to walk without
sweeping the dust or expiring with heat, but showing
them that if properly apparelled they could do work
hitherto held sacred to the other sex.

One thinks most of women's clothing because it has altered more than men's and has reached a more rational and practical stage than theirs. There are no open-necked summer garments of cotton for men. They have indeed kept to what they seem to like—hot and heavy garments all the year round with hard collars tightly fixed round the neck : only some of them are emancipated enough to discard these. But just as sick nurses adhered for long years to what they considered as the uniform of a Florence Nightingale, collars and all, men seem to have professional prejudices to consider. Tradition counts for much.

One thing countenanced by tradition both sexes are quickly discarding, the deep mourning of former days. It is almost inconceivable to the young to hear how the length of mourning was spaced out according to the nearness of the deceased relative : two years for a parent, six months for a cousin, and so on, ' half-mourning ' intervening at the proper date ; how the exact time during which crape was to be worn was decided by a mysterious convention known only to the adept, i.e. the dressmaker. Men did not suffer so acutely from these conventions, as their clothes had not to be greatly changed. But they had to wear their hat-bands to the regulation height, and in old days a bow of crape, and ' weepers ' on their sleeves on Sundays. Widows wore weepers for a long period of time and crape almost interminably, as we know from Queen Victoria's attire. Poorer people had to keep to dark attire ' in case of accident ', i.e. in case a relative of some kind should die. The deep black edge thought requisite on envelopes left little room for the script.

The games of my youth were few, but we children were left to play them ourselves and were not over-set by interfering grown-ups who never can understand what children are after. We played mild cricket (unluckily I was always made to field and my petti-coats came handy for stopping the ball) ; climbed trees, though these petticoats were a drawback and on one occasion hung their possessor ignominiously till cut down ; and rode our ponies, though without too much enthusiasm. For riding, my long habit was sadly in the way, and the tall hat I had to wear when growing up was uncomfortable. Still, ponies on the grassy hills were a boon, though I remember being thrown in the midst of shepherds shearing their sheep and being revived with raw whisky. Fishing for trout in the burn was all right, but we two young ones were entrusted with the precious baskets slung on the shoulders, and one melancholy day, after two dozen beautiful trout had been caught, did I not manage in scrambling along the rocky banks to lose my precious charge? To this day I blush when I think of it and of the cold looks of the disappointed fishermen. I never cared for burn fishing myself, for I couldn't be persuaded that the worms, however slapped, ceased to feel. The boys shot soon after they were twelve years old but John sympathized with me and did not care about killing.

Instead he and I wandered off, vasculums on backs, to hunt for rare ferns in remote little glens.

The greatest fun when days grew short, and especially when the perpetual rains of the late seventies laid hold of the country, was found in our log house. I cannot believe that anyone ever had such a well-built house entirely made by the big boys helped by the humble little ones. Wood, tarpaulin, moss, bricks for fireplace were all called into requisition, and before Boy Scouts were invented, fires were laid and made and delicious meals of a scrumptious kind (mainly composed of roast potatoes) enjoyed. There was the Song of the House and the Language of the House, both known by ourselves alone and thus a delightful secret into which no one ventured to enquire.

Of school games I know nothing, for I had no part in them since the other girls had none. Outside school games there was much later on the jump to lawn tennis, a new game entered into with zeal but not taken in the serious way that came to pass later on. The players were content with ordinary grass courts, not too well rolled, and small racquets, but everyone was good-natured, which they were not in games of croquet—a game irritating to the temper. But curling was being carried on lustily ; and it is a game I will tell of later on. It is played by all classes together, which in itself is a boon : no one is cross and everyone is excited and keen. I cannot help envying those who wield the besom. And the game can be carried on into old age like golf, which none of us ever played.

Walking was really our great amusement. We climbed hills, but as all of us had bad heads for heights we could not do any rock climbing.

As to indoor games, playing-cards were absolutely tabooed, and such cards were not even allowed to be in the house. But in our childhood we loved 'Happy Families', and draughts and chess were games for later times. There were also paper games such as 'Consequences', which all Victorians will remember as producing shrieks of laughter when the 'consequence' was peculiarly entertaining and personal.

On Sunday no games of any sort were, of course, allowed, nor indeed were walks more than saunters round the garden. But whatever others may have felt, I don't believe it was bad for children who had good homes to have a quiet day and to read Sunday books : the latter were a bit of a problem, for there were many books in the house, and not always parents to consult. I remember looking with some anxiety to find the name of God mentioned, as guaranteeing what was right. But the results were not always satisfactory from the point of view of our elders. I was distracted between the *Schönberg-Cotta Family* and *Adam Bede*, both of which seemed to meet my requirements. In the end I read the two but I felt regretfully that my beloved Dickens could not possibly be up to 'Sunday standard'. *Ministering Children* was filled with four-leaved clover which we searched for on summer Sundays while lying on the grass, and *Pike's Early Piety* we could not away with. *Jessica's First Prayer* and *Little Meg's Children* we read but they lacked vim. Grimm's and Andersen's Fairy Tales I loved. Of improving books *The Fairchild Family* was a delight, but it had even by our time become an antique. There were of standard books Borrow's *Bible in Spain* whose title gave it a quality which it hardly deserved, and of course the beloved Piggy Poggy (*Pilgrim's Progress*) and the hateful Foxe's *Book of Martyrs* which I dreaded, though it was read aloud to us religiously along with other tales of harried Covenanters. Gaussen's *World's Birthday* gave a succinct and rather fundamentalist account of the Creation. The books I loved most were those of adventure, above all those of Ballantyne and Kingston. Henty came much later. How one longed to be a boy and able to adventure ! A kind French governess who taught a brother and me passed us on from the *Malheurs de Sophie* to Jules Verne, and one adored his adventures, only somewhat spoiled to me by an older brother with a scientific bent of mind asking me whether I did not see the fallacies in the various exciting tales. I did not, and it vexed me to know that there were such, just as it vexed me when John Bunyan would say ' Now I saw in my Dream '. If it was a dream, could he not keep quiet about it and not spoil the story? I was all for truth, and remember as a very small child my dismay when a grown-up visitor to the nursery looked at my *Red Riding Hood* and carelessly said, ' I used actually to believe all these stories when I was a little girl.' There were queer theological books in the library belonging to old days, such as Boston's *Fourfold State* and one that intrigued us, Sibbs's *Bowels Opened*.

Before leaving the account of these early days it may be worth while to tell something of what the life was like outside the nursery and schoolroom.

The life of the workers in Scotland was hard enough though they did not look unhappy. They became, however, old men and women long before their time and suffered much from rheumatism. Also whole families went down from tuberculosis, 'went in a decline' as it was called, the one infecting the other. Many of the people round us were hand-loom weavers but also worked at harvest in autumn, for harvest in these days was a long process. The poorer children began to work at nine years of age, going to school just as they could, trying to avoid the days when fees were paid to the schoolmaster. When lads were hired out as 'halflings' they usually slept in a damp loft and had pork soup and porridge as their principal food. Fortunate ones were given suet dumplings. Sunday was a happy day on which they might have tea, bread and treacle, with skim milk cheese. Many of the villagers had 'pecks' or 'acres' of land in which they grew potatoes and corn.

The weavers made about 15s. a week, but often enough had to carry their webs for miles. There were several looms in each 'shop' and the floor of the shop was of beaten earth : the stove in the middle was replenished by the workers in turn.

There were plenty of games on the few holidays, such as 'Ball Shooting', 'Blind Barrow', 'Raffles', concerts and dances—all fairly rough, songs personal and possibly coarse, but cheerful. The markets and fairs were the great events of the year : at these there was much drunkenness, but they were greatly looked forward to. The ploughmen carried whips and, at some places, when engaged at the yearly 'feeing market', the thong of the whip was attached to the handle. Their dress was composed of white corduroy breeches, moleskin jackets with pearl buttons, but that was falling into disuse in the later sixties. The dances were often rough enough in my early youth, but later on nothing was more delightful than to go to a Harvest Home in a barn on a crisp autumn moonlight night and take part in Rory O'More, Strip the Willow and all the other country dances. I used to envy those who had such dissipations, for they were forbidden to us at home : one could only dance with the workers and servants, whose standards seemed to be less rigid than ours.

Shopping in the country was a pleasant thing for the shopper, especially if he or she (it was usually a she) was well off. The shopkeeper came out of his shop to greet the shopper, and after a conversation and probably in Scotland, a hand-shake, the proceedings went on. Inside the shop there was further conversation, for in those days time did not seem to count. My parents' visits even to the post office seemed to us children waiting outside interminable. The grocer's shop was our favourite, for the grocer, a dear old friend, always got out a string-full of sugar candy. The candy was crystallized on the string, and it was lovely to break off bits and eat them. Then he would say, ' just a sing-el fig, my little dearie,' and we had the fig, rather an aged one it is true. He was a very good man, an elder of the church, and he had much to tell our parents about the poor and needy ; but his graces before tea were long, and on one occasion he opened his eyes to see that his guest, the busy doctor, had taken his tea and made off ! The so-called chemist, who also dabbled in the early stages of photography and provided the necessities of sportsmen who were fishermen or shooters, kept tooth-brushes. But we were discouraged from using the latter since he suggested taking a few on trial and returning the unsuitable !

The interesting thing about country shops was that though the custom must have been small, discount was always given. As children we had little pocket-money and we delighted in going to pay the accounts at the end of six months (monthly accounts were never thought of) and receiving some of the bounty. I fear there was a good deal of bribery on the part of some people, but of this we knew nothing. Anyhow the custom was, if it existed, in a manner recognized. It has been modified, I imagine, not so much by laws against bribery and corruption, though they now exist, but by the establishment of the great stores which do not require to resort to such methods. There were in those days gifts in addition to ' discount ', which may or may not continue to the present time. But to my distress live turkeys used to be sent at Christmas time by tradesmen ; these were tied by the legs in a way which seemed to me, and was, cruel in the extreme.

The nature of shops has changed a good deal in other ways. In Edinburgh, where we lived in winter, there were no flower-shops (though the greengrocer sold a few flowers in summer) and my mother had to order flowers from a nurseryman in the suburbs. In London there was one special shop still existing in Marylebone, which we always patronized. But the absence of flower-shops and gay barrows of flowers made the greatest difference to the appearance of the streets. Then, more extraordinary still, there was the fact that tea-shops hardly existed. One could go to one or two shops in Edinburgh for a luncheon of a kind. I think soup was provided and possibly some other mild eatables. But I remember the excitement when a café was first set on foot in Edinburgh on a semi-charitable basis, as a sort of antidote to public-houses, and how popular it instantly became. It was indeed a commercial success. Before that time there were bakers' shops (very good of their kind) and public-houses. Where in the world did everyone lunch ? I suppose, following Lord Sandwich of old when at the head of the Admiralty, ' sandwiches ' of bread and meat were consumed on the premises by people who could not go home. When the A.B.C.'s were once started they became a real boon to womenkind,

LONDON SCHOOLBOYS IN 1894

SCHOOLBOYS IN SAME DISTRICT FORTY YEARS LATER

and once begun, such institutions multiplied. The advent of women into public life and into office work of all sorts was what really made the difference, for these women had to have food of some description, and they could not and would not go to public-houses, and such eating-houses as existed, mainly in basements, were far from attractive. The new tea-shops were really tea shops, and made tea and buns—no cream buns then—the staple form of refreshment ; it was later on that some more substantial fare was tentatively introduced. The first tea-shop that I remember in London was near Marshall and Snelgrove's—a delightful place it was, and frequented by us as children because a peculiarly attractive thick ginger biscuit was on sale. I have never seen that biscuit since ! I imagine that our nurse would not have ventured into the august precincts of Gunter.[1]

For a long time after my childhood, there was little opportunity of getting any form of light refreshments at country inns. One had to go into the commercial room and order a fairly expensive solid meal. But the advent of bicycles changed all that, and the woman was catered for in the way she wished and the man found he liked the same light fare. The motor-car has made still further changes, but this is a comparatively recent development. To sell tea a licence was required, just as it was to sell tobacco, and in the country the sign ' licensed to sell tea and tobacco '

[1] The Lyons Restaurants were started through the influence of two ladies in 1887.

c

usually meant that bulls'-eyes and peppermints were also to be had within. Sweet-shops were not the beautiful and numerous depôts that they later on became. In the country no one had money to spend on such extravagances. I heard of a child who was asked in Sunday School the meaning of ' licentious living ', and instantly replied, ' eating too many sweeties '.

Drapers' shops have changed enormously in the last half-century, mainly, I think, owing to the advent of ready-made garments. Not but that there were such in old days. ' Ready-mades ' were, however, poor in quality, made too often by sweated labour. Men's garments made to order were also, of course, made by similar labour, and in the most insanitary places: I cannot forget the work of the tailors in one-roomed 'houses' in London when I collected rents in the nineties. The man worked so hard that he hardly spared time to look up to speak to one, and the woman's work was equally trying. With the abolition of sweating came the factory with its well-cut frocks and other clothing. The difference this made to the appearance of the poorer people was immense and even the richer people could afford much greater changes in attire. The shops in any case quite altered. In old days one bought material for the most part from drapers, and even country shops had a good selection of material to choose from. I always remember the beauty of Lyons silks in the best Edinburgh shops. But there was usually little custom for made-up garments. The well-to-do never dreamt of buying such, the poorer people made things up at home as best they could, and it was not very well. Little girls' frocks, however, were, of course, home-made, large brown holland pinafores keeping them fairly clean and tidy. The multitudes of petticoats that they wore were also mostly made at home, but their stays and eiderdown petticoats were purchased in shops. Poor little souls to have to wear such !

There were tradesmen in former days whose work and importance have almost disappeared. Above all, the workshop of the smith—the smiddy, as we called it in Scotland—was a centre of gossip for the males and joy to the children, especially when they were allowed to stand near the forge and see the horses shod. Next to that came the wheelwright with his work of fixing on the iron rings to his wheels and making the hubs, and, best of all, occasionally the child's precious wheelbarrow. The glory of these old-fashioned trades has departed with much else that was picturesque, and we must try to console ourselves by thinking of the trades that have profited by the years. They are more numerous if less attractive to the sight.

No one over sixty could have been present at any of our recent national jubilations without casting back his mind to the manners and behaviour of the crowds of half a century before. Supposing we had been cast into a crowd of that date, what should we have found ? Plenty of good-humoured chaff, perhaps, but also plenty of rough horse-play. We should have been jostled by unpleasantly odoriferous individuals ; we women should most certainly not have been able to carry our handbags safely in the queer unpractical way we now do. Our menfolk would soon have been minus something, for even pocket handkerchiefs were considered worthy of attention by boys poor and ragged but skilful in the art of petty theft. One remembers how men thought it worth while to gain a few coppers by carrying out some menial work, for there was great poverty in those days.

Then there could not have been a crowd in the remotest degree resembling, say, that of the Jubilee week of 1935 in London without drunkenness and its results—fighting and disorder. Imagine only thirty cases of disorderliness for the whole of London's millions on Jubilee Day! The price of spirits has helped, but far more than that, the decent life which has resulted from decent education. Of course, we must not forget the modern inventions that have made sobriety essential for the bicycle-rider and the motor-driver. Who can do either in a state of intoxication, whereas many a time and oft we trusted to the wisdom of the horse—the long-suffering horse, ill-fed and constantly plied with the whip or checked by the bit—to circumvent the inebriety of the driver. Has mechanism contributed to good manners? It has apparently helped to make us better behaved. We do not now, as we did in old days, have to count our change carefully in bus and railway. It is often given us automatically: still there is usually no evidence of an endeavour to deceive either on the part of collector or passenger. And as to women's work, a high degree of intelligence is required by the girl who ' perms ' our hair, the cook who regulates her electric contrivances, the housemaid who mechanically spring-cleans and can deal with wireless and fuses. And all these things make life easier and cleaner, just as ready-made clothing makes people smarter ; while it gives them the self-respect that was often lacking in the worker, male and female, of half a century ago. Some of us watch the school-children making their way to their places ' by blast of horn ' (loudspeaker) on Children's Day, and notice the smart school frocks, badges and ties, wishing that all the children were up to standard. Some, alas, are not.

The change in manners is, I think, more visible in the public service than in private life. Do we remember travelling by bus or third-class train sixty years or more ago ? For those of us who were born in the more prosperous classes it was just ' not done ', and the reason was clear. The floors of the carriages were covered with ' spits ', and for some mysterious reason it was supposed that men must spit and women must wear long dresses that mopped up the dirt. The omnibuses and cabs seemed cleaner because the floors were covered with more or less fresh straw. But the company was far from select and often far from clean. On the omnibuses, men could climb a precarious perpendicular ladder to airy (if wet) quarters on high, but naturally women could not, hampered as they were by most inappropriate and bulky garments.

But if the workers have changed in manners, so have the employers, and that largely under compulsion. The 'favoured classes' may be too much favoured still, but they have somewhat more consideration for their employees. Think of what a ceremonial occasion would have meant in olden days. Carriages and lovely horses instead of motor-cars, liveried coachmen and footmen instead of neatly dressed chauffeurs. We remember with shame how the unfortunate coachmen and footmen were left outside during parties and balls to shiver unprotected in the cold and rain. Was it possible that they should be otherwise than tipsy and rough ? How splendid was a well-turned-out carriage and a pair of high-steppers, braced up by bearing-reins, and what a fiction it was : what miseries men and horses suffered to be beautiful and correct. The delightful ivory ' pass ' that for the great of the earth broke through the traffic is of the past ; Belisha beacons do their job unaided for commonalty and aristocrats alike ; and the Lord Mayor's coach is but a picturesque relic of ancient days, as are cockades and the tight liveries which left men's legs cold while their bodies were uncomfortably buttoned up. What horror would the footmanless vehicle have inspired in the bosoms of our ancestors ! No longer is it taboo for a woman of fashion to open the door of her carriage for herself— the solecism of former days.

As children we usually attended a church four or five miles off, and the drive there was a constant excitement. It was taken in a barouche—now, of course, an extinct conveyance, but a rather delightful one, for it was built on C springs, which meant pleasant going. It had two steps which let down, a hood and a curious front seat, the back of which pulled forward, and when the hood was up and the curtains drawn and the cover protecting the legs, it was practically watertight. The children, however, were placed in this front seat, and when the carriage had to be closed the only way of disposing of them was, to their delight, crowding them amongst their seniors' feet. This, and the fact that large Abernethy biscuits were dispensed on the homeward route, made a real adventure. The coachman had his own ideas of what was right and proper, being very like some of Sir Walter's characters. He had no scruples in declaring his views, and even on occasion stopping at an inn ' to see a friend ' and emerging wiping his mouth after the friend had duly regaled him.

We had to start early, as we had to reach the church long before the service began, for the horses must be put up and the man enabled to sit in his place in the church, resplendent in his blue coat and silver buttons. The church bell rung with a strange creak produced by the pulling from outside of the rope, which process we watched with anxious interest from within. The sound comes back to me with pleasant memories. The minister in his black Geneva gown ascended the pulpit and the precentor followed him, taking his place in his box below the pulpit, attired in a gown also, but a less

black one, for it was one which had been discarded by
the minister as having grown somewhat musty. Then
the name of the psalm to be sung was put up on a
sort of bracket in front of the box, and we all did our
best to sing it. We liked the sad tunes like ' Martyr-
dom ', to which countless Scottish babes had been put
to sleep by their mothers and nurses ; but all the
tunes were sung so slowly that they sounded sad rather
than joyful. Then we settled down to the long sermon, carefully divided into heads, which we tried
rather vainly to remember in view of subsequent
questioning. We could not but rejoice when ' Finally,
my brethren,' betokened a prospective ending, though
it was usually followed by ' Lastly and in conclusion'.
There was a pleasant odour of peppermints and ' Old
Man ' or Southernwood, which had been picked from
the cottage gardens to help in keeping the listeners
awake ; the males occasionally passed round the snuff
mull with the same object. The buzzing of a passing
bee diverted one's attention : otherwise all was still
and peaceful.

The great lady of the parish sat in a slightly elevated
pew surveying the scene from that point of vantage.
I wish I could describe her adequately for she was
well worth description. She had married young, but
been bereft of her husband, the laird, at the age of
twenty-two. With her had lived the Lady Nairne of
Jacobite tradition, who had written many beautiful
Scottish songs, such as *The Auld Hoose* and *The Land of
the Leal* ; but by the time I remember the authoress

GEORGE, WILLIAM, RICHARD, JOHN, AND ELIZABETH
From a sketch by their Mother in 1870

REV. GEORGE JACQUE
THE 'RELIEF' MINISTER

MRS. GRAEME
OLIPHANT OF GASK

had been for a good many years dead. The traditions
of the old house of Gask were, however, still continued, and our many visits there were among our
most valued remembrances. A few fair hairs from
Prince Charlie's head clipt off by the lady of Gask
herself, were duly shown to us, as were his bonnet and
the table at which he had breakfasted. Then there was
a walk to the chapel where Lady Nairne and the other
members of the family were buried, reached through
a dark avenue of trees. Once arrived the organ was
opened, and sacred music and psalm tunes were
played while we listened entranced. After that came
the visit to the dairy and the picking up of peacock's
feathers, and then tea for the children in the ' Prayer
Room '—the room in which family prayers were daily
held and servants catechized on Sundays. No one
was admitted to the precincts on Sunday, even if he
had come from afar ; it was a day of worship and rest,
and not of visiting.

The lady herself was, however, cheerfulness itself :
she was rosy-cheeked, smiling and bright-eyed. Her
happy face was encircled by a bonnet of the type of
her day, black in winter and white and black in
summer. On the same day in each year there were
certain changes. In spring the black bonnet became
light, the black cloak or dolman became white
trimmed with black lace, and the fires in the great
house were put off. In autumn the same ritual was
observed, though in the other way round. I can see
her swinging gait as she passed out of church, for

crinolines she still wore as of old. Indeed, her dress had not altered since the days when as a young wife she had passed her honeymoon in Paris and there got fashions which could always be repeated by county town dressmakers and modistes. Outside the church there was a frank embrace, including even our father in its ambit, and then the phaeton and its two ponies appeared under the care of the faithful tyrant John, and the lady gaily took the reins and also grasped a lovely whip on whose stem was an elegant parasol to protect her complexion from the sun. Not that she really cared anything for the sun and though in garden queer contraptions or shades were still worn by women under the very suitable name of 'uglies' I don't believe that she ever wore any such thing.

This seems to be getting away from the subject of religion, but not really so, for the lady was keenly interested in religious matters and doctrines, and she and our parents conversed much about them.

There were other churches around us which we often visited, since our father frequently took the services in the evening and held services of his own in a barn. He often rode to the more distant places, but to some we drove on a Sunday evening. There was one place in particular that we loved—it was a little church right away in the hills. The minister seldom if ever preached, since he had a deformity in the conformation of his features which prevented him from doing so, besides being very deaf. But he always pronounced the Benediction as a sort of token that he was responsible for the conduct of the service, and this was done in stentorian tones that roused the heaviest sleepers. Then when the service was over we were given glasses of wonderful milk with a deep covering of cream, for the glebe was famous for its milch cows. The elders were offered stronger beverages.

Religion permeated our lives, and the sense of sin and its consequences seemed to dog our footsteps when we remembered what it meant. But strangely enough the churches did not influence us as did the influence of home. Church in the country had a pleasant aroma of outside life and outside people, and the oppressive theology that was apt to overshadow our lives was blown aside by the fresh country breezes. In town, church, as a rule, just meant nothing to us but weariness of spirit. We had the deepest respect for the aged minister, who from his appearance was deemed to be a successor to the prophets of old, but that was all. After his death I went with my mother to see the body, which I seem to remember had a sod placed on it, and tried to feel that I did not mind ; but somehow I did, and was ashamed of my feelings and wished that she would not remain so long in the room. We were brought up to remember that death was an essential part of life, and must be faced without fear ; and it was the custom when it occurred around us, to visit the corpse while calling to express our sympathy with the mourners. This seems to me anyhow much better than the modern plan of altogether avoiding the subject with children.

Ministers truly played a great part in our lives and many were our intimate friends. It has become the custom to find amusement in the sermons of long ago in Scotland, and indeed there were many ministers whose sermons made us children find difficulty in keeping our countenances. But there were others to whom we were devoted. One of them was so remarkable that I should like to tell his story.

I often think of his account of his early entry to our town in the year 1835. He left the coach and walked down the one long street of grey houses built flush to the pavement with an open gully running on the side of it to carry off such drainage as fell in. Railways were non-existent, and on a grim winter's day it seemed to the young man, as he often said, as though he had reached the end of the world. Yet he had every confidence that he would spend the period of his life in this quiet spot, and the period proved to be long, for in 57 years he hardly left the place for a week at a time. The soft air of the west was lost to him for ever, and perhaps he was glad, for he had suffered tragedies there in losing father and brother by drowning in the Douglas water.

The 'Relief' church was made new, and it had its comfortable manse adjoining. It was actually superior in architecture to the grim-looking roughcast 'Original Secession' kirk just over the way, though wherein the difference in their doctrines lay few people could say. The young preacher was pleased to get the call, even though the stipend was then but £100 a

year, and he never ceased to be grateful that he was
allowed to live his life in a community that he loved.
He was a tall, good-looking, well-set up man with a
gentle way with him that no sinner, however black,
could withstand, and that aged and young alike
admired and loved. For the strange thing about him
was that he sympathized with the fun of the young—
half in secret it had to be—as well as with the sorrows
of the old. Children fell to him at once, especially
when he set his barrel-organ to play to them, though
the writer found it disappointing, in that no red-
coated Italian monkey appeared so that she could
give it nuts ! Of course, the minister had to be careful
in what he did or said, even to the very young, but he
had a dignified way with him, and used to lead off the
' Grand March ' at the opening of the village dance,
ignoring, what he knew well, that the end of the dance
would be rough enough. His dignity was possibly
upheld by the long black coat and clerical hat that
he always wore. None saw him otherwise attired,
even though he walked far over the moors to see his
very scattered flock. He remembered how a predecessor had been rebuked for casting off his coat
during a hot summer's day ! He himself used to say
that as in his walks every year he crossed to America,
so far as distance went, why should he want to go
elsewhere. Black gloves were worn for preaching or
on other important occasions, but in walking far
afield they were dispensed with.

There were two drawbacks to his complete happiness with the people he came to care for as a father for his children. One was his voice ; a strange impediment developed in his speech, and this had to be conquered, and conquered in great measure it was. How he did it he often told me. In those days, sermons had to be delivered extempore—'committed,' as was said—and no 'paper' was allowed. So this good man used to make his way to the hills and lecture to the shaggy Highland cattle who gathered round him, just as did every other animal. 'Never did I have a more attentive congregation,' as he used to say. His power over animals was such that he could bring a flock of wheeling crows around him and make some of them even perch on his outstretched arms. His pet cockatoo was, however, the cause of serious misgiving on the part of certain of his congregation : they felt it was hardly the sort of bird a minister should keep.

The other drawback was a much harder nut to crack. On his arrival it was still the custom to rebuke from the pulpit the sinners who had transgressed the moral code. He did it once, but felt so overcome with pity and remorse that he begged his session to allow the 'rebukes' to be given in private before them by him alone. There were in those days many who came under discipline, but the kind-hearted wife whom he had married soon after he was 'placed', had a comfortable kitchen tea ready for the mothers and their babies. The men could fend for themselves. But there was a further and more serious trouble that arose from a love of music that could not be eradicated. Now in 1835—but a century ago—music was looked on with the gravest suspicion in the Scottish Seceding churches. The young minister had brought with him his beloved violin (a precious one, acquired I know not how), and played Scottish airs and even— it was said—Scottish reels and dances ; he also occasionally played the 'cello. The good men of the Session met together to consider how this youthful pastor might be wisely but firmly dealt with, and finally it was decided to send to him a small deputation who could put the matter before him in its true light as tending to place temptation in the way of the weaker brethren. The deputation came ; the minister received them in the best spirit, acknowledging his error but asking that he might just play one or two tunes to them, it might be for the last time. They agreed, and having heard him, they returned to their fellows with the report that they had all been mistaken, for the instrument their pastor played was ' nane o' thae squeakin' feedles but a muckle sounding deep releegious-like feedle that played the Psalms of David ' !

So his fiddle was allowed to remain his loved companion, and his treat was to get a musical friend to come and play Beethoven's Sonatas one by one. Of these he never tired. And he was a poet, too—a poet who saw the beauty of God's world everywhere around him and who could put his feelings into words.

The doctrine preached was the pure word of the

Gospel with no pandering to modern views. It was a simple doctrine that suited simple people. No one who stood below him at the baptismal font ; no self-conscious father holding his babe in his awkward, unaccustomed arms, could forget the words spoken to him. The exhortation he had understood from child-hood, but then in low and solemn tones he was warned about the result of non-compliance with the Law of God and about the 'other place'—I can hear the minister's voice still in its vibrating whisper—that awaited the delinquents.

Yet he was merciful to sinners while in this life. There was one who certainly failed in the ordinary virtues of sobriety and yet ' was first on the floor on Communion Sabbath ', as her kindly elder said. There were others who received sympathy even if rebuke had to be administered. His people were solid country folk for the most part and carried out the old marriage customs of feet-washing and the rest. The first Secession church had been built by their own unaided labours after their ordinary day's toil was over, and as they passed round the snuff-mull they were conscious of the value of possessing a church all their own, over which the State had no dominion. The quaintly carved dove that used to look down from the pulpit meant that peace had been attained.

There was a ' jubilee ', of course, and how indignant the pastor was that he was given a new Geneva gown, ' when they should have given him his grave clothes.' Yet there was the good and faithful precentor to be considered—he who occupied a minor pulpit below him and inherited the less distinguished robes.

Rest came to the old minister when he was in his eighty-eighth year, for one Sunday his tall form—tall still—bent down in the pulpit and we saw that he could do no more. He left the church after reading the words of his text : ' Into Thy Hands I commit my spirit,' and that was the end of a long and honourable life.

D

THE SECOND DECADE
1872-1882

GROWING UP

THE early part of this decade was, on its public side, occupied with the discussion of a question not seriously thought of before by the ordinary man or woman : how the children of this land were to be educated, if indeed they were to be educated at all. The Liberal Government may have been Whiggish and uninspired in its policy at home and abroad, but it did a great work for its country as well as a brave one in introducing Mr. Forster's Education Act of 1870. It must for my purpose be taken as belonging to the second decade in my life, since the Scottish Act did not come into effect till 1872 and it was then that we children began to hear of this new and strange departure. Something had indeed to be done. England had neglected the education of her poor children disgracefully and in her neglect she was behind most other countries in Europe—of course, seriously behind Prussia. So far she had trusted for the education of the children to private charity with miserable doles from the State, and boasted that for the State to undertake this duty was alien to the feelings of Englishmen and would ' sap their independence '. Scotland was better off, thanks to the foresight of John Knox and the Presbyterian Church which made education the duty of each parish through its church ; and likewise to its Universities which kept a high standard going when the standards of university education in England were miserable. But conditions everywhere were miserable ; school buildings were hovels, teachers were scandalously paid, and it was only the real keen interest in learning which seemed to be born in a Scot that prevented absolute collapse. The Scottish dominie held the torch burning in the most discouraging circumstances.

The difficulties which came near wrecking the English Bill did not affect Scotland so seriously. There was not a huge Nonconformist population that objected to money going to denominational uses, and that wished the State to teach secular matters, leaving religion to be taught by its supporters. Presbyterianism was so strong and universal in Scotland that its teaching could be carried on if there were a conscience clause allowing for exemption ; and though there were many branches of it, these did not differ in essentials. School boards were set up in order to deal with the matter of education within their local areas, and for the first time women were admitted to the privilege of membership. The excitement of this new kind of election in the country is well within my memory. One little board near us had the local lady land-owner as a member : but she retired after the first meeting because it was decided not to open

proceedings with prayer. Other boards had to make
suitable arrangements with schools belonging to other
than the churches established by law, i.e. mainly Free
churches. And this became a terrible bone of con-
tention, not on doctrinal but on material grounds.
Many of the ministers were at loggerheads with one
another. The fights were not only about the disposal
of money, but also about the appointment of teachers,
for the Established Church trained some of their
teachers and the Free Church had its own ' Normal
College ' for its own school-teachers. The children
seemed likely to be forgotten in all these fiery disputes,
but in the end things got along, though not without
much criticism, not only from the various denominations but from the public who declared that education
was being made worse than it had been before ; and
the rate-payers and employers said that the population was being spoiled for ordinary manual work.

Now we children came into the picture, for we
heard all this being debated with great vehemence
and heat. Was it a good thing to have the individuality of the citizen interfered with ? Was it not better
to let people do what they ought to do on their own
account ? They would never in this world appreciate
what was given them free and unsolicited. Our
nurse wistfully told us how her mother had scraped
up the pence for the large family's education (though
she could only keep her at school till the age of ten)
and consequently how they profited from their hard-
won teaching. Everyone seemed to fear the worst :

servants who would not serve and ploughmen who would not plough. It is curious how we all dread the result of pampering when we have all enjoyed the pampering in our own persons, and what regard we have for the morals of the less prosperous beings ! I suppose we really thought that working people had morals more easily upset than those of the well-to-do. Not that the so-called better classes were alone in their criticisms. Our first tutor must have had a great struggle to qualify as a *medicus*, but I cannot remember his supporting the new ideas. He, however, left us for India soon after this time : he was very good in teaching the elements of knowledge and excellent at athletics, able to climb a tree like a monkey and to leap over crevasses without fear, a feat which he even induced one of my brothers to emulate. All this made him popular with us all. My younger brother and I had at odd times foreign governesses. Our mother had, however, a great prejudice against governesses, having suffered much at their hands, and this plan soon came to an end.

The most interesting point, to me, was that at last, owing to the new Act, women were about to be recognized as sapient creatures. The election for the first school board in Edinburgh was very exciting since two well-known women were standing as candidates. Now why and wherefore I became interested in this matter I cannot tell. It must have been due to some *zeitgeist* that was passing through the air. No one in my home was in the least interested so far as I knew.

The four sturdy brothers and above all the medical
tutor were violently against women coming into
universities. I do not remember what they thought
of ' public life ' in so far as serving on public boards
was concerned, probably they did not think at all.
Our parents were so engrossed in religious matters
that such things did not seem to concern them. One
of the lady candidates (the word ' woman ' was never,
of course, used) was a Miss Flora Stevenson much
respected by all Edinburgh society despite her being
considered somewhat ' advanced ' in her views. Now
it struck me, could I help this lady's candidature ?
It seemed difficult, but I had an idea, for I knew that
each householder had as many votes as there were
candidates and even if I could secure one it would be
a brave deed. At that time my father was suffering
from headache and he liked me to sit by him and
stroke his hair to set him to sleep. I waited till he
was not quite asleep but, as I thought, in a peaceful
state of mind, and then I screwed up my courage and
said, ' Papa, do you think you would mind giving *one*
of your votes to Miss Stevenson ? ' I can still remember the start of the peaceful papa, right out of his chair.
' What is the child speaking of ? ' he exclaimed in
amazement. The world to him was evidently turning
upside down, and so in fact it was.

Then there was the great question as to whether
women medical students were to be allowed to enter
the University with the view to graduation. There
were those who advocated this extreme view, but it

was opposed by all, or nearly all, respectable Edinburgh, especially the medical professors. The main fight centred round Miss Jex Blake, who fought valiantly if ineffectually. Naturally I did not know the details, but I did believe that my sex was being unfairly treated, and as it was impossible at table when discussion raged most strongly, to make my voice heard against four boys and one tutor, I informed them that I should write down what was the truth and that they would have to read it. I did this in a queer essay which I still possess, not badly written for a child of nine, entitled ' Fair Play, or a few words for the Lady Doctors '. The arguments were to my mind irrefutable. ' You men are all against Miss Jex Blake. Certainly it would not be right to behave that way (if it is true) if there was no necessity in doing it, but it is quite right when there is a necessity for it as there is now. There needs to be one rather bold woman to fight against men. You say women are weak and inferior to men, and when men get lazy and loll about, you call them effeminate. You say women do nothing hardly except to please themselves, and when women want to work you will not let them.' And so on, with many home illustrations and finishing with the ominous but far-seeing words, ' The women are determined to get to the top of the hill and they shall.' The strange thing is that the nine-year-old ' keeper of women's rights ', as she signed herself, ever got to have these advanced views. My mother had been to a meeting at which Miss Jex Blake spoke and being a clever artist gave me a very unflattering pencil sketch of how she looked, but this had no deterring influence.

Later on I came to know the Misses Stevenson who worked so valiantly for the cause. They were four attractive and wealthy ladies who, still young, managed to elude all suitors ; and as they occupied a large house near ours, we knew them by sight : later on they became real and valued friends with whom I often stayed. Miss Flora, the ablest and essentially a woman of the world, never failed to be elected for the school board and for long was its distinguished chairman. Her name is perpetuated in an Edinburgh school. Louisa, also a clever woman, worked for women's education and arranged for classes for women of University standing, before women were admitted within the University portals, as well as helping to set on foot a school for domestic science. Another sister was artistic and did much for the Kyrle Society, like Miranda Hill, Octavia's sister, while the last was housekeeper and kept all the domestic wheels running smoothly. Both food and drink were much considered and were of the best. But this is looking forward. In the early decade of which I write the women's movement was carried on amid many discouragements, and women doctors, like Dr. Garrett Anderson, started on their work with only a few brave spirits as patients. Before this decade was over, things were better, but not much better. Public health services for women and children had not begun, and women were not too anxious to employ women doctors, except for small children. I have often been told by those who ought to know, ' You see women doctors have not made good, they have made nothing of it.' Other professions opened to women slowly and almost by stealth. In reality this was the beginning of the great movement which was to develop fully next century and fundamentally influence social life. The foundations were truly laid by Victorian women and the next century reaped the advantages which accrued from their work.

Strangely enough the great Educational measure did not have the effect of strengthening Liberalism in England—rather the reverse—because it offended nonconformity. The Dissenters wished State-aided education to be compulsory on all, and would not recognize the claims of existing church schools, and the result was that difficulties crept in and later on developed further. Still the advantage of having public bodies on which all classes and creeds were proud to serve was enormous. For the first time, to everyone's surprise, women voted, moved resolutions and took their part as citizens. This and the abolition of purchase of commissions in the Army, which came about the same time and deprived the service of its aristocratic character, were violently opposed. The latter measure was indeed carried out by the prerogative of the Crown against the virtual opposition of the House of Lords. But the Education Bill had passed, and the Ballot Bill did the same in 1872, again amid tremendous opposition. Some of the opposition came indeed from good Liberals, like John Stuart Mill, who thought men should have the courage of their convictions and vote openly. One way or another, there awoke a new spirit amongst the people, for not only were men now allowed to vote freely and as they wished, but secret voting made it easier for women to vote, later on. At least it was held, truthfully or not, that the ' saving shelter of the ballot ' would give courage to the timid female, though as things turned out she was less timid than was supposed. The University Tests Bill, enabling students of all faiths to be admitted to the Universities of Oxford and Cambridge, was another great reform which came about this time.

All this has to do with the beginning of the decade— a decade which proved to be so important to the young. We children passed from childhood to youth and from more or less accepting what was given us to striking out on our own lines, different from those of our parents. Two or three family calamities made a deep impression on us and drew the family bonds closer. The first was the loss in 1875 of a very dear brother, aged sixteen—nearly seventeen. He was a clever boy—supposed to be the genius of the family— but more than that, he was a merry being, intensely musical, a wonderful mimic and bringing just the atmosphere of happiness and fun among us which we needed. A year later a terrible railway accident killed an uncle and two cousins ; and in 1877 our father died. He was considerably older than our mother, who was his second wife, and had of late years not been strong. But it left our mother to carry on alone, a task which was none too easy, without practical experience of managing land or money and with a family of boys of great individuality to bring up and start in the world. She was a very remarkable and attractive woman and grew in spiritual and intellectual stature as the years went on. And the years were many, for she lived as a widow for forty-eight years and died at a hundred years of age in 1925.

The early part of this decade was marked for us by a surprising and unprecedented revival in religion which had its main starting point in Edinburgh. This happened before our father's death, while we were still more or less living there. Such an event was sure to affect a family such as ours and make us dwell even more than usual on religious matters. It coincided, however, with a more advanced outlook on the part of my elder brothers and caused heart-searchings of a serious kind on the side both of parents and children, though these did not develop much before our father's death. The rest of this decade—or the most part of it—was marked by constant questionings and a general breaking away from old moorings. I don't think this made necessarily for unhappiness, because youth is so certain of itself that it enjoys raising new barriers and instituting new shibboleths which it little realizes are going to be as ruthlessly attacked by the generations to come.

This did not, however, happen at once : there was first of all a period of joy in discovering what books had to give one. The boys pursued the ordinary well-trod paths of school and university, with German universities included for the elders. Girls' education as stated took the form of classes at a day school, and then came a winter in Paris : a common combination. As usual a girl's education was thus extraordinarily scrappy. The classes that I attended were quite without relation to one another or to what had gone before. Some teachers were good and inspiring—others absolutely futile and incomprehensible. I often wonder whether there is not something to be said for this plan, which always reminded me of chickens finding the food they wanted by pecking around till they did so ! One emerged terribly ignorant in some directions, but really interested in others. And occasionally the systematically educated modern school-girl issues forth interested in none. In my day music was the one thing compulsory, and every girl learned to play the piano and hours of ' practising ' were often wasted. Gradually my brothers and I awoke to the delights of music, and especially of what was then called ' The Music of the Future ', meaning by that, Wagner in particular. That was a real awakening, quite separate from anything we were taught—a sort of revelation of what music could mean. And also a sort of protest, such as youth loves, for the older generation called it loud and meaningless sound. I can never forget what Tannhäuser and the Pilgrims'

Chorus and Lohengrin meant to us, though we never of course went to an opera, and hardly ever heard music properly rendered. There was still the Puritan dread of pleasure—even artistic pleasure—unless it were to lead to something useful to mankind. Could we use it for the service of God and of our fellows ? Otherwise it might draw us into evil ways.

Then we began occasionally to buy books for ourselves. One of the drawbacks to well-to-do youth—female youth at least—in these days was that it had no money to spend. If ordinary wants of food and clothing were supplied, nothing else was thought necessary, and all through one's young life this was a quite unnecessary drawback in a case where money was not unobtainable. Probably it resulted from our mother carrying on the tradition in which she was brought up. Later on my elder brother made the matter good, but it was a serious irk for a long time. Young men, of course, had to have their allowances till they earned for themselves.

So much has been written of late about Victorian childhood in a critical sense that one is apt to think of it as a period of pure repression and unhappiness. As a matter of fact, for those who had the good fortune to be born into a tolerably comfortable home there was indeed an order which might now be called institutional ; but it is absurd to say that this caused active unhappiness. The regularly arranged day, the insistence on punctuality and forms of an artificial sort, were tiresome, but not painful ; and they made for the sort of orderliness which helps incongruous individualities such as exist in any body of people, small or large, to get along together without rubbing one another up too disagreeably. Then in a family like ours, and there were many such in Scotland, the regular observance of the forms of religion—family prayers morning and night, church on Sundays, and so on, did not necessarily spell hypocrisy. It was true that there were many inconsistencies in the life ; prayers were often a form, and the household may have resented their bonds though they never dared to say so. But as in most cases prayers meant reading a chapter of the Bible, and though the chapters, taken as they were strictly in order from Genesis to Revelations, were sometimes unsuitable and often incomprehensible, they at least taught the listeners something of fine literature ; and this remained with them all their lives. One often recognizes in the speech of unedu-cated persons something which betokens that they have a grasp of expression such as Elizabethan literature gives, and remember how it has been obtained. Very frequently there is also to be found an unexpected understanding of some of the great mys-teries of life and death. It is the greatest loss to be without that splendid foundation of culture. We have also testimony to its practical use when we read of the help knowledge of Old Testament literature was to those like Lord Allenby whose work has been in Eastern countries.

Of course one is taking for granted that there was

something more than mere form in the religion put before one, and so indeed it was in our case, whatever it might have been in others. There were strange inhibitions about Sunday observance and keeping ' apart from the world ' in what seemed, and seems, an irrational way. But we knew that at the basis of these restrictions there was a deep reality. To cast off shams seems so simple, and as life tends to be conventionalized and fossilized, it is just as necessary to do this as it is for the snake to cast off his skin. But the skin had its use in its day, and so possibly had the conventions. It seems indeed as if each generation were bound to rebel against the previous one if any progress is to be made, and unluckily the process is painful.

Anyhow religion was a very real thing in our childhood and it affected us very deeply. The difference between doctrine and practice no doubt struck us acutely even when quite young. We were taught that there were only two alternatives set before us, and that it was a matter of infinite importance to decide which way should be chosen—one leading to eternal bliss and the other to eternal damnation. Yet how strange the attitude of our teachers and parents to these terrible facts ! I remember my youngest brother's dismay, when walking as a tiny boy with his mother one Sunday, they met a man marching along the street, pipe in mouth. ' That man is going to hell,' said the boy. And he was not only taken aback but really horrified by his gentle mother's words, ' You must not say that Willie : it is not for us to judge.'

Did his mother really believe what he had been told, or was she not honest or truthful—she in whom he had implicitly believed ? It was long before he got over that horrid alternative and was able to trust his mother again. Nothing she told him was quite the same as before.

My disappointment was connected with the destruction of books of fiction. Yes, they should be burned, said my father, and I looked forward to a lovely bonfire that never, alas, occurred. And more than that, my father openly read *Gil Blas* and Scott, though we were not allowed to read *Old Mortality* because of its attitude to the Covenanters, of whose sufferings we used to read on Sunday mornings !

Altogether for thoughtful children, the world was found to be full of mysterious complications and contradictions. We learnt the doctrines of Calvinism from our father : the distinction between Sanctification and Justification, between Free Will and Predestination, but even we children came soon to know that these doctrines that meant so much to our forefathers, who had indeed spent their birthright in maintaining them, were to us empty words. Our interests were quite other. We were concerned faintly at first but in a growing way with the conditions of our fellow beings. Could it be right that there should be in existence these miserable objects whom we saw when our father took us to see the historic closes and vennels of Edinburgh in order that we might learn about the famous robberies and murders, and see the debtors' refuge near

Holyroodhouse where he used once to visit a ne'er-do-weel connection of the family ? No, it was not right, but then we were told they were people who had not heard, or at least listened to, the glad tidings of the Gospel. There was, for instance, so-and-so, an old woman whose little room was perfectly clean and tidy, and she was contented just because she was good, and waiting the summons to her heavenly home in happiness. (One such I remember had fourteen cats in the room and said she was ' counting her blessings '.) We must have missions to teach people the truth and they would be as good. This was not wholly convincing because there were so many of the other sort, apparently making straight for hell, and yet we were not too much agitated about it. The old aunt who visited us was strong that it was the good people who should be cared for and did not approve of our mother's kindness to sinners ; to her all men were the same and she was ready to help all equally. To the indignation of her relatives she even sent a message to a poor woman about to be hanged for the murder of her husband's paramour, and who in her distress cried from the dock, ' My weans, my weans, what will they do ? ' Unluckily for my mother, her message reached the public prints—an unforgivable offence on the part of a young wife.

The Scottish logic of the Calvinists—so logical and yet so false—must have come hardly to the truly religious, but far from Calvinist, English mother. She sorrowed with all that sorrowed, good and bad, and

E

to the horror of the North Country relatives went
amongst those women who were termed ' fallen ' and
dared to say that there were those of the other sex who
had ' fallen ' with them.

How, one wonders, were people able to put their
heads in the sand and declare that those who rejected
the Gospel were beyond the pale ? What was there to
accept of Gospel in these close bug-infested rooms, with
dark stairs and smelling of dirt and all sorts of filth ;
for in those days there was no water laid on and little
light ? Do we hide our heads in the same way now,
though in another manner ?

In visiting the sick, a text was cast by pious people—
never by my mother—at the heads of the sufferers
and tracts were thrown from a carriage to the cottages
on the road. That last amused us children, but the
tracts were some of them rather terrifying. Many
were about the work of evangelists called, I think,
John Ashworth and Richard Weaver, of Rochdale,
and there was one dreadful one about the Hell-Fire
Club in Edinburgh and another showing a soldier
being flogged. He had been frequently flogged before his conversion but never after.

The temperance movement was affecting the
working classes fundamentally at this time, but I
don't think this applied to the richer people. It
was certainly a democratic movement, beginning with
unions of children and lodges of good Templars and
bands of temperance workers, culminating in the Blue
Ribbon movement. When the children of our small

town marched to our home to tea, they were armed with banners adorned with strange devices, such as ' Wha would hae a drucken man ', altered for the boys to the same sentiment as regards the wife. And our esteemed cook was cheered when she went to London on Boat Race day to see how the movement had, as she vainly thought, taken hold ! But there was no idea that I can recollect as to the propriety of giving whisky to tradesmen or other visitors or having wine at home. There was an enormous amount of drinking amongst the population, rich and poor, and one constantly met with drivers quite tipsy ; especially at New Year or on market days the streets were disgraceful. It says much for the workers of our land that this evil has, to a great extent, been combated mainly by themselves. It has made an enormous difference to society as a whole in our country.

There were still facts to remind one of the old days of the Rising of '45 and the earlier fighting in 1715, when all our villages were burned. The name Stewart had been suspect, and I remember one old lady known as Betty France whose real name was Betty Stewart, and in the big houses round there were many relics of Prince Charlie, who appears to have been a most untidy young man. Names were occasionally changed for other reasons, for a shepherd who lived above us in the hills was always known as Parker because he had been an ardent supporter of that eminent Whig, Charles Stuart Parker, who represented our county for some years.

Even in 1880 ' Sabbath Observance ' as it was termed was still strict. In a local newspaper of that year it was said that though church members observed Sunday in a sufficient way there was some driving for pleasure at a neighbouring town, Crieff, and that some of the young people of Auchterarder had been seen walking on the hills. However ' it was satisfactory to know that none of the farmers had ventured to do work on the Sabbath as had unfortunately been the case in some places '.

In those days there was more church-going of a conventional sort. It was considered the proper thing for farmers who had a certain standing, to go to church with their families in their gigs. In the very early days of my life this was done by the hill farmers in a farm cart lined with straw, in which, greatly to their joy, the children were set down. The cart was put up at the ' smiddy ', from which point of vantage the family set forth to walk. I don't think unmarried ploughmen, who lived most uncomfortably in bothies, went to church or, if so, it was very seldom, as is indeed the case still.

When a family or group of people are brought up in a tradition of protest against the usual views of their fellows, whether in politics or religion, there is always a risk of a certain self-consciousness and even a sense of self-sufficiency being developed. Our protest emanated generations back, rather than from the present day, and was mingled with an intense belief in loyalty to traditions. We had, we considered, a wonderful ancestry, and though the element of piety was only developed a couple of generations before, it was very real to us. And through the many generations previous to this, in the country in which we dwelt there was at least a history of good living or what we deemed to be such. One is old-fashioned enough to think this an advantage, though others think the reverse, and that it is better for each to tackle the problems of the world by and through himself. Of course, no one in this civilized world is free from traditions, but there are some who have fewer than others, and we had many.

On the whole the process of growing up is no easy one. Some of the most trying parts of life seem to come just at the time when one might be most happy. One hopes, but is not sure, that things are better now : then, it seemed that if a young woman were longing to be free and to do something whatever it was on her own, there was no chance of doing so. Schoolroom days passed and a winter in Paris was a pleasant interlude before settling down to country life, for the Edinburgh house was unnecessary after my father's death. The visit to Paris was in company with my mother and nurse, who now acted as my mother's maid. It was not a satisfactory plan for me so far as learning French was concerned, but it was admirable for my mother, who was able to do many things that she could not do before and to give expression to faculties hitherto latent. The main one was painting. She had quite special gifts in that direction, but as a girl living in the country, she could have but little instruction, and to her deep disappointment a plan to work in a studio in London while living with an old friend there, was frustrated as being not quite proper. So although it came to her in middle life, being able to work in a studio and copy at the Louvre was a pure joy. Later on she exhibited some of her work in the Scottish Academy. I had music lessons from an exiled Pole, and enjoyed them. He, poor man, felt bitterly about the woes of his country. He used to say, after an attempt was made on the emperor's life, 'Le Czar sera tué : mais—que voulez-vous ? ' The life so threatened indeed was soon to come to an end in the manner predicted. I had no special gifts in the way of painting but I also worked with a Mme de Châtillon—a rather well-known painter of the Victorian type—and sat with my mother at the Louvre, as well as having singing lessons and, oddly enough, some instruction in dancing, since dancing was forbidden and I never went to a ball. This class was somehow thought to be a continuation of what was formerly called calisthenics. But the atmosphere of Paris delighted us both. It was a bitterly cold winter : the Seine was frozen hard and there were great piles of snow in the streets. When the thaw came it was an extraordinary sight to see great blocks of ice being carried down. This, however, counted little to us in our warm surroundings. The shops were lovely, the picture galleries a delight, and

though we never went to the theatre, Sarah Bernhardt seemed to dominate the scene, and we came into
touch with a side of life we never knew before. We
bought her photographic pictures, and read about her,
and once by good fortune, she gave a reading for a
charity which we could conscientiously attend. When
the brothers visited us they did not have the same
scruples, and once I went to the Grand Opera and
saw *Faust*, an occasion never to be forgotten.

This winter in Paris did a great deal for us as a family
in liberating us from the shackles of Scottish Victorian and Puritan propriety. I even went to some
parties at friends' houses, for we had some friends in
Paris. This was not a great success, for rather to my
dismay a young man tried to make friends, a foreigner
of course, and even called with some excuse about
giving tickets for a show. However, my mother said
she would see him and she did so, firmly and de-
cisively !

I rather think my mother had some qualms about
our lives in Paris, and to make good we went to a
mission in a poor part of Paris and tried to help the
poor, who suffered much in the cold, as well as attending various Protestant churches or chapels. I look
back on this part of my life as a pleasant one, and I
certainly learned something from it. I got my first
long evening dress then and for the time being was
interested in such matters. My mother, a beautiful
woman, always liked her clothes, and took pride in
them, though she would not allow this ; she dressed

always appropriately and with dignity but still had to wear the doleful widow's garb of crape though my father had been dead some time. But this was modified in Paris, and the becoming white pointed widow's cap with its long tail behind was discarded in favour of something not quite so distinctive, but still pretty. Paris seemed to have recovered much of the beauty it had when she visited it on her wedding tour and admired (and I think copied in dress and coiffure) the beautiful young Empress Eugénie. There were still ruins left from the war and the Commune ; the Tuileries were but a shell, and other things reminded one of these sad times. But the spirit of the nation was indomitable, and the tales we heard of the siege were told as of a time long since passed, though it was really not long before.

The return to the quiet of a Scottish home with all its small interests seemed something of a débâcle. I rather think my mother (who had not a natural turn for accounts) had exceeded her income, since the Edinburgh house was still on her hands as well as the country home, and agriculture was going from bad to worse owing to the depression and bad weather of the later seventies. When the Edinburgh house was finally got rid of, things were better, but the sons had to be set up in life. Anyhow it was decided that we should live quietly in the country and go to London to join my elder brother for three months or so in the year.

This meant finding an occupation for most of the

year in an isolated part of the world, and though I always loved country life, it was a change to be grown up and on one's own. My first conviction was that I was not educated, and I thought of how this could be put right. I should have loved going to college, but college in those days was unusual for girls, and the idea was not encouraged. It was also expensive. For an only daughter to leave a widowed mother was indeed considered to be quite out of the question, and no one made the plan seem feasible. There was in those days a new movement for carrying on correspondence classes, and I joined in the scheme and read books like *The Decline and Fall of the Roman Empire* and Bryce's *Holy Roman Empire*. I also practised and read Italian with my mother. Had gaieties been allowed I should have had that recreation and fun, but they were not, and in pre-car and pre-bicycle days 'neighbours' were few and not easily got at. Altogether until towards the beginning of the eighties things looked black and grim : it was the least happy part of a long and on the whole very happy life. It seems to me, on looking back, that this is the only time in my life that I suffered from what is now called frustration, the disease which is supposed to attack unmarried women. Certainly I never knew what it meant later on : life seemed brimming full and running over. I should, of course, have liked to study for a profession, but that was an impossible idea unless one were in the sad position of ' having to work for one's bread ' and that would have been then a terrible state of affairs. Even a brother wrote of the melancholy fact after he had been to see Mrs. Langtry act. ' She was a lady and acted like a lady, but what a sad thing it was that she should have to do so ! '

No doubt with the growth of education and culture, the pursuit of other pleasures spread and developed. Especially was this so with athleticism. The bicycle— the liberator of young womankind—had not yet arrived but lawn tennis had begun, and in Paris I got a curious silk apron which went right round the dress, with a large pocket for balls, which was supposed to be suitable for the game. We girls all wore aprons of some kind for tennis, and full and long skirts : blouses came in later. This game gave an opportunity for mixing with the other sex and tennis parties soon developed. Altogether there was at length, undoubtedly, a breaking away, even on the part of serious people, from the idea that life was made for work alone and for getting on in the world and that mere pleasure was a dangerous thing. I don't think we entered much into the new spirit because of the deep religious principles that still made us fear being ' carried away ' by amusements as such. But our ground-work was religious, not mercantile or utilitarian as was much of the hardworking Puritanism of the early nineteenth century. Still we had the idea that to read a book of a non-instructive kind during the working day was indefensible, and novels at such hours were banned. In the country we began the

Reproduced by permission of the Proprietors of 'Punch'

TENNIS IN THE EIGHTIES

excellent practice of reading aloud in the evenings. My mother was a delightful reader and I usually span, or carved in wood. She had not been allowed to read novels in her youth and now the classical novels were a joy to her. So we got through Scott, Dickens, Thackeray, George Eliot, Jane Austen, the Brontës, Disraeli, and many old-fashioned novels like *Evelina*, as well as *Gil Blas* and Dumas. Of course, this was a matter of many years and a good many of the novels were read more than once or twice. In this hurried and restless age there seems to be little of this enjoyable entertainment, and it is a pity that it is so.

Nor was there the crowding into towns that followed later and had gone on earlier, and the rural population seemed more or less content to remain such despite lack of the amenities of life. But the same desire for leisure and the enjoyment of leisure that was seen elsewhere was beginning to influence the country-man. The weekly walk to market town and public-house would not suffice him always and the woman was not always satisfied to live a life of drudgery. Beauty still existed in the country, but in the towns there were no bounds to the destruction of beauty and the promotion of ugliness that took place through the nineteenth century. Bad houses were built and they were ugly as well as bad. Men seemed to have lost the sense of beauty that is supposed to characterize the civilized man : and Scotland seemed to me to suffer more than England from this evil. The atmosphere even permeated the home, and it was difficult to combat, though no doubt it was beginning to be combated at the time when the younger generation at last became sensible of it, and rather inadequately tried to find something better.

In 1880, to everyone's surprise, Disraeli's ministry ended and a new Liberal Government under Gladstone took its place. Disraeli had stood indeed for imperialism, but he had also accepted the fact that new conditions existed and that the new democracy must be considered and appealed to. 'Jingoism' was, however, disliked and foreign policy was not a matter of much interest to the populace, especially to the country people.

Liberal politics were always interesting to me but a good deal of the political talk in the late seventies struck one as being rather clap-trap. In England there was more 'show' in elections than in Scotland. I remember one election in a part of England where we often stayed, at which there were four grey horses in the carriage of the sober Liberal candidate, the ladies being decked in blue and white. Indeed there was a perfect procession of horses and men. As the issue was Free Trade versus Protection, loaves were elevated on poles, showing the 'Gladstone loaf' as compared with the meagre 'Salisbury loaf', and there were inscriptions on banners such as 'The House of Lords Mend it or End it' (so often said in the last fifty years !), 'Why should the Labourer wait ?' (for the vote), and so on. The members of the House of Lords 'which claimed Divine Right to

govern ' were ' following their leader into the sea, in
which they and their privileges may be engulfed '.
Despite the verbiage, it all seemed simple and clear
in the days of the Liberal Revival of 1880, and the
issues were apparent to all. It was pointed out that
labourers were demanding the vote ; indignation
existed with the House of Lords and its blocking
measures (though the speakers were many of them
directing their steps surely and clearly towards that
much abused but long lived institution), and the great
names had only to be mentioned to be cheered to the
echo : Gladstone—the G.O.M.—and Bright were still
living and active forces. ' We do not ask what is
expedient for this party : we ask what is *Right*.' Do
we indeed ? And the ' genuine working man (no one
has seen a Tory working man) asks who had ever done
business with any man who would not like to hold a
bit of land ? ' The pathos of it all comes over one.
If we had only known what was right and had done
it as we so glibly declared we were doing, all might
have been well.

When a young woman reached the later teens she
seemed to enter a new phase of life. So at least it was
in those far-away days. A long dress with a slight train
even in the daytime was *de rigueur*. Bustles were no
more, but there were curious sorts of padding to make
the figure the desired shape (so different from the
present slimness) and stays moulded the waist to what
was considered a seemly size (say 21 or not over

25 inches) for a tall girl well developed. The first formal visits were made to country houses, and a small trousseau was required. The solemnity of the visits was impressive, for the great still preserved their place in society almost unimpaired. Footmen, none under six feet high, abounded ; and they marshalled the guests to carriages, while maids and luggage were provided for in omnibuses. Luggage was portentous, for the voluminous skirts of satin or moiré required much room, and no one thought of the unfortunate porters who had to carry the boxes. The fitted dressing-case, without which no lady travelled, was a constant care, for it seemed always on the eve of being lost. Then morning prayers were something to be remembered. There was the row of chairs set out for the gentry to which they advanced while an enormous array of servants stood to attention. Immediately everyone turned round as at a signal, and knelt. The guests had walked into the room in order of precedence, and so had the servants : there was the regular and well-understood precedence of the house-party and also the possibly more intricate order of precedence of the maids and valets, which depended on that of their masters and mistresses. No under-servant was allowed to speak at table till the upper servants departed for the housekeeper's room, there to complete their meals. Young servants had to be up betimes and get their work done before there was a chance of their meeting the gentry in the house, and they had to be ready for morning prayers. All

the servants were marshalled to church on Sundays—
the men in livery and the women in black frocks and
bonnets. One girl told me that she had sometimes
hidden under the bed to escape the ceremony ! Our
dear nurse was now my mother's maid and mine, and
she never failed to make friends in the stiffest company.
Without a maid in a great house the unfortunate lady
visitors would be lost, as it was impossible to get
attention for these unusual guests.

At eleven o'clock exactly, the custom was for all to
rise and go to bed. The butler and footmen stood by
the door and the gentlemen handed lighted candles in
old-fashioned silver candlesticks to the ladies. So
armed, all wended their way through dark passages
and to their candle-lit rooms. A fixed bath was
almost unknown, but the housemaids brought up
great cans of water from downstairs, hot and cold, and
there were bright fires burning so that it was quite
cheerful. Coals were cheap in those days. In Scotland
they were usually about ten or twelve shillings a ton,
if one were not too inconveniently placed as regards
coal pits.

We often stayed with family connections in a large
house in Warwickshire and when there, I used to go
with the châtelaine to visit the cottages and schools.
It all shocked my Scottish democratic mind considerably. The school-teachers were subservient to
the last degree, and, of course, the children were the
same. I disliked going into these schools. Then we
went round the labourers' cottages armed with soup,

or giving promises of soup, and I felt all the time that to give these people proper wages and decent houses would be the real cure for their many woes. The labourers were receiving 10s. to 12s. a week and it was explained to me that though my hosts were able to pay higher wages (for they were rich) it would not be fair to other neighbouring landlords to do so, since if it were done they would not be able to carry on their farms. This was, of course, the time of great agricultural depression that had come to a head in 1879 when a soaking summer ruined the crops, and I can remember seeing the blackened sprouting 'stooks' standing out in the end of October. There was a certain amount of pilfering, which was severely dealt with, but one could not wonder at rabbits being snared or pigs illicitly fed. Often enough, poaching was the only way in which meat could be procured. Small punishments were administered for offences, such as omitting the delinquent's name from a Christmas feast.

It was from South Warwickshire that the marvellous news came that the labourers were actually asking for a rise in wages, and, impossible to believe, forming a labourers' union after the pattern of the artisans'. Then, more marvellous than ever, they were said to be on strike and actually making speeches. I must say this surprised me when I saw the men.

For a time this incredible strike which took place early in the seventies was the talk of London, and then it was found that there was an 'agitator' at its head,

whose name was Joseph Arch. This extraordinary
man had actually travelled away from his native
village in South Warwickshire to the next county and
even beyond and had ventured into the manufacturing
areas which were not so far away. He had heard there
about strikes and combinations of men who made their
demands as boldly as their masters. He returned to
his village not long before we used to go to that
county, and found talk of real starvation on the wage
of eight or ten shillings a week. Since the slump in
agriculture was on, the farmers insisted that ' they
could not give higher wages for the rents they paid
to the landlords would not allow them to do so '.
There was some truth in this, but the landlords were
long in admitting it. Still the people observed that the
farmers lived well and also that the landlords lived
luxuriously. Hunting foxes and shooting immense
numbers of pheasants were the main amusements.
What, said Arch, of a strike ? He was a volunteer
preacher of Methodism—one of those of whom George
Eliot wrote from her knowledge of Methodism, obtained through her Methodist aunt, and Warwickshire
home. By some miraculous means (for there were no
written circulars, and calling day labourers together
was like proclaiming a revolution) a meeting of about
a thousand labourers was held under a great chestnut
tree which thereby became famous. The idea of forming a union was taken up with enthusiasm. Branches
of it were formed and Arch was its only support, until
suddenly some famous Londoners, including Auberon

Herbert, the socialist brother of Lord Carnarvon, so original in his views, took it up, as did Dilke and others. The landlords were horrified, and Disraeli, then Prime Minister, supported them so that it became a political question : the Liberal party on the whole stood with Arch, though when Cardinal Manning came forward as his supporter, the Methodist preacher was decried as an agent of the Jesuits. In the end, though the Union did not bring about great reforms, it did result in attention being drawn to the plight of the English agricultural worker and to the necessity of enfranchising him so that he could make his grievances vocal. This was done by the Reform Bill of 1884, though few believed that the English labourer could properly exercise his vote.

Our hostess in Warwickshire was a good woman in the religious sense, and went so far as to see and talk to Arch, explaining to him his errors. I think his Methodism appealed to her : her coachman was an ardent Baptist preacher who used to baptize people in a stream in the park ; and though she was a church-woman, she saw to her livings being held by low church clergy and approved of my mother and me going occasionally to a ' Little Bethel '—Methodist, I think. The service was to me touching : very simple and homely, and the singing was led by an orchestra of strange instruments, bassoons I fancy, and fiddles. The life of the English peasant was extraordinarily elementary and the gulf between him and his overlords was immense, probably greater than

in any civilized European country. It was the time
when Disraeli (who liked to assume the rôle of a landlord) used to preside over the ceremony of giving a
prize of a blue coat with brass buttons to the venerable
labourer who had for the longest number of years
contrived to support the largest family without having
recourse to parish relief. It seemed a strange reward
for having lived a long life of penury, and was naturally laid hold of by Joseph Arch, who stated that one
of those proud rustics had after all to seek the shelter
of the workhouse where the wearing of a brass
buttoned blue coat would probably be forbidden. It
is not wonderful that it took generations to forget the
life then led by country men and women.

If country life was strangely limited, I don't fancy
that town life was so very different as far as food and
clothing were concerned. I can never forget, when
we were young, the effect upon me of going to London
to visit our relatives as we children did every year, and
seeing the poor people there. We had a long journey
in the Limited Mail (a train limited as to coaches,
which in early days had luggage on the top) ; it left
Edinburgh in the afternoons and reached London at a
preternaturally early hour, when our poor aunts had
to be up to receive us. The first class carriages were
very comfortable, having pulling-out seats on which
we slept. By the decade of which I write I daresay the
boys sometimes travelled third class, but I usually
went with my parents who would not have thought
of doing so. In those days it was one of the things

that 'were not done'. After the Paris time, when money was rather concerning my mother, judging from one of her letters, she had evidently suggested our travelling second or third class, along with our former nurse. There was, however, immediately an urgent protest from her eldest son. He begged her to assure him that she would not think of such a thing. If she did it, it would greatly distress him. Of course, third class in those days meant 'travelling hard'. There were no cushions on the seats and often the compartments were not fully separated. But I think by the beginning of the eighties things were better. Second class was fairly comfortable and in it servants always travelled. In Scotland anyhow travelling third class made one subject to meeting drunken people, and the floors were abominably dirty as spitting was everywhere prevalent. Men spat on the kitchen floors as well as on the streets, and made things disgusting for all their neighbours. These minor evils are often forgotten. It always seemed to me odd that women never spat, and though they indeed never smoked—or at least only very old women smoked—that did not wholly explain the matter. Smoking was then of course held to necessitate spitting. The railway carriages were cold, for the only means of heating was by tins of hot water at one's feet, and the tins were often freezing or else so hot that one's shoes were ruined, or if not ruined, made to creak.

The buses had lovely straw on the floor and so had the cabs—and we liked the smell of it and the pleasure of

sinking our feet amongst it—but the trains had none.
The guard was always preternaturally attentive, and
was rewarded by half-a-crown before one reached London.   In day journeys to London, there was a halt of
twenty minutes at Preston (or York, if travelling that
way) for food, which was eaten hectically in the railway
buffet by our servants and ourselves when moving *en
masse* as a household.   I have a vivid memory of these
desperate rushes for food and drink all through our
journeys, for, of course, there were no restaurant cars
and luncheon baskets had not been evolved. We passed
through the level country of the Southern Counties
with surprise, when we were very young.   And our
nurse used to say to us, ' look at it : it is like a billiard
table,' and so indeed it was to our northern eyes.
The southern speech and manners always impressed us
too, and the appearance of the houses.   Oddly enough,
Scottish people often feel more at home in France
than in England.   The French ways are more like
Scottish in some particulars and our nurse always
said the older people were like her grannie—mutches
and all—and she felt quite at home in Paris, more so
than in London.   But the English, she had to acknow-
ledge, were more polite than the Scots.   ' Tuckets ;
here' was replaced by ' Your tickets if you please :
thank you ', which surprised us.

Once in the London cab, with piled-up luggage, we
were pursued by poor men, hoping for a few pence for
helping to disgorge our effects and carry them to our
rooms. These men would run for miles from Euston or

King's Cross to Onslow Square or Queen Anne Street, our usual destinations. Of course, the old horse that drew the ' growler ' went none too fast, and the driver to my grief kept checking its mouth or whipping to get any motion at all. Then we passed through such desolate streets. Seven Dials, or Soho, was a centre of poverty and wickedness where one used to see fights in the streets between women as well as men. The days of Dickens were not far off and there were plenty of ' characters ' not unlike his. The cabbies especially, with their many capes, were full of talk and rough in the tongue when fares came to be discussed. They were frequently enough drunken, and one had to look out for that and choose one with the appearance of sobriety, for collisions were frequent. The hansom drivers were of another class and had superior ways and superior horses. One felt ' someone ' in a hansom, and by this decade, ladies could drive in them alone. The great point was to choose a good horse and spin along with it. The bus horses were not bad, but they had a hard time of it on the slippery roads. The drivers were red-faced and stout, with many rugs to protect them, and excellent conversationalists, I believe, with the lucky people who managed to climb on the knife-board. How this was managed I always wondered, for it looked hard enough to climb the horizontal ladder to the ordinary seats on the top of the bus, which were placed sideways so that people sat back to back. Natur-ally women never attempted the feat, and the ' better classes ' seldom travelled in buses if they could afford

anything better. The conductors, like the drivers,
were characters in their own way ; they stood on the
step with nothing but a strap to hold on to, and tried
to persuade the travellers by foot to enter their portals,
by encouraging words such as ' Benk, Benk—only a
penny '. If you did enter you had to be very careful
of your pockets. Honesty is a virtue that has greatly
developed : for in old days small change had to be carefully counted. By the end of this decade we sometimes went by bus, more particularly by a big one, with
an extra trace horse for the hill, that took one up to
Hampstead. The railway went only as far as Swiss
Cottage, and after that there were fields where now
are all the streets from Fitzjohn's Avenue to Finchley
Road. We often paid visits to our friends in Hampstead which in those days was quite countrified. There
was what our nurse called a ' boss tree ', i.e. a tree
with a hollow in it, in the midst of the fields which
we had to cross in walking, and we always hurried past
it, especially if it were getting to be dusk. By the end
of this decade, however, there were, of course, the
Inner and Outer Circles of the Underground Railway,
and this took one a good deal nearer one's usual des-
tination. Gower Street was famed for being the most
sulphurous of all the underground stations and near
the exits a chemist kept a mixture, termed the ' Underground Mixture ', with which to resuscitate unfortunate
people overcome by the fumes.

When we were children we were, of course, taken to
see the sights of London, such as the Crystal Palace

A City Omnibus in the Rain

and Mme. Tussaud's. When I was very small the
Chamber of Horrors thrilled me and kept me from
sleeping, but later on we adored it. The Crystal Palace
also thrilled us children, especially as we were allowed
to buy some trifle from the booths. One drawback
when we were taken out in this way was the absence
of tea-shops or places where we could go for luncheon.

Sundays in London were chiefly spent by us in
church-going. We always went to hear Mr. Spurgeon
at least once in a visit, and were driven there in our
aunt's victoria. She had an excellent coachman who
was also a lay preacher, or at least a speaker at meetings,
for he used to talk of ' me and Radnor ' (Lord Radnor) as fellow speakers.

There were naturally no picture galleries open, nor
any places of amusement, so that Sundays were not so
very different from what we knew in Scotland. The
underground railway stopped during church hours—
whether in the hope that the men would go to church
or to encourage travellers to do so, I know not.

THE THIRD DECADE
1882-1892

YOUNG WOMANHOOD

In 1884 my mother took a house for a few months in London, and by this time the 'aesthetic' movement was in full swing, in dress, furniture and music, for the so-called 'music of the future' was now all the rage. This brought about changes in domestic life of a notable kind. Up to this date labour-saving was unknown in private houses. Hitherto these houses seemed to have been built and furnished with the view of making them as difficult to run as possible. Unlimited servants were required to keep them reasonably clean, and the servants' quarters in May-fair, where we were living, were disgraceful. Men-servants slept in the pantry where they washed the dishes, and the kitchens were damp and dark. Of course, in those days, no difficulty was had in securing menservants any more than maidservants, of whom there was an unstinted supply, at wages which were low. Servants had to be numerous for the life that was usually led, and the mass of furniture that had to be tended.

In the country there were rows of oil lamps that had to be carefully cleaned to keep them free of smell, and though gas was mostly used in town, it was not the kind of gas we know of now. The general improvement of gas lighting with the aid of incandescent burners came later, and so of course did electric lighting. But while in Paris in 1879-80 we had seen some arc electric lamps as a wonderful new development, and when visiting an uncle in 1882, I wrote to my mother that I had been taken to the little Savoy Theatre to see Gilbert and Sullivan's *Patience*, and that the theatre was beautifully done up in yellow plush and lighted with ' Swan ' electric lamps ' enclosed in frosted glass which gave them an extremely pleasant effect, something like the first streaks of dawn '. The aesthetic D'Oyly Carte had indeed shown great enterprise in lighting the theatre electrically by this date. The stage had no less than 824 lamps to illuminate it, and there were 370 more in the house. One must not forget, too, that in those days each installation had to have its own plant, dynamo etc., which was expensive, and that the fittings were still primitive. Lord Kelvin and other advanced people managed to have electric lighting in their houses by 1881, and Sir Coutts Lindsay got electric light installed in the Grosvenor Gallery, the centre of the new artistic movement. Probably the new invention induced the gas-lighting companies to improve their plant, in case they were displaced by their rivals.

To visit the ' Grosvenor Gallery, greenery yallery ' was our delight, hoping as we did, to see there some of the ' new ' visitors in artistic garb. The movement of course went on quite independently of the aesthetes so-called, who were following in the steps of Oscar Wilde and his admirers, and the result was interesting, as it affected all classes of the community. I remember when I went to London about 1880 the excitement of finding my uncle and aunt's very Victorian rooms done up in greens of various hues with artistic wallpapers, for Morris papers were coming into existence. The movement was taken as a joke by the older-fashioned people—but it was a real revulsion from the heavy, ugly Victorian furniture whose only virtue (and it was a great one) was that if expensive it was usually well made. Of course, there was a great deal of veneer and I suppose shoddy work, but as a rule, the drawers ran well, and hinges acted as hinges should.

Real ugliness has an effect on children, and it is well worth while making things round them beautiful. I can never forget the ugliness of our schoolroom in Edinburgh. The rest of the house was well furnished, with good rosewood and Utrecht velvet furniture in the drawing-room and rather beautiful marble mantelpieces and glass-drop chandeliers. But it seemed as if the refuse had gone upstairs. I think smell is remembered almost more than sight, and I can never forget the disagreeable smell of the ugly brown cardboard slabs placed on an iron stand on which our atlases rested. The carpet was of a dim crimson and the one armchair for our tutor of a sort of crimson rep. In the country everything was different : it was simple but sweet and fresh, and even as one entered the house there was a fresh scent such as I like to think of still, but which I cannot describe. Clean chintzes covered the chairs, and we had home-made scones instead of baker's bread and plenty of milk in old-fashioned white jugs adorned with raised ferns.

Certainly we owe a deep debt of gratitude to those who showed us how, without great expense, beauty and bright colouring could be brought into the home. I remember the delight we had in choosing one of Morris's papers for my brother John's lodgings in St. Giles', Oxford, in 1888, and a couple of years later helping him to furnish a small house. At this time also, we began to read Ruskin and to be impressed by his views on art, as well as on ethics and economics, though the impression was much more vivid as regards the first. I came to see a beauty in the trees and hills that I had never seen before, and to feel, what terribly oppressed me, a sense of despair when I thought of the multitudes who saw nothing of these beauties, and lived in the dark alleys I had visited in London.

As I had plenty of time, I took to practising the piano vigorously and had lessons from a very competent and delightful instructor, Mr. Lichtenstein, in Edinburgh. My practising was done before breakfast, and I remember one morning I found the piano dumb. The explanation appeared when I examined its inside organs which were stuffed with paper by a brother whose bedroom adjoined, and who did not wish his slumbers disturbed ! My mother and I played duets and with some friends we managed some quartettes for two pianos—mainly symphonies of Beethoven. This home music seems to have now disappeared : perhaps wireless has taken its place, but there is not the same fun in it, even if it is better.

While in London, my mother and I visited on Sunday evenings at a hospital for the epileptic and paralysed, and I helped the patients to sing hymns. The hospital is now a great and famous institution, but in those days it was composed of some rather charming old houses joined together. Though beautifully panelled, they were infested with rats, which used to run across the beds of the paralysed men. Strangely enough, the patients did not mind their uninvited visitors and even fed them. There were male nurses only in the men's wards, and though I knew nothing of nursing in those days I felt that things were not what they might be. And the men had fits continually in the midst of our hymns, which was rather disconcerting. Long after this I came to know a good deal about the management of hospitals and nursing from serving on the governing bodies of more than one hospital, and taking part in nursing movements for the registration of nurses by the State and so on. Of course, nursing standards have changed beyond recognition, and so have the hospitals themselves, and especially the nurses' quarters. But, though the modern world will hardly believe it, there was a homely feeling about the old system, with its simple appliances, that anyhow seemed to make for happiness. When things were bad, as in many infirmaries and poor law institutions they were, the result was, of course, disgraceful.

On looking back upon one's early life, the things that strike one as forcibly as any, concern the changes that have taken place as regards mobility. In our earlier days journeys were a problem, even after the time when an ' electric telegram ' was sent as a matter of course to say ' arrived safely '. This telegram was our first thought on reaching Euston on our annual visits to London. Of course, in starting from the country any journey was rather a complicated affair. First of all, one had to be sent to the station in a carriage, with luggage in a cart, not always available. Then one had to go to the county town by a slow train in order to change into the express. To me these drawbacks were nothing to the pleasure of travelling at all. One was only too ready to face them.

But what made a prodigious difference to the ordinary young person was the introduction of bicycles. In 1879 I wrote from London of an extraordinary sight, a lady attired in a sort of riding habit tricycling, unconcerned, down Oxford Street. That was the beginning of what developed during the next ten or twelve years, till in the nineties, bicycling, not tricycling, became the rage. We all tricycled more or less to begin with, but found our progress not what it might be, and several of us had accidents ; my uncle, Sir John Burdon Sanderson, a very serious one on

Basingstoke Hill : we had lesser ones. A woman had to take her courage in her hands to mount even a safety bicycle, for it betokened something fast, and our full skirts and petticoats were not well adapted for the work. Mercifully coats and skirts came into vogue before long, perhaps incited to do so by the new form of locomotion, and along with them came sailor hats ; and hence the lady cyclist in the end presented quite a good and tidy appearance, though various means had to be adopted of so fastening her skirts on her legs as to prevent them entangling themselves in the back wheel, or worse still showing her legs to the public, an unforgivable offence.

Thus it was that the young woman found her liberty and with it the power to make friends of both sexes, for young men and women bicycling together, though not thought quite proper, came to be tacitly per-mitted. That, however, belongs to a few years later. In the eighties long walks were the order of the day. I never managed more than twenty-five miles or so, but my brothers walked seventy and even over a hundred miles on end. A seventy-mile walk was to the top of Ben Lawers and back to our home : one of $103\frac{1}{2}$ miles taken by the two younger men was from Ballater to Cloan. They used to arrive tired and rather footsore, but were none the worse for their expeditions. We were all used to walking from child-hood, as our father encouraged this and made a point of showing his disregard for the notices that ' Tres-passers will be prosecuted '. We had days out as

G

children, climbing the higher of the Ochils, and taking tea with shepherds or else carrying our luncheon. The elder people—the men, at least—always carried flasks of whisky as a necessary accompaniment, just as it was in curling and other winter sports. Somehow women, weaker as they were reckoned, never required these aids to exertion ! Our mother took a prominent part in all these expeditions, and in great measure directed them with considerable force of character ; but I never remember her dressed otherwise than in her full Victorian skirts—very likely of silk—reaching to the feet, and voluminous petticoats, as well as a Victorian bonnet : never a hat. This did not impede her progress at all, and she continued to walk till well over seventy. In her youth she was reputed to have sent her English friends home in invalid carriages ! One wonders that the excess of underclothing lasted so long, seeing that in the eighties the woman's movement was moving apace. Women were taking medical degrees and the women's colleges were flourishing but any hope of such an avocation was, for me, nipped in the bud. My brothers were scattered, one remained in Edinburgh as a lawyer. John moved to Oxford after having graduated and after a tumultuous time of controversy with his teachers in Edinburgh. He had thereafter some opportunity of study in Jena and elsewhere in Germany, while Richard settled in London.

The absence of the brothers, with whom one's life was so closely intertwined, made a good deal of dif-

ference to me, even though they returned as frequently
as they could. I got interested in the affairs of the
little town near us, and we had lectures which were the
source of much anxiety, for either the lecturer or the
lanternist was apt to fail, and the hall was terribly
cold. However, certain lectures (endowed by Combe,
the phrenologist) on Health were enormously popular
and always crowded. One wonders if this would be
so now. It was indeed in the more remote districts the
beginning of the teaching of how to live healthily, now
become so universal. It was followed by ambulance
lectures in connection with the Order of St. John,
given in 1885 by my brother John, who at the time
was doing some very interesting experimental work at
Dundee on the air in schools, sewers and slum houses.
He was at last freed from attendance at those Edinburgh professorial lectures which so bored him, and
was starting on his own original work with a con-
genial friend, Professor Carnelly, a promising scientist,
who died early. These ambulance lectures caused the
greatest excitement in Auchterarder, especially as a
skeleton was brought to illustrate them. All classes
of people attended, and the lecturer was most realistic
in his methods, even showing, practically, how to use
the stomach pump ! He had interesting demonstrations of how bacteria developed on jellies, and he was
indeed the first amongst us to show in a popular
but convincing way the necessity of preserving cleanli-
ness in wounds. I never attended more original
lectures, for he had no idea of following the beaten

track or the syllabus laid down. Later on there were many other lectures on First Aid and Nursing, in connection with the St. Andrew's and Red Cross Associations, but these, being the first, seemed the most exciting. I had attended First Aid lectures when in London and passed my St. John's examination at the Polytechnic in Regent Street and received my certificate from Princess Christian. I did not realize how much I was to have to do with the movement later on when the Voluntary Aid Detachments were started two years before the Great War.

During the later eighties we had plenty of visitors at our home at Cloan, and amongst others, Herbert Asquith (as he was then called, for he became 'Henry', his second name, after his second marriage) and his beautiful and singularly charming first wife, Helen. She was intelligent but devoid of ambition and only anxious to live happily with her family. I can see her with her splendid boys who played in the garden at Hampstead, and her little girl, who took part in a charade. When my brother was ill she insisted on having him to stay with her and be nursed into health. Of course the two young men of like tastes and not dissimilar ages were constantly together. My brother and Asquith sometimes also travelled together and once they went as far as to Italy and France. 'H. H. A. proved an excellent travelling companion,' Richard said, though ' his French was but a trifle better than mine, which wasn't saying much '. Asquith lost his very remarkable mother in 1888.

ASQUITH, 1885

Asquith's style of speaking, at this time, was clear and concise as later, and admirable in delivery, and yet he did not move a country audience, for they thought him cold. It was difficult for these young lawyers to adapt themselves to the people they had to address, and I have sat through many rather chilly meetings in the country villages. Sometimes a distinguished Queen's Counsel, like Sir Horace Davey, would endure the enthusiastic ' For he's a jolly good fellow ' with a long-drawn look of agony on his face, and obvious dread of the chairing which might follow !

A very interesting young man who visited us was J. K. Stephen, the son of a distinguished father and himself author of *Lapsus Calami*. His untimely death, resulting from an accident, was tragic. He was standing on a windmill, eighty feet from the ground, and the arm of the mill struck him on the head. My brother had the highest opinion of his legal capacity and often discussed obscure legal points with him.

Mr. Andrew Carnegie came to live at a country house not far off, and we saw a great deal of him and his attractive young wife. He had interesting guests, whom he asked us to meet, and amongst these visitors was Matthew Arnold, who took me in to dinner and astonished me by his knowledge of the neighbouring fishing streams, since he did not personally know the neighbourhood. To my surprise, he seemed even to know the little ' burns '. I enjoyed his talk very much, as I had always had a great admiration for his work and felt it an honour to meet him. He had the stiff, rather highbrow Victorian face one knew so well from pictures, but he was delightful to me. The dinner party was slightly marred for some by a favourite dog getting loose amongst the hats and coats of the guests and reducing the former to pulp ! Not all appreciated the joke.

This was the beginning of a real friendship on my part with Mr. and Mrs. Carnegie ; the former used to say to me as to many others, ' I shall not leave a fortune as a curse to a child of mine.' As we know, he did his best to carry out this dictum, even after his adored daughter was born. He was most generous in respect of the library in which I was interested, and long after this when he instituted the Trust for the United Kingdom and bestowed a couple of million pounds upon it, I was pleased by hearing that he wished me to be a trustee, since he usually considered that women's sphere was elsewhere than in the tangle of public life. Oddly enough Labouchere, though an out-and-out iconoclast, shared this opinion.

The Herbert Pauls were other visitors at this time. He had a mordant tongue, and was extraordinarily witty and clever in repartee. He was rather a terror to many people, owing to his incisive sayings, though at heart he was kind and affectionate. His wife was and is everything that is delightful, and smoothed over difficulties. But he was hardly a good candidate for a middle class Scottish constituency. He certainly was not what the Scots call 'hearty' and extreme short-sightedness made him frown and fail to recognize people. For sheer ability he had few equals.

I think by 1888 electric light in private houses had become more or less common. Anyhow, I remember a large dinner party in Grosvenor Square, given by Lady Aberdeen, where the light suddenly went out and candles placed in anything that was handy had hastily to be collected in order to light the tables. I fancy this was not unusual in the early days and it made a pleasant diversion for the guests who liked to think they were not subject to such disasters in their gas-lit rooms.

In these days, i.e. in the late eighties, there was a terrible amount of bad feeling amongst statesmen and ordinary folk alike, and there was also anxiety about the dynamiters who were at work ; there were several explosions that caused great alarm. We were living in Clarges Street not far from Sir William Harcourt's house, and as he was Home Secretary at the time, it was guarded by several policemen, and somehow we were always anxious when we passed through the narrow foot passage, at that time leading to Hay Hill by Lansdowne House. The Tories were especially abusive to Sir William Vernon Harcourt. I remember hearing that the latter said to Lord Charles Beresford, who had been speaking in the House, 'Well, Charlie, you don't look like a statesman' and that he was met by the rejoinder ' Nor do you look like a Weathercock ! ' alluding I suppose to his Home Rule propensities.

I always enjoy hearing an eloquent speaker on whatever side of politics. I think for beauty and timbre of voice, the finest orator was not a politician at all, but a minister, Charles Haddon Spurgeon, who died in 1892. He made himself absolutely audible all over his great tabernacle, and if unattractive in person, he was able to carry his hearers with him by his immense sincerity ; his sentences rolled out in a beautiful sequence. I don't think I ever heard a better speaker. I always thought he must have come near Bright in eloquence and in persuasive powers, and when I hear sermons broadcast, I long for him to be alive, though indeed he would have had to place a limit on their length.

John Morley, as he then was, came to Cloan in October 1888 and I have pleasant and interesting recollections of him. He spoke to me a good deal about George Eliot, for whom I had a great admiration, and emphasized her immense sympathy with suffering and her own look of pain. He was much devoted to her and described her appearance as ' bishop-like ', though I am not sure what that meant. He said, however, that he had got real guidance from her and from John Stuart Mill, but not from Carlyle, whom he had visited. These two could never have been sympathetic, for their philosophy of life was so different. He felt about George Eliot that she wrote as a psychologist, and said that psychology got old,

MATTHEW ARNOLD, ABOUT 1870

JOHN MORLEY, ABOUT 1880

while human nature did not do so, and therefore the Brontës and Mrs. Gaskell would probably survive her as popular writers. Victor Hugo had visited him, in reference to his review of the *Toilers of the Sea* and about the same time he met Renan. He had a great admiration for Hugo, and said he felt better after reading him, for his atmosphere was fresh and healthy as compared with Dumas. Wordsworth he considered the poet to live with. Then came the sort of question that constantly arose with Morley : whether men like Gladstone and Bright, by their example and devotion, or the poets by their writing, do most to elevate mankind ? We must have belief in humanity and look for the good, but both consistency and logic are impossible in politics. Morley recommended me to read Burke above all for guidance on this subject, especially as concerned the American revolution. As a poet, Wordsworth, he considered, was paramount. Shakespeare had much of garbage as one sees in the *Merry Wives of Windsor*, etc., but Gaboriau was the author to read after one had made a bad speech !

Lifts were dangerous contraptions in those days as they were not always well protected, and soon after this when Richard had Morley and Dicey as guests at Members Mansions, where he lived, the former very nearly showed the latter into the well of a most dangerous lift. Mercifully Richard saved him in time : an unfortunate servant lost her life in the same lift not long after this escape.

A little later I met Morley at the Asquiths, in Hampstead. The talk there was about another of the problems he loved to explore. The subject this time was
one which he often discussed in later years—which
one would rather have been, a great political, a great
pulpit, or a great legal orator. Morley fell heavily for
the second, which was very characteristic, and he
quoted Savonarola as his ideal. In the pulpit, he said,
you have the widest aims and the widest scope. As to
the latter it seemed to me dubious, but I fully sympathized with his view, as I still do, as regards the
aims to be held before the speaker : only I rather fear
that the pulpit has not now the same weight that it had
fifty years ago, much less than in the time of Savonarola. The discussion went on to consider the other old
question of whether one would rather see two sides of
a question or no. Men who do the great things in the
world concentrate on one side and see it alone. Is it
not selfish to see but one side ? And as to the great
things to be done, we must be true to ourselves and these
questions will solve themselves. One could never be in
Mr. Morley's company without such discussions arising
and the Asquiths' house was the best *milieu* for good talk.

At this time John Morley was drawing up a political
programme, and I think Richard had tried rather
vainly to bring him into touch with Sidney Webb with
whom he had formed a friendship.

Later on I saw much more of Morley and had many
interesting talks with him. But that was for the most
part in the succeeding century.

In looking back it seems as if ' the middle eighties ', as they developed, signified a time of wonderful cheerfulness and hope. On the intellectual side there was the movement dominated by Professor T. H. Green and Arnold Toynbee of Oxford, which made for an outlook on the universe which was not only satisfying to reason but also encouraging to those who wished somehow to work for their fellows. This movement, which was founded on the idealistic philosophy dominated by Hegel, influenced us all greatly. Green's *Lay Sermons* and his *Prolegomena to Ethics* and Bradley's *Ethics* were books we read, and from them we proceeded, like many others, to further philosophic studies. It was the beginning of a great deal of serious work on my brothers' part and a certain and minor amount on my own. But on the practical side, one tried hard to see how to bring one's theories into practice, as Green did in the city of Oxford ; while Toynbee's influence went to the founding of Toynbee Hall and many other settlements and clubs for working men and women. A writer on the more distinctly religious side who meant a good deal to us younger ones was Hale White, who wrote under the name of Mark Rutherford. His first books recorded the life of a dissenting minister, who had to leave the church and suffer much in doing so. They were written in a simple but lucid eighteenth-century style, and for those who had in their own way to pass through equal difficulties, they were very moving. It was indeed the age of problems now forgotten, but gradually we seemed to be able to see light shining through the darkness and to have some hope and certainty for the future.

Then our interests were greatly extended through the work of the brothers. The elder, Richard, got his first chance of making a name in the Courts in 1883, after the usual discouragements of a young barrister, and by 1884 Gladstone spoke appreciatively of the young politician, while the President of the Scottish Liberal Association suggested his name for a Scottish constituency, and under pressure he agreed to stand. The election came earlier than he expected (in 1885) and he was elected through a new working-class electorate—the 'hinds' of East Lothian—by an immense majority. This signified a change in the direction of rural matters that was almost inconceivable to the old aristocracy which despite bad seasons still held its sway in the country, if not in towns. It naturally created a good deal of feeling as regards Liberals who were usurping the place of the rightful owners of the soil, particularly when 'carpet-baggers', i.e. young English lawyers, came to the front. This feeling became acute during the next years when the Irish question cropped up and many of our neighbours gazed at us with surprise, amounting in some cases to horror. The 'Invincibles' were a terror during the operation of the Crimes Act of 1882, and for a long time explosions were dreaded, specially in London.

Yet it was a time when housing and sanitation, so disgracefully neglected, began to be thought about seriously, and there were Exhibitions of a more or less improving sort, like the ' Fisheries ' in 1883. This oddly named Exhibition was, I think, the first of a new form of entertainment to which Londoners could go *en famille* in the evenings, and which proved a valuable development in the social life of the time.

The year 1885, when we became personally interested in and excited over politics, had not been a happy one for Mr. Gladstone, since then came the tragedy of Gordon, at Khartoum, which brought about a passionate resentment against him on the part of many English people. The Irish question, and the County Franchise Bill enfranchising the labourers as occupiers of rated dwellings, seemed to engross his whole attention, to the detriment of other important matters. He was temporarily replaced by Lord Salisbury, but that government lasted only till the new franchise was in operation. There then arose a new socialist movement, or what developed into such, owing to the opposition of the House of Lords to the extension of the franchise, and a divorce became evident between the working classes and the middle-class liberalism which so far had held the field. This divorce continued, since the Government had as yet no idea of what was required to make the life of the working man tolerable. The very fact that compulsory education existed gave an opportunity of discovering how miserable was the condition of the children, yet feeding and clothing in any practical sense were looked on askance. Also before the election there was much

unemployment and indeed sheer starvation. We
used to see the processions of miserable-looking unemployed men in London and there were meetings of
angry protest.

Now it was that the Fabians, who professed to advance slowly but surely, came into evidence. They
were no revolutionaries but they worked hard, using
every opportunity offered by the existing machinery
of Government to gain their ends. We came into
touch with the leaders through my brother : particularly with George Bernard Shaw and Sidney and
Beatrice Webb and some others of the intellectuals.
Then there was Henry George, of a less intellectual
type but an ardent apostle of land nationalization.
My brother John and I were much attracted by this
scheme, but Richard would have none of it. It seemed
to us younger ones that if the land could be national-
ized, our economic difficulties would vanish.

Though Gladstone was in power in the end of 1885 a
solid phalanx of Parnellites held the balance and the
position was precarious. Parnell was dissatisfied with
the Liberal offer of ' the greatest possible extension of
self-government' and went so far as to place his hopes
on the other side of politics. Hence the position of the
Government was difficult and became more so in the
next 1886 election.

It is necessary to mention these political events since
they caused a change in the orientation of one's life,
and it was the same with the lives of many others of
whatever political hue. It was as though one had got

away from the dullness of the drab life which was the
lot of so many unoccupied women into something that
was not only real but full of excitement. I could not
give any help in the 1885 election, as my mother and I
had just had a serious carriage accident in which she
was terribly hurt. But I did so in all the other elections which my brother fought for the next twenty-
five years, and also became treasurer of the Scottish
Women's Liberal Association and sometimes spoke for it,
even though I was not always satisfied with its outlook.

There seemed a great deal of pretence, one felt, in
many of the political demonstrations. Perhaps those
earlier in the decade were most unsatisfactory, but one
did not know so much about them. What one wanted
was to help one's neighbours in a way which should
neither be influenced by the denominationally religious
or ascetic attitude of mind characteristic of the Church
nor by the hard outlook of the cold economist on the
other hand. We did not so much want to do ' good '
to our neighbour as to develop the sense of a concrete
life in which we should all play our part. That is, we
did not wish to exist as isolated units but as part of an
organism which should develop in the right way. We
found that the new ideas seemed to meet the needs of
those to whom the ancient shibboleths of the Church
had become tinkling cymbals. Had I been a University
student I could have discussed these matters with
my fellows ; as it was, one had to grope one's way
alone. It was rather difficult to make clear to others
what these conceptions meant, but it seemed to me that

through settlements and work of that kind, points of contact with others would possibly be found, and in 1884 I got into touch with the work of Octavia Hill, while my elder brother lectured for the Working Men's College, founded by Frederick Denison Maurice, and also for many other such institutions, even though he had become a very busy man.

The whole thing may seem commonplace now, but I don't think the immense changes that occurred amongst the more serious part of the community during the eighties have been sufficiently realized. Anyhow, they took place in the society in which we moved, and certainly this was the beginning of all sorts of so-called philanthropic movements with a different orientation from the past.

In Scotland, for instance, a movement called the Social Union was set on foot, which was typical of the new outlook. Hitherto, good works had been done mainly by the Churches, or by those influenced by orthodox religion, while this had the wider compass that characterizes many similar movements in the present day. The promoters of it were anxious to start housing reforms in Scotland, where the conditions were much worse than in England, and that is saying a good deal. A deputation headed by Professor Patrick Geddes was sent in 1884 to discuss the matter with Miss Octavia Hill, and it happened that the day on which they called I also had gone to see Miss Hill, on receiving an introduction from a younger sister of my mother's, who knew that I found life unsatisfying and wished to help me. Miss Hill told the deputation that she would have to train the lady who might start work in Edinburgh. They were nonplussed until Miss Hill turned to me and asked if I would help. I was rather taken aback, as I was young, about twenty-one, and had no experience. But at last I consented and this ended in a good deal of work in this direction and a successful start being made in Scotland.

For me it opened up a new vista. I had always known my poorer neighbours in Scotland, but that was in the country, and now one learnt how the working classes in towns actually lived. The plan of sending well-to-do children away from home while still quite young seems to cut them off from the knowledge of the people amongst whom they are to live and to make their future lives lop-sided. Where I worked there was much sweated labour and families were living in small single rooms where the man did tailoring, while the woman bore her children, sewed and cooked and tended her little ones. It was often hard to take the rents, though they were only 2s. to 3s. 6d. a week, very different from modern days. In the older houses, despite the efforts valiantly made to get rid of bugs, they swarmed. The system of house management was excellent and the ladies were able to re-house the well-behaved tenants as occasion offered ; but one saw the immensity of the problem, and the means taken seemed to me (who had imbibed a good many radical ideas) inadequate without State help, and to this Miss Hill demurred, since she believed

H

that it would introduce a deleterious political influence. She always caused us in our elaborate and
excellent accounts to make a statement of rates
separate from rent so that the tenants might realize
what they, in fact, were paying as rates imposed.
On the whole, we owe an immense debt of gratitude to her, for she first showed how property of the
poor type should be managed, and she drew attention
to the great need of seeing to this. She was indeed a
very remarkable woman ; her countenance was noble
and she had a commanding manner, along with sweet-
ness of disposition. She was truly one of a generation
of women of whom the country has great reason to
be proud, and she would have made a real mark in
Parliament had she been eligible for election. Her
alliance with Ruskin had ceased before I knew her,
but there were still remnants of the Ruskin influence
in the Maypole Dances in Paradise Court. To these
we shepherded the children, but they seemed, to my
matter-of-fact Scottish mind, rather out of date and
foolish, and I much more enjoyed taking the children
(who had many of them never seen a country field and
who thought I tended the greenery as they did their
little flower-pots) to the park of a kind friend. When
I asked a child if he had been in the country, he
replied, ' Oh yes, Miss, I've been to Waterloo when
'Erbert was going away,' and the children asked me
if I had to water the green field *every* day. It all
depressed me terribly and I could not forget it when
I got to the loveliness of the Scottish hill lands.

I have given these personal recollections in order to show what the young women of the so-called leisured classes had to contend with in Victorian days. But now I should like to say something of the sort of life that was led by us all, and what the outside world was like.

As a matter of fact, the distrust of State interference was really breaking down, perhaps by the subterranean influence of the Fabians, and Miss Hill, like Dr. Chalmers in Scotland, was of the older school. The younger generation wished the pace hastened. The Charity Organization Society was in full swing, under the direction of fine men like Charles Booth ; but with the Hills and Maurices (they were related), the economic outlook was tempered by the new feeling for art and beauty, which was to be not for the select few, but for all mankind. Hence societies like the Kyrle Society, which brought art to the home of the people, and, above all, the National Trust Movement, for procuring open spaces, were sponsored by women like Miranda and Octavia Hill. Octavia had a very sensitive side that made her easily upset when the little things of life went wrong, but she had devoted fellow-workers who were ready to meet these strains.

This work could only be done by me in London and by visiting Edinburgh, as I often did, staying with various friends there. I wanted to do more for my immediate circle, and one thing that weighed upon my mind was the lack of books on the part of the young people of the little town and district in which

I lived, since there was no public library. I set to work to get one instituted, with a good deal of discouragement but with real help from one or two valiant souls, more especially from an enthusiastic lawyer in the town and also from a splendid mill-owner. We got a little library of well-chosen books successfully established, and had courses of lectures in connection with it. As I was secretary, all this entailed a good deal of work and correspondence, but the scheme grew and finally developed into a much larger one, in connection with an institute. By that time there were many helpers : first Mr. Andrew Carnegie, and then a neighbouring and very generous landlord, but to begin with we eked out the funds by means of bazaars. Hardly anything of the kind gave me more pleasure than getting the library set on foot, cataloguing it and working with friends and neighbours who were only too ready to help. The library was on the whole serious, very unlike the ' twopenny libraries ' of the day. I remember one working man going through the three volumes of Schopenhauer's *World as Will and Idea*, volume by volume, and Darwin's *Origin of Species* excited a young chemist so much that he could hardly sleep. We had to ' vet ' the books very carefully, for the ministers were some of them watchful. My brother John had generously given me a set of George Eliot's works and on the strength of it I had asked a well-known minister in Dundee to lecture on her writings. Unfortunately he termed the lecture ' The Religion of George Eliot ' and there was a real outburst on the part of the Free Church minister, a Highlandman of the stricter sort, seeing that George Eliot, in his belief, was an atheist, besides other things unmentionable. After his denunciation from the pulpit, I asked the librarian what was the result. He said ' all the Elders came to borrow the novels in order to see what the pernicious books were like ! '—so that the good man's end was apparently not attained.

Readers were fewer in those days, but they paid for the privilege of reading books and many country people waded carefully through volumes of serious works and were ready to discuss them. I suppose we did not get hold of the real novel readers who abound in the present time : indeed we rather definitely discouraged them, so far as modern novels were concerned.

Mr. Carnegie's help was everything to me. He wrote from New York in 1890 : ' Please spend the enclosed £25 for new books. Am delighted to hear that your library is flourishing. One of the arrangements we always talk of making, when we are to be in Scotland next time, is to renew our acquaintance with the Haldanes. Indeed I sometimes feel as if I should like to go on a pilgrimage to see your mother ; one of the type of grand Scotch mothers of which Ruskin says : " Nor is there anything among other nations to approach the dignity of a true Scotchwoman's face in the tried perfectness of her old age." I always think of her, and three or four others like her when I read that passage which I keep above my desk always.' My mother was not Scottish but she deserved all that was said of her and more.

Housing work was regarded as but one side of the bigger work of making life in Scotland, as a whole, more interesting and beautiful, and it was, in these days, a good deal under the influence of Professor Patrick Geddes and some artistic friends, and combined with work for developing children's playgrounds, flower growing and so on. Handicrafts like wood-carving became a special interest, and I worked at that with the rest, and helped to get up classes for it, even at home. Indeed, before the educational authorities took up such matters, we all tried to set on foot the very classes that soon came ' under the code ', as it then was called. We had, I remember, embroidery classes, cookery classes and what not, as well as courses of lectures on literary subjects, and for many years I had a Home Reading Union circle. This excellent scheme provided syllabuses and notes for circles of readers, in a way which was prophetic of the well-known B.B.C. study circles, and, whatever it might have been with more sophisticated readers, the mill-workers who formed my circle were intensely interested, and we read quite a fair amount of history and poetry, and even tackled elementary geology and physics, besides collecting the traditional history of our parish. Some people derided us as blue stockings, but I have had many testimonies to the use this elementary form of adult education proved to those who became mothers of families and workers in various sorts of industries. Many went abroad, mostly to Canada, and took their books with them. We had expeditions to spots of historic interest on Saturdays, each one taking her own food and paying for her transport. I have preserved some of the essays written by one specially gifted young woman, and they are quite remarkable. Though she had merely her small weekly wages, and, owing to circumstances, had a heavy weight of responsibility laid upon her (for she had to bring up two children, not her own), she collected a tiny but carefully selected library. She married, but unhappily died when her baby was born. I often think of the help she and other members of the circle gave me, for I got more from them than anything I gave. I have kept some most interesting letters, written by old members of this union long years after, and they convince me of the need for education after school days are passed.

The general idea of adult education, which was to be one of the main interests of my elder brother's life, was indeed at last coming to be known, even in Scotland, where the academic traditions endured so long. There was up to this time actually very little in the school course to make a boy or girl feel that the teaching dealt with matters of daily life and environment. Handiwork, carpentry and gardening, or teaching by touch and sight were hardly thought of; cookery was neglected, and the standard of housekeeping was very low. On leaving day school there was nothing supplied by the State excepting rather unattractive night schools for the three R's, including book-keeping. The evening school was dark and dim : even long after this in 1903 when I was elected member of school board things were not very bright. I can never forget on one evening how a deputation of young men ' waited on us ' to say they would like instruction in building construction : I can see their eager faces now, looming out of the darkness, and re-member so well the feeling that we were but feeble guardians of our trust. However, they got their class and one of the deputation has risen to a position of importance in his profession, more I fear from his own work than from the help we gave him.

During the latter years of the eighties, politics and education were not the only sources of interest, for philosophy rivalled them with my brothers and myself. I wanted something to do which would occupy my spare time in the country and give me the sense of not wasting it. Hence, about 1886, when I was twenty-four, I undertook a large piece of work along with a very able young woman named Frances Simson. It was to translate three solid volumes of Hegel's *History of Philosophy*. The volumes were completed and pub-lished in the years 1892, 1894 and 1896. It taught me a great deal, for one got interested in the great men dealt with ; but it was rather tedious work and certainly exacting, and I felt ill-equipped for it, since I had not lived in Germany or had a University education. But having put my hand to the plough, I went on, and there was great pleasure in discussing points with my brothers and others philosophically minded. Possibly this intense interest in such matters resulted in a certain aloofness from the interests and amusements of everyday life, and this, with our exceptional devotion to home, may have caused a certain separation from one's fellows. If so, it resulted really from our family upbringing and traditions, which caused us to concentrate on things speculative rather than on those of everyday life. But it made us happy and insensible to the ostracism which came about on the part of our Tory neighbours when the Home Rule question became acute. I do not suppose that there was any other well-to-do family in the county in exactly the same position, and I expect we were deemed highbrow and self-sufficient. Up to this time the landed party still held the management of county affairs, and certainly of social affairs, in their own hands. County councils were not yet and school boards hardly counted.

It is difficult to define the attitude of the normal Scot to the governing landed classes, such as it was in the last century. For there was no subservience, such as existed in England, and yet the holding of great tracts of land carried with it a respect which was really traceable to feudal days. The laird was some- one to whom respect was due, and this respect was given ; though I am bound to say the lady had scant share in it so far as her powers were concerned. What caused this special relationship of proprietor to

tenant to disappear was not poverty—for in olden days
the lairds were frequently poor—but the sense that the
owners of land were getting away from the people.
The boys were sent to English schools and joined the
English Church, the life ceased to be in accordance
with feudal ideas as they were understood, and the
lairds preferred to sell their estates to the newly en-
riched, rather than live a dull and penurious life at
home. Then democracy was taking from them their
old traditional employment of governing the country,
and why should they stay ? The newcomers frankly
looked on their ' places ' as pleasure resorts and not as
the real centres of their lives. In watching the development of a country one sees the orientation altering
from year to year : a few old families, one is glad to say
(though it may be unjustifiable), hold to their own land
and accept the new conditions. But most are selling
their possessions to be used as schools, convents, homes
of rest and so on, leaving the newly-educated and
quite competent population to carry on in its own
way. The young generation have a different set of
values and the stuffy lives of the lairds of olden days
have no attraction for them ; while the family
treasures mean little to those who have discarded an
outworn sentimentalism. To us of an older generation
it seems as if something of value were missed, something which belonged to a common humanity. On
the other hand, I suppose there is gain of a material
sort to the community at large. I remember long
ago the Webbs foretelling that the country houses

would be used as they so often now are and that town
houses would be divided up in flats, just as has happened, but at the time I never thought it would
happen in my day.

The first idea, when my brother Richard thought of
standing for Parliament, was that he should have con-
tested the division of Perthshire in which we lived. He
would have liked this, as his ancestors had represented
the county often in olden days, and, Radicals as we
were, tradition counted, as it always counts in Scotland. However, after he had held one very successful
meeting, the sitting member for the whole county,
who had been abroad (the county was divided
under the Redistribution Bill) chose the Western
division, saying to my mother that it was absurd for
one who had no property in it (for then he had none)
to think of representing it in Parliament. Our
mother, who was like a lioness on her cubs' behalf,
replied, ' No, he has not a foot of ground but he has
Brains which is more important ! ' I did a good deal
of canvassing in East Lothian from time to time, and
the ploughmen's wives were keen when they realized
that I was not ' the Primrose League '. The question of women's suffrage had now emerged and
naturally as I held strong views on it I was glad that,
in contradistinction from most of his party, Richard
did the same. A Bill to enfranchise single women was
introduced by private members as early as 1883,
and this he supported. Of Liberals, Lady Grey and

the Asquiths were then against it but Lady Aberdeen was always sympathetic and very helpful.

This movement for the suffrage was taken up keenly by many of my friends and there were some ardent supporters, like Lady Carlisle who presided in London over the main society which advocated a whole-hearted suffrage. Some of those who worked for it then would certainly have been militants had they lived to see the Pankhurst movement in operation. If Lady Carlisle was one of the keenest of these there was opposition of a kind which was difficult to meet on the part of eminent women like Mrs. Humphry Ward, who wished women to do useful parliamentary business through committees, without actually becoming voters or members. Many of our Liberal friends thought the change would mean a Conservative vote and were therefore cool. But gradually the foolish jokes with which the matter was met in the House of Commons disappeared ; though not entirely so till the question took a really serious strain. For some reason, it was thought by many that prostitutes would vote *en masse*—though for what or for whom I never discovered. It was never suggested that men of ill life should be disenfranchised.

The years at the end of the eighties were not as peaceful and full of cheerfulness as the earlier ones. Not only were there the terrible political difficulties over the Irish question, which ended in the split between Gladstonians and Unionists, but there was the menace of unemployment once more. After the

CUNNINGHAME GRAHAM, 1905

first reading of the Home Rule Bill in April, 1886, the
break in the party became momentous. Men were
blackballed at the clubs, and hostesses had difficulty
in knowing whom to invite to their houses. Indeed,
liberalism had changed its character, and whiggism,
in its old form, was at last no more.

The distress amongst the poor people was certainly
very great at this time, and appeals were issued by
prominent individuals like Manning and Spurgeon.
But the Government held aloof, although there were
nine Labour members in the House, including Arch,
the first agricultural labourer to be such. The idea always was that these Labour representatives were
agitators and that they were egged on to extreme
views by Socialists. One heard this doctrine constantly reiterated. Street meetings were held and
Trafalgar Square was closed. The unemployed, however, made an attack upon it, and after the affray, two
of the fighters, Cunninghame Graham, then a member
of Parliament, and John Burns, remained in custody.
The former, a Perthshire laird and a friend, sent for
my brother to bail him out. He went at once to the
aid of his boisterous friend who was so wonderful to
look at, for he had a distinction which could not be
excelled by any Spanish hidalgo. Cunninghame
Graham afterwards described his experiences during
his months of confinement. He told us how his real
regret was to miss the daffodils of March and the early
spring flowers, and how his job was to carry coals upstairs. One would like to have seen this magnificent

equestrian, who looked so splendid as he rode in the Row, give dignity to this menial occupation, as he certainly would have done to any occupation he was set to.

It was Jubilee year in 1887, and in the midst of bonfires and rejoicings many felt that other things should have been in mind. Sweated labour came to the front through a Board of Trade Report next year (1888), and conditions under which the manufacture of cheap clothing went on shocked all decent people. All this certainly impressed the younger people deeply, and movements arose in which we took part as we could, in order to improve conditions especially for women. Mrs. Humphry Ward's *Robert Elsmere* had a great influence and there was a real desire to do as her hero did, work in the East End and there find salvation. ' Slumming ' it was called by the profane, but it meant something very real to me and many of my friends. Was it right to spend so much on Jubilee celebrations when there was so great a need ? The question was hard to answer but at least educational and housing reform were slowly going on, and local government took the place of the old administration by justices in Quarter Sessions, which was always a step in the right direction.

In London there was at last a real interest arising in these social questions, and many of my young women friends made their way to the East End in omnibuses or hansoms, to try to do something for the poor, and a magazine called ' 1888 ' (and dubiously well written) was started. There was also the influence of Professor Drummond to be remembered. Drummond, the author of *Natural Law in the Physical World*, had a remarkable series of meetings, some in the Speaker's House, attended by what is now called ' society ' girls whose consciences had been moved to do something for their fellows. Lady Rosebery helped with money and Lady Aberdeen with enthusiasm and advice. Then in Scotland we set on foot a benefit society for women, that is a contributory friendly society, such as men possessed. It was started on the best actuarial lines and I worked very hard to get it going by visiting quantities of printing and other large shops, but it had not the sort of backing possessed by the great friendly societies, and when the latter resolved, some years later, to open their portals to women, we were glad to fall into step and merge our efforts into those of the Order of Foresters. I think we did a little to hurry on the movement of enabling women to have a part in the great thrift societies that were not merely collecting societies, but were managed and governed by the members themselves. I addressed many meetings of workers in the various women's trades, on the subject. After the change, the Women's Court in Edinburgh had a successful career in its new guise, and I attended the High Court of Foresters, as a representative, at Chester, and altogether got much knowledge of the working of friendly societies as well as of their use. We felt, I hope fairly, that our initial efforts had not been in vain.

The Railway race about this time was a small excitement at Cloan. It was thrilling to go to the little station and hear which train for London—East Coast or West Coast—had reached a certain junction first. It seemed marvellous that no accident occurred but all went well. In earlier days we loved to visit the railway station and be allowed by the kind porter, David Graham, to work the signals. As, in those days, there was no block system and much competition on the part of the railway companies, I cannot conceive how there were not more accidents. Trains were given a certain time to get ahead and if there seemed any danger a red handkerchief was waved. It is amusing, in present conditions, to see in family letters the advice to our mother 'not to hesitate to have the express stopped at Auchterarder'. Expresses in those days were specially stopped for anyone of consequence who desired it and this privilege was often taken advantage of.

Trade seemed better by 1889 and people were on the whole more cheerful, thinking things were going to improve. In 1889 also education was reaching the populace and there were demands for making it free and for extending it through extension lectures and technical training. The newly established County Council for London had men on it like Lord Rosebery, Lord Hobhouse and Lord Monkswell, and philanthropic educationists like Mr. Quintin Hogg gave a fillip to popular enthusiasm for better streets and a cleaner town, for People's Palaces and reformed housing and food.

Lord Rosebery as chairman used to start forth from Mentmore to his work at 9.30 a.m. armed with his bag, like other city men. It was the first start of the great body which was to do much in promoting a sense of citizenship in the metropolis and it was very important that it should have a good send off, as it had. There was a very just feeling that Parliament had not done enough for the people and that now local effort must play its part and show a really progressive spirit. The Church took it up in the form of a Christian Social Union and Scotland shared in the new spirit and had now her own Local Government Board.

The long drawn Parnell Commission had a dramatic scene when it was found by Sir Charles Russell that a broken-down journalist named Piggott had forged the letter alleged to have been written by Parnell, but of this I shall speak later. Then there was the Dockers' Strike. Dock labour was wholly unregulated, un-skilled labourers were paid about two shillings a day and those who got that were lucky to be taken on at all. John Burns and Ben Tillett came into prominence in bringing to light the dockers' grievances, and public feeling supported the men against what was truly regarded as sweating. Long negotiations followed, with Cardinal Manning as a negotiator, and at last the men came out triumphantly. There were, how-ever, other strikes, and though sweating was still undiminished, labour was beginning to assert its rights and conciliation boards began to be talked about.

I

The real effect that Walter Besant made on his readers has also to be taken into account. In all advancement made at this time, his work was specially valuable and had the material result of causing the People's Palace to be built in Whitechapel. His book *All Sorts and Conditions of Men* was immensely popular and had a far-reaching influence.

While living at Cloan, a minor interest of mine, about 1890, was to start an incubator, then a new-fangled device. Mine was a queer affair like a table, heated from beneath by a lamp. The first incubation brought out one solitary chicken, the second several, and the lonely number one took charge of the next brood, in spite of its turning out, to our immense surprise, to be a cock! After that I sold my contraption successfully and waited till a better system was devised.

That year my mother suffered a great deal from rheumatism and we went together to Bath, where we were joined by my brother, John, from Oxford. He and I scoured the country very happily and I took swimming lessons, and went to work in an old library, mainly occupied by a strange collection of old gentlemen. I was busy with my translation of Hegel's *History of Philosophy* and had to refer to many books. Bath seemed to me not to have changed very much since the days of Miss Austen, and I was invited to take walks with other young people, just in the same way that her heroines walked—gentle walks they seemed to a Scotswoman accustomed to tramping moors and fens.

As to politics on the Liberal side at least, the first year of the last decade of the century was a time of gloom. The Irish question was ever present, and we were all committed to Home Rule, and yet one saw no light or hope. I was in London a great deal, since a great sorrow had come into my brother's life and he liked me to be with him. We had many devoted friends. Henry Asquith was constantly with my brother and of him he spoke in nearly every letter. He had applied for silk later than Richard, though his senior, and therefore to their joint amusement the latter was able to send him the first brief he received as Q.C., which happened to be one in Common Law and therefore his special work. An entertaining article appeared about the two, which was termed 'A Race', for at that time they were much together in the public eye. The forms and ceremonies of 'taking silk' amused and interested my mother who had great legal traditions and sent lace ruffles (which the recipient did not wear) to go with his silk stockings. I do not know if the same custom still rules of sending cards to the judges in a certain form, going in full-bottomed wig and silk and knee breeches to get the patent of procedure from the Lord Chancellor, and being asked, along with the other novices when within the bar, 'if they had any cause to plead'. My diary states that it was so then.

Irish Home Rule had received a devastating shock after the divorce case in which Mr. Parnell was concerned, and its disastrous consequences, and this was accompanied by a serious financial crisis in the city, which in 1890 added to the general depression. Young politicians felt it hard to keep up their courage. The Eight Hours Bill was being discussed, but for the most part it got little encouragement. Nor indeed did Scottish Home Rule, though it had a half-hearted support from the Liberal side.

When in London in the early nineties I saw a good deal of Lady Grey, Sir Edward's first wife, who often stayed at my brother's flat and was sometimes with us in the country. She was a very remarkable woman— not easy to know, though with a deep vein of senti- ment below a rather stand-off and sometimes cynical manner. The two young people, Edward and Dorothy Grey, were I think in the later eighties one of the handsomest couples I ever knew. She was splendidly built and apparently very strong physically, and both loved to live an open-air life. Nothing seemed to tire them. At Cloan we walked up Ben Voirlich or other hills and it was a pleasure to see their devotion to one another and their pride in one another's strength. We drove in a wagonette in these pre-motor days and in it went to Loch Leven (where Queen Mary was imprisoned), which was beyond walking distance ; but we walked back part of the way. Sir Ed- ward was modest, realizing that he had not in his youth had the education of his friend, six years his senior, and honestly sought his guidance in his reading. The young husband and wife conscientiously read

together serious books like Gibbon's *Decline and Fall* ;
and Thomas Love Peacock was then one of their
favourite authors. Indeed they were together learning
many things which the ordinary man and woman
entirely missed, and more than making up for any
early neglect of education. Lady Grey had a wholly
modern and then unusual hatred of shams, religious
very specially, and the shibboleths which passed with
most of us irked her, and she did not fail to show this.
She made friends with those who interested her,
regardless of ' class ', then so much considered, and
had a real desire to live, when in London, in the East
End among those whom she could help, or rather,
she would have said, who could help her. The plan
came near eventuation and she consulted a woman
who had already done this and had studied deeply in
economics. It was an annoyance to her to have the
cynical advice that her place was to be a leader in
society, and that it was there that she would shine and
be of use, rather than elsewhere. The reply was, I
think, unjust as well as cynical, but her beauty and
manner suggested it no doubt, as well as the life that
most probably lay before her.

Despite the fact that she had not an ingratiating
manner with bores and those she thought shams, she
would, had she lived, have taken a prominent part in
the social, political and philanthropic life of her time,
even if she had not been what is called a popular
hostess, for she had a distinct ambition to do this. She
died as the result of an accident the very year her

husband came into office. She enjoyed, in particular, her talks with John Morley and she was a real help to us all in a time of great trouble, just because of her genuine sympathy.

By this date, as Home Rule was in the background, the younger men in the Liberal party (now rent in twain and become on our side ' Gladstonian ') grew impatient, and were on their own account working out schemes of social reform. It was hardly to be imagined that at his advanced age their leader was likely to do this. They felt that the old liberalism was out of date, and wished to press for consideration the reform of the land laws, education, women's suffrage and so on. This feeling grew in intensity as the years went on. Gladstone's immersion in Home Rule had given the party a deadly blow.

For all of us younger people, the necessity for doing more to ameliorate the conditions of the working people was oppressive. I find a letter of my own, saying that the sights I saw going to the Opera House at Covent Garden ' made me quite sick ' and that people *must* drink to forget their misery. In Scotland the figures giving the deaths of infants under one year of age were disgraceful, though curiously, considering the conditions under which people lived, not as bad as in England where it amounted to 150 per thousand births. The housing in Scotland was immensely worse than in England, for 15 per cent. of the population were living in single-roomed ' houses ' while in England there was only a small proportion of people who were doing so. Drunkenness was bad everywhere, but worst in Scotland, and it is no wonder that there was a steady increase in the returns from duties on intoxicants which helped to keep up Budget surpluses. Mr. Goschen's budgets reflected the prosperity of the time. There was also great growth in betting and gambling practices which affected serious minds. The revelations about the Baccarat Set in high life also gave the decade a bad name and there was a great development in speculative companies. A notable one was that to make an underground railway from St. James's Street to Holborn. The development of the social services was seen in the new London County Council, with its rather advanced programme. There were at least a majority of ' Progressives ' and John Burns advocated what he called ' Practicable Socialism' which made a good cry, so that socialism thus became something less to be feared than it had been so far. Sidney Webb was its principal supporter and he gave it a certain intellectual flavour ; though his programme was advanced enough. Sidney and Beatrice Webb became our friends, and visited us at Cloan. There was always great discussion as to which was the abler, but no conclusions were arrived at, for both were extraordinarily able and yet more extraordinarily diligent. They made one feel heartily ashamed of one's idle hours when one saw how they worked from morning to night, producing volumes of carefully verified matter. They had great influence on politics on both sides because they saw nearly as much of Balfour, the Bishop of London and the Conservatives as they did of Liberals like my brother, though there were indeed those like Asquith who turned a deaf ear to their theories.

When at Cloan in 1892 Mrs. Webb was busy over the subject of Trade Unions for women, then but a hot-house growth as she said; and she was also much concerned about more factory inspectors being appointed, especially working men. And thus they brought in a new and practical way of looking at these problems, though it was then thought by many people that they were wishing to interfere too much with the 'liberty of the subject' and making people too subordinate to the machinery of the State. Some of their greatest work on Poor Law and Trade Unions came later; but their personal influence (possibly helped by the attractive lady progenitor of it, though we dared not say so) was very great on those who were to be the statesmen of the future. I remember Beatrice Webb first explaining to me the amendments to the Employer's Liability Act, afterwards to be incorporated in law.

On quite other lines General Booth of the Salvation Army was doing his best with the scheme he adumbrated in his *Darkest England*, and he spoke with fervour and great effect. He had a hard fight—often a physical fight—to carry on his work, though in time it became popular. There was the even more important work of his namesake Charles Booth who wrote on 'Life and Labour' in London, made enquiries into the causes of pauperism and advocated a scheme of old age pensions to which little attention was at first paid.

In 1891 I went to a Hyde Park demonstration by the launderers of London, pressing for better conditions. It was attended by thousands of women and was addressed by Cunninghame Graham, John Burns and Miss Abraham (afterwards Mrs. Jack Tennant), who was later a factory inspector and who has done much useful social work.

We hardly realize how little attention was in those days paid to the Trade Unions and the Labour movement on its political side. The Unions, in many cases, were not recognized, and there were strikes, railway, colliery and seamen's, on the question of recognition. The tailors and omnibus men struck, the latter on account of under pay (6s. 6d. a day for drivers and 5s. for conductors) and of course the action of workers who refused to work with non-union men, was called intimidation. The London County Council however was taking up the workers' grievances and also demanding, as part of its forward policy, the setting up of public parks and taking over tramways and fire brigades, all of which sounds commonplace now. Mr. Goschen's surplus had provided money to make elementary education free, and a good deal was done in the way of factory legislation. There were no women inspectors as yet, but there was some attempt at dealing with sweating, and the inspectors were soon to follow.

One often thinks that this new movement for seeking help from local bodies rather than from the strife of party in Parliament meant more than we realized then. Looking back on the social reforms of the last half-century they seem to have been more closely bound up with local government than Parliament, which merely set the seal on what had already been thrashed out and decided. In those days people used to say with Besant, what has government done for you ? It speaks of good houses and sanitary officers and honest food and yet people are still living in filth and eating rubbish. Can we not arrive at some better machinery ? And yet, especially in the country, when we began to speak of county councils and to suggest doing away with the little local parish boards, there was an outcry from them as well as from the big people who controlled county matters uncriticized because there was no public with the power to criticize. After this the human beings with whom dealings were had, were men who had been placed there by vote. Women as yet had no place upon the councils, but as they had taken their places on school boards the first barrier had been broken down. The next, their admission to councils, was not to come for years, since the election of Lady Sandhurst to the County Council of London in 1889 was declared invalid.

It seemed as if this were a time of rather remarkable women, and a good many with whom I came into touch come into my mind as well as Beatrice Webb. One was Mrs. J. R. Green, widow of the historian, and herself a writer of history. We saw a great deal of her, and she had all the charm of an Irishwoman, with a tremendous sense of right and wrong. She had at her home in Kensington Square delightful gatherings of interesting literary men and women, like Jusserand, and she was a welcome guest at Cloan.

Then there were all the suffrage supporters like Mrs. Ashton Dilke, Mrs. Amos, Mrs. Eva and Mrs. Charles Maclaren, and the wonderful Miss Cons, who made the Victoria Hall, a music hall on the south side of the river, develop into the famous ' Old Vic '. Lady Grey joined Miss Stevenson and me at some of these meetings, for dubious about women's suffrage at first, she came in the end to support the movement. Mrs. Besant impressed me very much, in 1895, with her account of her work in India. She herself was dressed in Indian attire, had a coloured servant and was living at the centre of theosophy in Regent's Park. But what I remember impressed me most about her was her defence of the caste system as obviating the struggle for ' getting on ' that we have in England, and her account of how much our English dining habits disgusted the people of India who felt that eating was a thing to be done privately.

Perhaps one should also mention some of the women who were reformed-dress supporters. I met some of them, like John Strange Winter (Mrs. Stannard), and Lady Harberton. The former formed an Anti-Crinoline League, why I did not fathom, since people were attired in narrow skirts and pads, if not bustles. The divided skirts advocated by Lady Harberton came in another way uninspired by her ; first came knickers, for a time called divided skirts, with real skirts above, though shorter than in old days, and these were followed by the frank shorts of the real athlete. It was the necessities of games, not convictions, that brought the change of garb. When my brother John and I were bicycling in the Highlands we found in a little town a regular *émeute* circling round a lady in knicker-bockers who had an irate male companion. It took a great war to make these practical garments usual and popular.

This was also the period of the 'Souls' many of whom were distinguished people of quite a different calibre. They were men and women of the world who helped to break down many stupid social shibboleths and who formed an attractive society, though without any definite bounds. My brother, though never a member, became intimate with many of them and enjoyed their society. Hence I used to meet some like Mr. Harry Cust, Editor of the *Pall Mall Gazette*. A great joke was perpetrated by some of the 'Souls' by issuing an exact simile of a leading article which was sent to friends. It was extremely well written in true *Pall Mall* style and purported to be a report of proceedings in which Asquith and my brother were supposed to have put Balfour into jail in the capacities of Scottish Secretary and Lord Advocate. Morley read the article and a good deal of fun resulted. The *Westminster Gazette*, the famous successor of the *Pall*

Mall, was published I think in 1893, and I met Mr. Cust the day before its first issue, at a dinner party.

To return to famous women, there was Mme Novikoff, who was supposed with some truth to have had great influence over Mr. Gladstone concerning the Russian question. She had parties at her house in Regent's Park, but by this time her influence had waned and she was becoming a rather tragic spent star.

Then there was Margaret Llewellyn Davies who, after working in her father's parish in a poor part of London, took up the Co-operative movement very strongly, more especially the Women's Co-operative Educational Schemes, which did much good work. When in London she had a club in Lisson Grove for lads and girls together—a startling new departure then, especially in so poor a neighbourhood. She asked me to help her once or twice a week, about 1884. My mother insisted on sending the butler with me to the scene of action and fetching me back, perhaps with some reason, for there were many thieves about; but it made the matter irksome. I was truly alarmed when once or twice Miss Davies could not come to the club and I was left to grapple with it without her very efficient aid. The club was held above a fried fish shop and the smell of fried fish shops in London always reminds me of it even now and gives me certain queer qualms. Miss Davies was also interested in women's Trade Unions and in having a Union mark on goods produced under Union conditions. She talked much of this when later on in 1892, she came to Cloan.

One of the attractive Victorian ladies who did much to beautify the world, especially the world of childhood, was Kate Greenaway. She was influenced by the Morris and Grosvenor Gallery movements but she had a peculiar charm of her own which has left its mark on picture books and which for a time influenced children's dresses before the practical short frocks and knickers came into vogue. After that they looked affected. My mother and I sent her branches of ' bird cherry ' which she wanted for some reason, and I have found a letter written in May thanking us for it and telling how though the spring was vanishing, the wild roses are out and the pinks : it was like June instead of May she said : rather pathetically, she concluded that she had been painting all day and was tired.

I was never a scientist nor even a very efficient laboratory boy, but during the last years of the eighties and for some years onwards, I had great interest in helping my brother John with his experiments on the carbonic acid in the outside air. The experiments were done amongst the evergreens, both at midday and midnight and in winter time, so that this entailed going out amongst the bushes with my apparatus and then weighing the tubes, through which the air had been drawn by an aspirator outside, in a laboratory which we rigged up in an attic inside the house. In snowy weather the task was none too easy, as the aspirator often froze ; but it was great fun, for one felt that something practical was being done, and though

I had no experience of such work I gradually learned how to do it moderately well. It was a change from reading and translating philosophy in the country, and I would have sacrificed much for this particular brother who did much for me. When my mother and I went to Italy in 1898 I was able to do experiments in the tunnels (greatly to the alarm of my fellow travellers) and also to dash into, and out of, the Grotto del Cane, near Naples, in order to get a sample of the gas that poisoned the dogs. John was infinitely patient and as he explained everything carefully he was delightful to work with.[1] I don't think anyone can have had brothers as kind and helpful as I had, for the elders were always advising me with my philosophical work and discussing its bearings, whereas the youngest looked after my temporal affairs, so that hitherto they have never troubled me.

No doubt most girls are like Maggie Tulliver, who went out fishing with her brother Tom, not because she would naturally have fished, but because she moulded her life by his, and I suppose I was somewhat the same. The moderns may do otherwise. The only approach to a quarrel amongst us was one between Richard and John, over the problem of Achilles and the Tortoise, and as they were driving together on their way to a tennis party, they landed in a ditch, so excited were they over the subject. Hence they never quarrelled again ! When we were all together at Cloan, there seemed no end to the subjects we had to discuss,

[1] Later Professor J. S. Haldane, F.R.S.

between politics, science and philosophy. One's life no doubt became what the Germans call *zersplittert*, but if that does not make for efficiency (and it does not), it makes for great happiness. I always hope that the young will make a point of having plenty of interests, even if they can but pursue some. Of course, in my case I was exceptionally placed, being in touch with so many people who were experts at their own business, for we had many interesting visitors ; but the drawback was that I had no special reason to concentrate, as a young man would have had. I went to and fro to London and met interesting people there, more especially the Asquiths and Greys and occasionally the Aclands, Buxtons, Munro Fergusons and Birrells. My mother was not strong enough to travel much, but she was quite glad that I should do so and join committees for political and social matters, of which there were many.

For some reason, ' the nineties ' have always had a bad name, but as a matter of fact, a good deal was done for the working people of the land through an Act—if an inadequate one—on the Housing of the Working Classes following on the Royal Commission on the subject. Above all came the Employers' Liability Bill, besides other minor legislation concerning the notification of infectious diseases and the extension of technical education. There was a succession of strikes, including even strikes amongst Government servants, such as police and postmen, and there was the beginning of an agitation for an eight hours' day.

These things were important from a national point of view, but as far as the ordinary men and women of the country were concerned life was influenced, as much as anything, through the introduction of the ' safety ' bicycle in the beginning of the nineties. Now at last, not only were men able to get about easily and cheaply for their business and pleasure, but women were able to do the same, and for them it counted more than for men, because they had not even the penny-farthing bicycle that looked so formidable to ride but which did its turn. I feel that the inventor of the new bicycle ought to have a national memorial erected to his memory and that women should largely subscribe. No young woman of the present day realizes the sudden sense of emancipation that it gave, and this applied especially to the countrywoman who, if a housewife, often never got more than a mile or so from her home. To the women of the well-to-do classes, so-called, it meant a revolution in their mode of life, enabling them to visit friends at a distance and above all go easily to a neighbouring town which they had only been able to visit now and then. Even when the parents were wealthy enough to keep horses, these were seldom to be had when required by the young people.

At first anxious mothers hesitated before allowing their daughters to go out with male friends ; the sense of added safety owing to the companionship modified their feelings of propriety, and they were assured that the thought and attention required to guide success-

K

fully this strange machine obviated any desire to carry on frivolous conversation. They forgot, of course, the occasional mishaps, which in the first years of cycling were more than occasional! Soon everyone went happily alone, just as they might have done to walk. For some time, the machines were too expensive to be in common use but that was temporary.

One of the good results of cycling was to promote temperance, since few men could ride a bicycle successfully when drunk. And also it made for good country inns because hitherto the roadside inns were used only by men and there was little to be had but drinks of beer or spirits. Now that women came on the scene, reasonable food was supplied as well as temperance drinks and plenty of tea, if not coffee. Coffee unfortunately was generally bad.

Another movement in the early nineties arose from the growing popularity of the game of golf. Tennis had so far been the only game suitable for women since something more exciting than croquet was required. Golf took women—of course only one class of women—farther afield and helped to develop a healthy physique : its special benefit was that older women could play as well as younger.

Really the 'naughty nineties' got their name because of what was called the fast set, and these had little contact with the respectable middle-class life which one knew best, much less with the working classes. The latter were mostly occupied with developing the new organization for carrying on successful strikes in order to increase their scanty wages or diminish hours of labour. There were also other interesting developments at this time, such as the coming into use of the telephone on certain main lines. Of course this did not in any degree mean the setting up of a telephone service as we understand it, which a little later made such a change in social life. There was also a matter that interested housekeepers, the introduction of frozen meat from abroad. There was naturally the greatest objection to this new form of food and no one who could afford to do otherwise would use it or let their cooks use it, and butchers came under suspicion for selling this pernicious merchandise.

THE FOURTH DECADE
1892-1902

THE END OF THE CENTURY

THIS, the last decade of Queen Victoria's reign, had opened in rather a depressing way for the party to which we belonged. The June election of 1892 brought a Home Rule majority, it is true, and Gladstone became once more Prime Minister, Asquith being his excellent Home Secretary. But the great man's majority in Midlothian had fallen from 3000 to 690, and this represented the same fall in the spirits of his supporters. There had been many set-backs to the enthusiasm for Home Rule that he had managed to evoke earlier in his campaign. I was in East Lothian helping my brother, but it was difficult to know what to talk about. Small-holdings as a topic was none too popular, and the mention of it in a meeting brought serious heckling upon one's head. Disestablishment did the same, for the Church of Scotland was strong in East Lothian. Local Veto, or indeed any interference with the drink trade, was coldly received. This was the first time I heard ' Collectivism ' spoken of at political meetings. I expect it was derived from Fabian influences and not from the orthodox Liberalism of the day. Joseph Chamberlain as what Mr.

JOSEPH CHAMBERLAIN SPEAKING AT INVERNESS ON THE
HIGHLAND LAND QUESTION

Gladstone called a ' Dissentient Liberal ' certainly brought a new element into the party which he was to join. He supported Old Age Pensions and, before 1892, had the satisfaction of seeing Lord Salisbury's Ministry pass important Acts such as those for Coal Mines Regulation, Allotments and Agricultural Holdings, and he even ventured to declare his views in the Highlands. My friend Edith Munro Ferguson sent me in a letter a clever cartoon, representing him as a Highland orator.

Of course Gladstone dealt with Disestablishment. I heard the speech in Edinburgh, in which he spoke of it ' as at the end of a long vista '. It was indeed a long vista, for it has not come to pass at this day, and the Church has gained strength rather than losing it by the changes which have come about in its character during recent years. Gladstone still preserved his wonderful commanding presence as he went about in Midlothian with his host, Lord Rosebery. The latter had lost his wife, Hannah Rothschild, to the grief of very many, in 1890. My brother knew her well : I only slightly ; but she was kindness itself when we did meet. Her Jewish funeral made quite a sensation in Edinburgh, conducted as it was with the strictest rites prescribed by the race. She had been interested in a benefit society for women of which I have spoken, and consented very unwillingly, being possibly slightly superstitious, to insure her life for what was called ' Funeral Benefit '. I can't remember why we fixed on this rather lugubrious request excepting that by paying a sum down, the monthly contributions of ordinary membership were avoided and the money went to the society which knew no claim would ever be made. As a matter of fact Lady Rosebery died a few months after she joined our society.

I saw Mr. Gladstone at Colinton, which was in his constituency, just before the election in 1892, and he looked worn and was wearing goggles since he was suffering from his eyes. But he seemed to regain his full vigour when in Parliament, and as regards his Home Rule was both uncompromising and formidable. The younger men felt that they had not much chance of formulating a policy of their own. It would have been impossible, had one not seen and known this great man, to realize what he meant to his generation or how a man well over eighty could possibly hold a position so predominant. One wonders whether to marvel most at Gladstone being Prime Minister at eighty-five, or at Pitt holding the same office at twenty-four, that is, sixty-one years younger. The former was certainly the most remarkable man with whom I came into touch in these or any times. I don't think anyone can express fully to later generations the immense force of the man and the sense of power that he gave one. It always seemed to me that in his time no one could have behaved in the Cabinet in the way that was done in later days. I can't believe, for instance, that in Gladstone's time Christian names were ever used in conclave—a plan which always seems to me wrong, even in mild charitable committees—and as for smoking, it would have been absolutely out of the question. I don't know whether the ' Sir ' with which Mr. G. was always addressed, was peculiarly his perquisite or not, but it was invariable with the younger men. I was much in the Ladies' Gallery and often during the Irish controversies of the eighties and on March 24, 1887, I heard Gladstone speak on the Coercion Bill. He seemed so old at that time, yet Sir Henry James (afterwards Lord James of Hereford) said after a visit to him, ' That old man will live fifteen years and carry his Bill before five are out.' He lived as a matter of fact for eleven years, but more than a quarter of a century had to elapse before Home Rule was granted to Ireland.

I remember my brother describing how Gladstone looked and behaved when Goschen was speaking. Richard was seated just behind him—a place he often occupied—and could see the nervous twitching of his hands and hear the deep ironical cheers that reminded him of the deep roar of a lion in its den. He was indeed leonine in every way. On asking for leave to introduce the Coercion Bill, W. E. G. and Balfour spoke and then Dillon. Richard spoke after Dillon. He was unprepared, and like many in the party, under the influence of the excitement of the occasion. However, his speech gave satisfaction to his friends and Gladstone always remembered to express his appreciation of a young man's efforts. Feeling was terribly bitter at this time and stories were told about him of the most revolting kind, even, I regret to say, by our own

MR. AND MRS. GLADSTONE, about 1897

acquaintances ; and all who told these tales, as usual, vouched for their truth. Sir Horace Davey and Sir William Harcourt's son were blackballed at Brooks's Club and no one dared to put up a Home Ruler, even in that home of Liberalism. The young lawyers like Asquith and, I suppose, my brother, suffered in their practices, and our neighbours in Scotland were shocked and in many cases cut us, though the little town near us was all in sympathy. One adventurous young lady wished to hide behind a tree at Cloan so that she might see the dreadful Home Rule visitors, but the fear of her father's wrath prevented her from doing so !

I suppose the time when Gladstone was most worshipped by the populace of Scotland was in the days of the struggle for the vote for the workers, which came under the Franchise Bill which had been rejected by the Lords but finally passed in 1884. In 1885 he spoke in Perth and of course we all drove the fifteen miles from Cloan to hear him. Sir Donald Currie, the member for the county, was our guest. It was a wonderful meeting and impressed me immensely as one of the earliest of the great meetings I have attended. Sir Donald returned to Cloan with the G.O.M. by rail, stopping the train at Auchterarder, our station. He told us how directly Gladstone got into the train he fell upon his Homer : but still he awoke to an interest in Auchterarder because he recollected from his knowledge of church history, its connection with a famous ecclesiastical case which preceded the Disruption of Established Church in 1843. This showed a remarkable knowledge of such history in Scotland.

After my brother got into Parliament in 1885, I sometimes came into personal touch with the Gladstones, especially at the time at which Lord and Lady Aberdeen lent them their delightful house at Dollis Hill, outside London. On one occasion in 1889 I lunched with them there, just after Mr. G. had been on his western tour which greatly affected his voice. He was not supposed to speak much, but he did talk a great deal, joking about the ducks which were served at luncheon as being different from the ' dooks ' as he called them, of the Upper House. (His sense of humour seemed to me slight !) He also spoke of the wonderful change in the prices of houses, instancing Carlton House Terrace. He didn't like Lord Rosebery, then a young man, settling in Berkeley Square. He being ' the most handy man he knew ' had chosen ' a house the most unhandy '. This surprised me greatly, but I imagined that he was judging Berkeley Square by Carlton House Terrace or St. James's Square, the home of most great Parliamentarians of that time. What always struck one with Mr. Gladstone was his enormous vitality and the eagerness with which he discussed every topic. He was keenness itself about what Mr. Carnegie had written on the spending of wealth, with which he fully agreed. With Mrs. Gladstone I had a good deal of talk at Dollis Hill. She was constantly anxious for her husband's health, especially of his speaking out of doors from a four-in-hand. She and her son had arranged to sit on either side of him, so that one or other might prop him up as required. She loved being at Dollis Hill and being able to come out there with a kitchenmaid to cook for her, and told me much of her work for girls, etc. Finally she wanted me to take her seat at the Parnell Commission, then going on, and gave me her husband's card which would allow me to have her place in the well of the court. I went there, but after a time Mrs. Gladstone herself appeared. I was about to leave, when she told me to stay, and as the court was crowded to its utmost limits, she got me shown to what was practically the witness-box. I was shy but she so kindly patted me on the back and said ' It's all right, I'll take care of you '. I heard Kerry, Sexton and others examined and cross-examined and felt as if I should have confessed to anything under the sun, were I subjected to such a gruelling ordeal. As I wrote to my mother : ' You can't think how horrid the Attorney-General looks when he thinks, or seems to think, that the witness is lying. I felt I should have said anything they wished.' Mrs. Gladstone had been delayed by an interview with Millais about his portrait of her grandchild. I had other opportunities of attending the Commission which was causing such intense feeling and, in particular, I was there at the opening of Charles Russell's most remarkable speech for the defence, and saw Parnell and Davitt, though I did not hear them examined : nor was I present at the final Pigott dénouement. The secretary of the Commission, Mr., afterwards Sir, Henry Cunninghame was an old friend.

I describe in my diary how Richard told me of a conversation he had with Mr. G. regarding Disraeli in a time of great tension. He said : ' He was a very bad man but he had great debating power. He accused me of misrepresenting him when I could not trust myself to mention his name.' Gladstone had challenged Dizzy to quote instances of his misrepresentation, but merely had the reply that it was a common thing. ' Would he then instruct his secretary to give details ?—no result '. He had told Lady Salisbury on her speaking somewhat apologetically for giving a place to Disraeli in the Cabinet, that of course it was inevitable. Gladstone's memory of speeches delivered sixty years before astonished Richard. Mr., afterwards Sir, Thomas Raleigh used to give amusing accounts of the sayings of eminent people, having in a wonderful degree, the power of mimicry as well as a sense of fun. He saw a good deal of Gladstone at Oxford and described his modes of speech. There was for instance a discourse on a brown leaf : ' Mr. . . . has presented me with this leaf and is very pleased to describe himself as an admirer of mine. I find my admirers are divided into two classes and those classes balance one another. There are those who give me what they imagine I would like and those who take from me what I have and enjoy.'

I heard Gladstone introduce the Home Rule Bill of 1893. His voice was weak but the peroration was finely delivered. He also spoke in a debate on Uganda, not too clearly. At this time Lord Randolph Churchill was beginning to be ill and I could see that he held his hand on his heart nervously.

Mr. Tom Raleigh, just mentioned, though silent in general company, was often intensely amusing. Once at Cloan my mother and I took him to a local charitable entertainment which proved to be somewhat vulgar. My mother was very uncomfortable and wished to leave the hall, but Mr. Raleigh said ' No, don't go, I am enjoying it too much and it would look so conspicuous if we were to march out '. He never, though a grave Don, let us forget ' That awfu' footba' Club ' and liked to sing the chorus about the man who kicked his wife out of bed—the song then being sung— asserting that he went to hear it under my mother's auspices !

Gladstone was always uncompromising and for- midable when any personal question arose. He would not, for instance, have Acland as a Whip because he had been a clergyman. The 1892 election was a hard blow and he looked worn and is said to have remarked ' I shan't be in at the death ', i.e. the passing of the Home Rule Bill. News of his diminished majority in Midlothian came to him when at luncheon. He finished his meal and went quietly to the other room and said : ' By the way, Morley, I have thought of a point in connection with the (Home Rule) Bill.'

It was almost as if he were acting a part. Sir Algernon West, whom I often met, was always looking out for outside information to convey to his chief. He was touchingly devoted, and used to say ' I would sweep his chimney '.

When Mr. Morley was at Cloan he told us that Gladstone said of the Duke of Argyll, ' You know he became suspicious of me because he thought I wanted to disestablish the Scotch Church—as if I cared whether the Church were disestablished or not.' Certainly when I heard him in the Albert Hall in Edinburgh he shewed little enthusiasm one way or other. John Morley told us that when Mr. G. was Lord Rector of Glasgow University, Principal Caird asked him if he did not grudge the time given to the comparatively dull academic sphere. He got up with a frown and said ' Politics are dull, not Learning '. The same day he made one of his great speeches. Morley spoke to me with emotion of the affecting scene when his portrait was presented to the great man. He was in tears. He talked of his complete simplicity and of how he had left him bareheaded on a cold November day. He always read for half an hour before he went to bed, which seemed to me an excellent plan and one to be followed ! Morley was most anxious to be the person selected to write Gladstone's Life, but at first it did not seem likely that he would be so. He was much gratified when eventually this came to pass.

Having said so much about Gladstone, who died in 1898 but resigned in 1894, I should also speak of the other great man who passed during this decade : a man of a very different type. He died in 1891 but he passed out of practical politics after the O'Shea débacle in 1890. Charles Stewart Parnell is one of the tragic figures in history, and though I never really knew him I came across him in those early days of Home Rule excitement. His sharply cut, sallow, bearded face is indelibly fixed on my imagination, as are his deep-set eyes, but even more than that, the queer twitching of his narrow fingers as I sat behind him at a dinner given to him by the '80 Club. This was in 1888. I heard him speak rather often in the House. In March (1887) there was a remarkable debate which I heard on a motion for the adjournment of the House, when Parnell called Balfour ' the mildest mannered man that ever scuttled ship or cut a throat '.[1] He had a real gift for invective, though not properly speaking eloquent.

One of the most striking speeches was delivered in July that year, 1888, on the motion for embodying the Allegation Bill which gave Parnell a great opportunity of declaring his innocence. He spoke about midnight, in a condition of great emotion. I can hear his words ringing through the chamber : ' You call me an honourable member. Were these things true I, who

[1] The attack was made over the arrest of Father Kettle, an Irish priest. Mr. Parnell said of Mr. Balfour, the new Secretary for Ireland, that this mildness of his manner would not make him escape from the judgement history would assign to him as one who in his short tenure of office had been guilty of more errors and displayed more callousness and indifference than any of his predecessors.

am termed an honourable member, should be dis-
honourable and dishonoured.'   Then why, he demanded, does the Government desire to investigate
many other matters as well as these forged letters ?
' It would investigate what Tom did, what Dick did
and what Harry did, before they investigated what I
did.' This white-faced and tragic looking figure made
the deepest impression upon us all in the Ladies'
Gallery. I was seeing the various Irish M.P.s a great
deal, Justin McCarthy and others, and was assured
that the incriminating writing was quite unlike Mr.
Parnell's. I was told by them that, though so strong
in speech, he seldom swore, but that he did so over Sir
Wilfred Lawson's motion to appoint the Select Committee. It was not as a rule Parnell's eloquence that
impressed one, however, excepting when intensely
moved, as he was at this time.

When at Cloan, Morley told us that he met Parnell
in the Lobby one night about 6.30, when the Allegation Bill was coming on. It was late owing to other
business, and he asked Morley if he thought he could
be away for an hour. ' Why ? ' asked Morley. ' Oh,
there is talk of gold being found at my place in Wicklow and I am not satisfied with the assaying machine.
The man told me that if I came at seven I could see
another one ! ' Mrs. Paul had been taken in to dinner
by Mr. Parnell at the Buxtons' house and he talked of
his bad memory and difficulty in remembering dates
(which indeed appeared rather frequently and sometimes tried his supporters). Mr. Gladstone took him

BALFOUR, ABOUT 1885

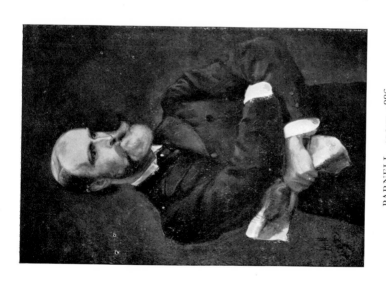

PARNELL, ABOUT 1886

into a corner afterwards and appeared to be haranguing him on historical grounds : he listened in silence. I don't think Parnell knew any history. Richard sat next to him at the '80 Club dinner and Parnell told him that either Ireland must rule herself or have a despotic ruler, if that were possible. Former leaders had been too weak. He asked for information as to Lord Spencer's association with the Land Bills before he made his speech. Then he told him about his great interest in the gold diggings in Wicklow, for one day while shooting he found some ore and returned home to get a spade to dig up what proved to be gold. He had escaped from an attack made on him by Balfour, in order to see to an assaying machine, but returned in time to reply. I think that was another occasion than the one spoken of by Morley.

Another Irish leader, Mr. Dillon, paid us a visit to Cloan in 1887. He spoke of Chamberlain's efforts in regard to what he called forestalling Gladstone concerning Home Rule, negotiating the Kilmainham Treaty and attempting to get Parnell made Chief Secretary, also revising an article written by a Nationalist in the *Fortnightly Review*. Chamberlain, he said, even offered to go to Ireland with Dillon if the Nationalists would give him a platform, but this they refused as it would mean deserting Gladstone. Dillon talked of the lack of leaders in the Nationalist Party, owing to the lack of education amongst them, and said he was not a democrat, for he saw the dangers of democracy as exemplified in American wire-pulling. He considered that the

L

Irish Party, as such, would succumb as soon as its objects were attained since its great interest and sentiment were holding it together—indeed at present it was a virtual tyranny. From the English point of view he suggested that a Parliament should be granted to Ireland for an experimental period of ten years—an odd idea. Dillon was apparently reactionary in many ways, disliked trains, telegrams and daily papers. Indeed he was a real diehard and thought that the Irish Parliament would, to the surprise of English Radicals, be conservative since it would represent agricultural interests. He gave us an amusing account of the experiences of his companions and himself in Kilmainham Gaol. His cell was only 8 feet by 6 feet and it contained a small bed and a chair, and the window was too high for him to see out. Parnell, however, had a furnished room. They suffered much from having three guards outside, who talked and disturbed them at night. One night Parnell put his palliasse against the door to deaden the sound. At 6 a.m. the Governor came round and the guard pointed out the leader's room. When the door was opened the palliasse fell into the Governor's arms and he was much alarmed, thinking the prisoner had escaped and left an infernal machine behind him. The guards used to call out every quarter of an hour ' All's well ', which was also disturbing. One prisoner in the infirmary at last threw out a bottle of medicine on the guard, calling at the same time ' All is *not* well '. Dillon's view was that if the leaders were imprisoned further, it would leave the peasantry ungoverned and more crime would result. In Forster's time prison appears to have been a rather agreeable place. Mr. Dillon acted as librarian. To their surprise, the Moonlighter prisoners, who had been accustomed to earn 9s. a week, were allowed £1.

Mrs. Lauder Brunton, who was a Stopford, a sister of Mrs. John Richard Green, and very Irish, was a friend of ours : she said she must confess that Parnell was not very agreeable socially. He came to a dinner-party an hour and a half late and all he said after having all the dinner re-served to him was, ' Sorry I'm late—I had a letter to write.' His treatment of his followers seemed to satisfy them—at least they were absolutely deferential to him and apparently never objected to being ignored.

Tim Healy was always delightful as a conversation-alist. I enjoyed meeting him at dinner in 1887. But like many Irishmen he was emotional. When a clause in the Crimes Bill was being discussed about, I think, making it a crime for an evicted tenant to reoccupy a holding, he made a strong appeal to Lord Hartington to which he did not respond. Healy thereupon burst into tears and said that he prayed God that those who showed no mercy might, at the Day of Judgement, find none. He became a great favourite in London society later on, and especially at Gray's Inn, where he was a Bencher.

Another later Victorian of whom we saw much in the nineties was George Meredith. In the latter part of

his life he was much of an invalid.   My brother visited
him constantly, and my mother and I occasionally went
to see him and his daughter in the little house at Box
Hill.   They also came to stay with us both in London
and at Cloan.   A visit to Cloan was in September,
1890, after they had been with friends in Glasgow,
and Meredith was better in health than he had been
for some time.   He was a picturesque figure in his
brown velvet coat and red tie, and was as ever full of
talk.   It was quite unnecessary to entertain him, for
the wonderful sentences poured from his mouth and
we had but to listen.   The little burn that passed our
house attracted him greatly, and he loved to walk by
it in the early morning and to talk of the sound of the
stream tumbling down amongst the stones as one of
the sweetest in nature.   He delighted, he said, in the
' nymph of the waters ' and a hedge of scarlet tropaeolum in front of the house immediately had its simile :
' Woman resembles the tropaeolum : she is a parasite
full of beauty.   Therefore let her remain a parasite
catching the fleeting tail of facts—unravelling the
mysterious tangle of hints ' and so on.   His speech was
always after this style, though it was difficult to recollect the exact words.   His daughter and I thought
his views of women, which were ostensibly ' advanced ',
most inconsistent, for greatly to Mariette's disgust, she
was kept with her chaperone within the grounds of
his cottage.   She copied out his manuscripts in case of
fire and these in pre-typing days were kept in a case
usually supposed to be her dressing-case about which

there was always great anxiety. He was then just finishing *One of Our Conquerors*, and explained that he had to make his hero mad and then kill him.

Meredith, while with us, met our much loved old minister, of whom I wrote before, who had come to his parish in 1835 and remained in it for 57 years. He was then an aged man, but a great lover of poetry and fiction. The old minister patted Meredith on the back, saying 'You're just a laddie'—which pleased him. Meredith told us how John Morley and he had walked in the Lake District and how he had seen a lamb in a pool and written a Wordsworthian sonnet on it. Certainly he was a true nature lover, despite the apparent artificiality of his conversation. I remember his enthusiasm in his early morning walks in St. James's Park in London, over the double cherry, which was in full bloom at the time and whose loveliness impressed him. But one always felt that one could not catch up his conversation which seemed to flow on never-endingly. I cannot forget the effect when he marched up and down the platform of our little station at Auchterarder, while waiting for a much delayed train, declaiming to the astonished stationmaster and porter sentence after sentence of Meredithian eloquence on everything on earth and above the earth, not one word of which did they comprehend.

In 1895 I remember lunching with his daughter, later Mrs. Sturges, and having some serious talk with him. He spoke of Carlyle as a great romancer, but not as an historian and he teased the governess about

Judenhasz and later about Christianity being kept separate from life. I tried to find out what he thought of the Scottish or Kailyard school, then in great vogue, but he had not read much of it. He admired Crockett, however.

George Meredith wrote to me on September 9th, 1890, about a plaid which he had wished me to order for him. Those who remember him well, remember how gracefully he wound his plaid over his shoulders, and how it fell over his spare form in folds. It went well with his soft brown hat and tweed clothes. He had recently had a loss in his family. He wrote : ' The Auchterarder Plaid enrols me in the Clan Haldane. And of course the gift is accepted most gratefully, though it is a gift that yet more impoverishes than enriches. For do you not see how it robs me of power of ever imposing another commission on you ?

' I beg you will tell your mother that her letter comforted me. Any word of hers would do so, for she is of the order of good women, to whom we men that have had a full taste of life would kneel—and I do.

' My girl and I send her our best respects. We send the next best to the Member for East Lothian. We shall not forget the view of the range of the Grampians. Believe us both to be most warmly and gratefully your servants and friends. I would bid you if you think it would please the worthy curé of your town, to commend me to his recollection.'

The last sentence refers to the aged minister, with whom Mr. Meredith made friends. He said in 1901 that he often intended to put him into one of his books as a character. In 1902 he was not very well, was deaf and read incessantly, and in 1904 Richard and his daughter used to walk beside his donkey chair. He looked older, Richard said, but was very much interested in things, and affectionate. Later on, however, he went to see him with Mr. Asquith and he was brilliant in the extreme : they had a wonderful evening of talk.

Of minor Victorian celebrities I saw much of Lady Dorothy Nevill about this time, for she asked me to lunch with her whenever I spent Sunday in London. Hers was one of those elusive personalities that belonged to a former generation, far more than to our own. The whimsicality of her ideas seemed so entirely a part of her ever-enduring youthfulness and daintiness that they distracted the mind from the goodness of her heart and the shrewdness of her judgement. She was a real Tory of the old school, and hated, or pretended to hate, what she called my ' horors ' (*sic*), i.e. Liberal or Radical statesmen whom she believed to be my friends. Only, when she met them in the flesh, she usually fell to them. She really liked everyone who was of interest to her. Her letters were odd and scrappy, careless as to spelling, which she despised, but most entertaining. She hated cruelty : ' I have been today to a wonderful sight of frivolity carried to its utmost. You will despise me but I like seeing everything from high intellect to the utmost frivolity. I went to see a shop showing the newest devises (*sic*) for hats for Ascot, amongst other terrible creations was one for *200* guineas sent to a Princess from Bucharest made of nothing but the tender plumes of those dear birds. You cannot imagine the ghastly array of enormous hats to be put on such terribly empty heads. It is sad to think of all the emptiness of heads and bodies now going about, apparently able to talk and chatter in their own way. And what is to come to us in a short time—no one seems to care. L. G. (Lloyd George) seems to carry all before him and he has got the lowest of the low with him and they are in 1000s compared to our poor pathetic middle class.' And again she asks me to see that she got a good place at a meeting, at which my brother (to whom she was devoted) was to preside. 'Mr. Gosse gave me a ticket but I have begged him to get me a seat near the Speaker's, not with the lower friends of the people. I like to be aristocratic while it lasts—and I hope the humble may manage to be exalted on this occasion. I was so grieved not to see your brother in purple and fine linen take his seat.' Though she hated the 'horors' (Radicals) she used to say they were the clever people. 'The upper class are—though I ought not to say so— very . . . [words failed her] they seem to take no interest in anything but golfing. It makes me quite sad when I go to any of the museums and see not a soul there. . . . Not one soul of the higher class visible— in fact I never heard of any one of them knowing the place, and for this we are spending millions.'

She could not bear pretence, being herself ab-solutely devoid of it. I remember hearing her say

LADY DOROTHY NEVILL IN THE OLD DAYS

to a traveller to the South Pole, or some such place, whom she suspected of suffering from being the lion of the day : ' Ah, *I* don't know any geography beyond Australia ! ' Possibly it was true, for she never aspired to knowledge of any accuracy in things that seemed to her not to matter. ' I don't pretend to be a bright specimen—like you ! ' she would say to those she thought self-important.

Lady Dorothy was a real friend whom I missed and so did her friends in the London Hospital to whom she brought from outside an unusual breath of gaiety and fun. She used to advise me to make friends with those younger than myself, as she did herself, and in spite of her gloomy forebodings in writing she kept her gay spirit to the end.

Even towards the end of the century there were enormous differences as regards the manner of life of the people of these and other lands, and one often thinks how we should be irked by many petty inconveniences which would meet us every hour. The telephone we are apt to think of as a nuisance, as it often is. But we know of our irritation when it is off work and of our gratitude to it in cases of accident or illness. All Scots were proud of a Scotsman, Graham Bell, having invented the telephone in 1876, but there was much litigation concerning its use and the United Telephone Company was not allowed to use wires in streets or underground as late as 1888. In 1885 there were only 3,800 telephone subscribers in London, and

10,000 in the rest of the country. The unsettled policy of the Post Office and difficulties with local authorities kept things back till it took over the Company's business in 1911. By this time even the little towns and villages had got the telephone and matters went on apace. I remember the excitement when this first occurred with us, and when a mischievous nephew put through the message to the local butcher (not thinking that the service was really in working order) : ' I must tell you that we have all become vegetarians so your instrument is of no use to *us* ! '

Then as regards mobility, the changes are inconceivable. In 1936 at holiday time in summer, it is estimated that there were 12 million people transported by the railway companies to seaside and other resorts between Friday morning at 8 a.m. and midnight on Saturday—that is to say, more than a quarter of the total population of this country. I have no figures for the end of last century, but the holiday movement must have affected but a fraction of that number. Besides this, motor-cars, which did not exist then, are crowding the roads, so that one gets the impression that no one remains immobile unless invalided. It is strange to think of the changed ideas regarding the way in which to spend a holiday. Up to near the end of last century, Sunday school treats in the rural districts meant the loan of ordinary farm carts with boards for seats and horses with well burnished harness, in order to go to picnic, very possibly to a neighbouring farm or gentleman's house, five or six miles off. It is difficult for a true Victorian to believe that these quiet expeditions did not give more real pleasure than expeditions by motor-bus and train to places far off, where there is no human contact, and for which days of preparation are needed. But the Victorians may be wrong.

The impression one had of the social life of the intelligent sort at this time, as represented by those like the ' Souls ', was that it was taken up with one side of life and used its powers for personal enjoyment : intellectual interests were carried on regardless both of other people and other lines of work. That, at least, was how it seems to have impressed other people, who did not belong to the select company. For them conversation was at a high level, without the priggishness of the blue-stocking or the solemnity of the salons. Hence it was a delightful society for those who shared in it and an interesting contrast to the more serious society of the Webbs, Reays, Aclands, Pauls and Morley; or of Graham Wallas, who was writing his interesting life of Place.

There were excellent plays of a popular sort in the latter years of the nineties. The delightful Dorothy Baird was acting in ' Trilby '. Mrs. Patrick Campbell was in her glory, and I went to the first night of ' Little Eyolf '—to me an entirely new kind of play.

The *Westminster Gazette* too had made an excellent start under the able editorship of Mr. Spender and the cartoons of Gould done about 1 p.m., quite quickly, were a great asset to the paper.

With a Liberal Government in power—popular or unpopular—there was a good deal of social life, much of it among the young politicians being led by Miss Margot Tennant, who was making up her mind as to the suitor she meant to choose as her husband, and both the successful applicant and herself visited us together at Cloan. Beatrice Potter, another famous and beautiful young woman of an entirely different type, had already made up her mind and she was now Mrs. Sidney Webb, and leading a different sort of society. The new Home Secretary, Asquith, was doing useful work, and there was much to be done, for 1893 was a year of great suffering, especially in Lancashire. The Home Rule Bill was still the King Charles's Head and it involved infinitely long discussions and some fracas in the House. Besides this, there were labour troubles, and in South Yorkshire, at Featherstone, there was a riot in which two men were killed. Keir Hardie was a portent, appearing as he did at the House in cloth cap and with a brass band to lead him, and the I.L.P. was formed with its doctrine of the Right to Work. In 1894 Gladstone withdrew from politics at the age of eighty-five. His tragic leave-taking of the Queen he served so faithfully will be remembered. Both were old; she was ten years younger than he but age had told on her more, and she had not the great mindedness to part with him in a fitting manner. Without consulting Gladstone, Lord Rosebery was put in his place, with Sir William Harcourt, to lead in the Commons, but the Government lasted but one year and an election in 1895 gave conservatism full power for the rest of the decade and more. It was a real landslide for the Liberal party, though it saw progress amongst the Socialists.

Harcourt is credited with the saying ' We are all Socialists now ', and it was true in his case more than in most, for he introduced the Death Duties Budget, which has made for socialism more than most of the measures which have been credited with the crime. As regards death duties, my brother helped him greatly and though the two had differed rather seriously before, they became unexpectedly reconciled, and later on they worked together and in the end were almost affectionate.

On the 17th of February, 1894, Richard, who had been a faithful confidant in all his friend's anxieties and had done his utmost to help him, though often a friendly critic of the lady, who gave him so much anxiety, acted as best man to Herbert Henry Asquith. Both bride and groom looked strangely nervous, but bridegroom and groomsman were carefully dressed for once—Richard by Smallpage and Asquith by Poole. Mr. Gladstone, who was, of course, present, looked magnificent though infirm.

This wedding made a distinct difference in the social side of the party, for Mrs. Asquith became a leading force in its running. The party indeed was to be in the wilderness for many years, but it was going to change its character in a way one only realizes in looking back. So far it had been largely middle-class and non-conformist : it, or its leaders rather, were now to mix with all sorts of people, welcomed so long as they were interesting to talk to. Dinner parties on Sunday now took the place of simple Sunday suppers, and instead of keeping alongside the growing Labour or Socialist party it was, I always felt, getting away from it. It is always difficult to appraise these things, especially at the time, but I think those who, like myself, went to the various parties given for Liberal women realized it. It shocked me when a lady reporter asked me who were these ladies, pointing out certain guests. I replied Mrs. So-and-so and Miss So-and-so. ' It's not that I want ', she said, ' it's Coronets ! ' And there were, strange to say, coronets still among the Gladstonian Home Rule Liberals, though mostly new ones.

Perhaps this new orientation of our party had some connection with the lighter outlook of society in general. The stiff Victorian attitude was passing away as it had to pass. But the fact that the Liberals had a Prime Minister in Lord Rosebery, who won the Derby, gave them, for a time, a certain *cachet*. My brother was rather unexpectedly not in his Government, though he had been a close friend and consultant in political matters for years past, but it was better for himself that he was not so. We all felt that Lord Rosebery was not putting his back into the work, and those outside could not do much without him. All the women's political societies, to which I belonged, were discouraged. Rosebery's sleeplessness had probably a good deal to do with this apparent apathy. I remember that he said one day he had slept three hours, as though a wonder.

The winter of 1894 was exceptionally cold and there was plenty of curling at Cloan. But the cold was hard upon the poor and the luxury of the rich contrasted with the poverty around. It was said that at one of Lord Rosebery's receptions the flowers alone cost £1000, and this seemed inconsistent with the tenets of the old Liberal party.

An election took place in January, 1895. My youngest brother, his wife and I were living at Dunbar and we did our best for Richard, canvassing among the labourers, for we knew it would be a stiff fight. The fishermen were always difficult, but the labourers and miners were still faithful friends. We began in this election to use the new-fangled safety bicycles made for women and so superior to the slow tricycles we used to favour. But our mother drove from Perthshire to East Lothian in a wagonette, with her own horses, and being fairly well at the time, was able to be present at the declaration of the poll and she saw her son—no small weight—successfully carried shoulder high by the crowd afterwards.[1]

After this I got my second volume of Hegel finished, and began to work at a little life of Frederick Ferrier, the Scottish philosopher, for the Famous Scots Series.

[1] This election was disastrous for the Liberals. The Opposition came in with a majority of 152.

This brought me into touch with several delightful people, including Ferrier's daughter 'Coggie'. My brother Richard had been much exhausted between his own heavy law work and his other work on death duties, but he joined the Tweedmouths and Morley at Guisachan and later went with his brother to Weimar and Göttingen. His stay at his old university town was always a pleasure, especially as he saw his much-loved German governess, Fräulein Schlote. I also arranged about the publication of a small book of extracts from Hegel, called the *Wisdom and Religion of a German Philosopher*. I fear it was only valued by the initiated, as such books usually are.

I had in 1890 an opportunity of seeing something of the old Germany, with its famous men, because my uncle, Sir John Burdon Sanderson, had to attend an International Medical Congress in Berlin, and he and his wife invited me to go with them. The journey was both crowded and hot and hardly any food was to be had : also one of the party had monkeys with him and there was a terribly heated argument as to what category they came under, as no mention was made of any such passengers : we went over the lists to see whether 'affen' could be counted as dogs, cats or horses, while hoping they might be exempted altogether from taxation. Officialdom reigned as I found later on, when I got into a first class compartment with a second class ticket, between two stations close to one another, and meaning in my innocence to pay the difference. We had, as a matter of fact, to go before the authorities and pay a fine.

At Berlin we had the opportunity of seeing and meeting the great scientists of the day—Virchow, du Bois-Reymond and many others. We took tea with the last mentioned in his lovely villa at Potsdam and found him very lame with gout and characteristically ill-tempered. We were told that to keep him in good temper Gaede had to do an experiment with a blunt instrument while pretending to use a sharp one as directed by his chief. John and I tried to do some translation into English from an important book which he had written, but the results were disastrous, since nearly every word was altered by the author. His view was that there were two living physiologists—himself in Berlin and Ludwig in Vienna. For them niches were to be kept in some public building. I regret to say that at the great party the champagne was rather liberally partaken of, but we ladies departed early. Caprivi was at the Court Garden Party and pleased me by asserting that in England, women appeared to be abler than men, instancing Mrs. Humphry Ward as the greatest living novelist. I visited many of the social centres of various kinds, and was immensely impressed by them, just as I was at Essen a good many years later. I also saw what was then the wonderfully good equipment of the common schools : our country had not nearly so many maps and pictures, not to speak of teachers' museums. Then I learnt a good deal about the ' Versicherung ' system, which was the origin of our Health Insurance system set on foot by Mr. Lloyd George, who later

M

invited me to act on some of the committees regarding it, and even suggested my becoming a Commissioner, which would have been a whole time job and therefore impossible for me to undertake. He deserves much credit for the way he pushed it through, in spite of enormous difficulties with doctors and friendly societies alike.

In 1893 with my younger brother William and two friends, I had an interesting journey to California. America was extraordinarily different then from what it was when I visited it twenty years later. It was the year of the Chicago Fair, and Chicago was crammed with people, struggling to get about in cars far too few to hold them. One had to cling on to them like limpets, hoping for the best. Of cabs there were none. But our excitement was when we got to the Rockies and were told that our train was likely to be 'held up' and we must be prepared for the worst. Everyone set about searching for arms, and quite a supply appeared. One very fat gentleman remarked, after producing two revolvers, that he had lived too long to be without them. The engineer had a Winchester rifle, and the express-man, who occupied a car in front and was responsible for the safe in which the bullion we were carrying was placed, prepared himself for a struggle. The sheriff and a local judge were also of the company, as they had news of the trouble. There had, it turned out, been a terrible case of ' Holding Up ' shortly before, when the engineer, express-man and others were killed, and the same gang was waiting for any train at a place called Midvale, where there was a hut. The robbers had, however, gone to a sort of restaurant for food and been recognized and, being in Indian territory, they were pursued by the Indian (Flatheads) police. After a fight round the hut at Midvale, in the course of which the unfortunate restaurant keeper and one Indian policeman had been killed, they were surrounded. None of us knew that there had been an attack till we reached this place and passed the vans containing the dead bodies. It was strange to see the whole thing—the hut with mounted police riding round, armed with Winchester rifles : the sheriff and the most unjudicial-looking young judge, who told us all sorts of tales of this wild neighbourhood and of the cowboys and their doings, so that one felt as if in the midst of a Bret Harte novel. The newsboy who perambulated the train with very expensive papers begged us to buy, for as he said it would make no difference in the end : one thief might as well get the money as another ! The sheriff told how his wife had wept at his departure, and how he had told her just to bury him where he lay, which strangely enough did not comfort her. The robbers had, we heard later, escaped from the cabin by night but were pursued and one was shot dead. The other had got off, but was wounded. The judge expected that he would have to condemn him to death, unless lynching settled the matter, as he seemed rather to expect. There was no chance for him in the mountains, without either horses or provisions. We spent a Sunday in a town which was little better than a mining camp and went down one of the mines. I had rather a terrible impression of what a ' hard ' town might mean. There was great noise in the gambling and dancing saloons on Saturday night and one China-man was killed in a fray. The wooden huts had no apparent sanitary arrangements and some had omin-ous notices inscribed on them, such as ' Scarlet Fever here '.

I cannot think that the Yosemite Valley can be as attractive now or since the time when we drove in coaches, the driver flicking up a rattlesnake with his whip, and when on reaching an hotel we were all dusted down with long-handled feather dusters. The dust was appalling but the scenery was mag-nificent.

Towards the end of the nineties the scene became overcast by the dread of war, for on December 29th, 1895, Dr. Jameson—a Scotsman known to many of our friends—who was Administrator of Mashonaland, conducted a body of troops of the British South Africa Company across the frontier of the Transvaal on the way to give armed support to the residents in Johannes-burg, who were resenting the Boer rule : he was surrounded and forced to surrender. We all know the result—how, as happens in such cases, the English believed that their people, ' the women and children ' of their race, were in danger : the Boers that their territory was being laid hold of. The Kaiser sent an ill-advised telegram of congratulation to President

Krüger. Though Jameson was summoned home and punished, the feelings that arose became more and more hot, but all this belongs to history.

This was the beginning of a great division in the political life in which we were moving. One side was led by Campbell-Bannerman and the other by Lord Rosebery : the first believed that the Conservative Government, led by Chamberlain, was leading the country astray, influenced by the mining capitalists, whereas the other more or less supported Milner, who went out in 1897, and felt that the demands of England must be supported.

Rosebery, in spite of an admirable biography, was one of those enigmatical characters who have never been properly estimated. I never knew him well, but could not but be proud of a few written words of esteem, for I think he was one of the ablest men of our time, though also a spoilt child of fortune. My brother saw him continually and worked for him assiduously in his Imperial League days. As Rosebery came into a room, he looked round with that strangely self-conscious manner which was so characteristic of him, and which seemed to betoken his outlook on the world. That is to say, he never lost himself in his cause, as did his great leader, Gladstone, and there-fore, with all his eloquence, did not persuade his audience or carry them away as did the other. His eloquence was marvellous : the words were carefully chosen and balanced and his delivery perfect. I often heard him speak. Even his ordinary notes of convention were never conventional, but examples of concise, polite and original expression, written in his beautiful script, such as might be given as examples to the slap-dash young writers of the present day. His books had the same quality, perhaps, of over-polish.   The gods seemed to have given him every gift and yet, with all his success—Prime Minister, winner of the Derby, devoted followers who would have cut off their right hands for him and who were waiting for the lead that was to carry them to victory—with all that, his life was in a sense a failure : he was never able to give the lead that was required and his party became divided. Yet while he was in full force, he gave a glamour to political life. As to his speeches they were full of wonderful phraseology. There were constant aphorisms that stuck in one's memory. Sometimes, however, he seemed just to fall short of the perfection he aimed at. His address on Cromwell, for instance, was said very truly by a good critic to have been ' brilliant but not great '.

When Richard dined alone with Lord Rosebery, as he often did, they used to start for his nightly drive at 11 p.m.—the carriage as usual set out with pos-tilions. He greatly admired our mother and said that a letter she sent him ' was of the finest tone and must be preserved amongst his documents ', and one special talk she had with him about Scottish wit and Sir Walter Scott impressed him greatly. With my brother he would sometimes sit at the back of the house in Berkeley Square talking till midnight. It was tragic that while Grey remained ' cool and efficient ' in the later times of stress in 1902, when there was a supreme effort made to render the Liberal party efficient, Rosebery, whether from ill-health or otherwise, withdrew from the forefront of the struggle and uttered as from outside. This was the time when Campbell-Bannerman spoke of the 'methods of barbarism' and Rosebery of ' ploughing a lonely furrow '. But even when he made a great speech, such as that at Chesterfield, Rosebery's manner was better than his matter, and there was little result despite the splendid resounding and often wise phrases.

Even when old and frail, his mind was as acute and his words as caustic as ever. Lord Novar told me that on one occasion when he asked him the political news, he had said : ' Politics are dull as ditch-water.' Rosebery quietly replied : ' Ditch-water is interesting and instructive when looked at through a microscope ! ' A cynical but true remark.

Sir Alfred Milner went out to South Africa in 1897, after the report of the committee inquiring into the Raid was published. I remember him first in 1885, when he was writing for the *Pall Mall Gazette*. I enjoyed my talk with him very much, but a very conservative lady—a relative—who overheard our conversation, thought him terribly advanced, which seems strange considering his after-career. He was a friend of my brother's, and Richard thought highly of his power and clear mind ; but I always felt that he was certainly not the man to deal with Krüger. I always wished a Scot had been sent out who would have understood that queer ' thrawn ' character from old experience. I met Lord Milner last at Windsor Castle and had an interesting talk with him. But that was long after this.

If politics were somewhat dim from 1896, science was progressing. There was, of course, the boom in regard to the new pneumatic tyres on wheels, which made such a difference : a lifting plane actuated by a light engine had also been invented. My brother gave me a lovely Elswick bicycle, which was my constant friend as long as I bicycled at all. The old Northfleet was discarded.[1] Gas had got its new incandescent mantles which enabled it to compete successfully with electricity. Röntgen Rays were also discovered about this date, and it was now that the law by which every mechanical locomotive had to be preceded by a red flag was abrogated, and in celebration of this great event a procession of cars was to proceed from London to Brighton, and crowds collected to see the start, which was but a start for many of them, for most failed by the way. France still held the field in the car industry.

One thing which entirely ' went out ' about this time was the old-fashioned driving expedition. My

---

[1] This was a theoretically efficient bicycle on which gears could be changed at will. Both Sir Edward Grey and I did our best with one of the make, but the gear chains kept entangling, and I was often left stranded and had ignominiously to come home by a horse-drawn vehicle.

mother and I delighted in this annual tour in a phaeton
with luggage strapped on behind.   This year (1897)
we visited her old homes in Northumberland and
walked over the moors of Otterburn and saw the old
house of Biddleston : stopped to pick flowers and to
visit friends.   It is difficult to believe that dashing
through the country at railway speed can make up for
the pauses to pick rare flowers or see fine views.

The dispute of 1897 at the Penrhyn quarries
resulted in bands of Welsh quarrymen going about
singing hymns.   We heard them in a well-known
Hampstead church and there was much sympathy
with the men.   The Workmen's Compensation Bill
was under discussion as well as the eight-hour-day
for engineers, so that such matters were forced on
the attention of all of us who belonged to the Liberal
party.   It always seemed to me that these social reforms
required more attention than they got.   For my part
I was interested in our local efforts to improve the conditions of the workers with whom I came into touch.

It was Jubilee year once more and the Diamond
Jubilee this time.   The House of Commons stand was
at the end of Westminster Bridge and from that point
of vantage one saw the scene well.   The Queen—so
small and homely in herself—looked absolutely royal
and commanding in her simple dress of black and
white.   There was no doffing of her mourning for the
husband who died 36 years before.   We lunched in
the House of Commons and spent a long time on the
Terrace, meeting Miss Gully there.   Then there was

the Thanksgiving Service at St. Paul's and one saw
the Speaker Gully's Procession, and him in his old
and decrepit car going to present his address at the
Palace. The Naval Review was another wonderful
sight. The year was cold and wet but, marvellously,
' Queen's weather ' favoured the celebration.

In 1898 there was fighting in Egypt, ending with
the battle of Omdurman, and the country rejoiced in
finding in Sir Herbert Kitchener a soldier in whom
confidence could be placed. Then the Dreyfus case
was the constant theme of discussion, and those in
touch with the great Jewish families, like the Roths-
childs, heard much about it. I remember at a garden
party it was resolved to send a congratulatory telegram
to Maître Labori, his counsel. On the social side,
Rhodes, ' neither a great moral hero nor a scoundrel,
but a very powerful statesman of the young colonial
type caring for trade more than show ' as someone
concisely put it, was a dominating interest. Like
Richard, he was much with Rosebery, and my mother
and I were anxious about the conservative bent of the
Liberal party, though Campbell-Bannerman and not
Asquith was the successor in leadership after Gladstone's resignation. Then came the great event of the
year, the death of the famous statesman. A quarter
of a million people passed by the bier as it lay in
Westminster Hall, by a decision which had no pre-
cedent in history. Men spoke in broken voices,
Tories and Liberals alike. My brother wrote : ' One
cannot express what one feels about it all. It gets

deep down. His death is as noble as his life has been.'
Lord Rosebery and he went at midnight to stand for
a little by the coffin as it lay in Westminster Hall.
' The service was fine but I would have liked to have
seen the Abbey full of people who loved him instead
of the many who abused and miscalled him while he
lived. The 90th Psalm was the best part of the service.'

A personal loss to us this year was the death of our
dear old nurse, ' Baba '. She was truly a part of our
lives and her love was a great gift to her ' children '.
We got permission from the Sheriff to bury her in a
cemetery soon to be opened as the churchyard was
overcrowded, and we four—her children—held the
cords that let down the coffin into the land which, as
our mother said, was like that of her Master, ' land
where never man was laid.' We owed much to her,
and as is said on the inscription placed by Richard on
her tomb, ' we have much reason to hold her in grateful
and affectionate remembrance.'

Our London home was now in Whitehall Court,
overlooking the river, where my brother took two
flats which together were called a ' maisonnette '.
The front rooms had lovely views. Here he had many
guests, more especially Edward Grey and, at least once,
Lord Morley.

The spring of 1898 was mainly spent in Rome,
where my mother painted and I went about with an
Italian lady. There we witnessed an interesting

ceremony, for the Pope [1] for the first time came into the open and received 20,000 pilgrims. The ceremony in St. Peter's was very impressive, as was the sound of the wonderful silver trumpet on the elevation of the Host and the dead paper-white face of the old Pope as he was carried in his regal chair. The crowd was tremendous and at one time I thought I was going to be crushed against a pillar. Lord Rosebery's villa at Naples, which at his request was visited, was very lovely in its spring verdure, but he was not there. Later on I saw him as he spoke with his usual eloquence at Perth when he opened a new library and attended a banquet—all deeply interesting to me.

It was next year (1899) that war broke out and politics took a new trend. Also parties became once more divided, and this time in a different way. The names given to the two parties were the Independents and Little Englanders, i.e. those of the Liberal party who sympathized with the views of Milner and Rosebery, and those who held to the older liberalism of Campbell-Bannerman. But the Conservative Government was safely in the saddle. Neither of our parties was perhaps very inspiring or satisfactory. Mr. Gladstone had so concentrated on Home Rule that other things had been left aside, and Rosebery and Harcourt were frankly Whigs. Great fortunes had been made in South Africa and Americans came to spend their fortunes in England, and the prosperity of the country was more financial than real.

[1] Leo XIII.

Anyhow all of the well-to-do lived in a different way. The old dinner parties at home were changed into dinners in restaurants, and the week-end habit became rampant. Bridge was played by day as well as by night, though not in our family surroundings, and we had to leave our dinner parties when the game began or else find kindred souls to talk to. Then women's clubs began to function. The first I went to, as the guest of Flora Stevenson, was the Albemarle, a mixed club well run, and there, amongst others, I met Canon Ainger, who, to my dismay, talked of Crockett as 'a vulgar dog', distinguishing him from Scott. One knew Crockett had his faults as a writer, but I never thought of vulgarity as one of them. Our Women's or Ladies' Club in Edinburgh was started soon after this and being admirably run was a consistent success. I acted on the committee but the success was due to the chairman, Lady Novar, and an excellent secretary, Miss Meiklejohn. The old idea that women were unclubable gradually vanished : poor souls, they had little chance of communal life in the old days, when preserving the Home with all its manifold contents, sacred by tradition and sentiment if not by actual value, was a solemn duty to the Family and made the women into mere keepers of museums of mementoes. The spring cleaning of these unnecessary possessions took up six weeks of every year : and drove the male members of the household nearly frantic.

At one of the many dinners given by my brother this year ('99), I had Lord Curzon on one side and

Mr. Massingham on the other, both opposed to women's suffrage, now becoming a hotly discussed question, but both deeply interested in the Greek war. A number of brave and patriotic men had offered themselves for service in Greece. Curzon rather cynically proposed that ' the present Poet Laureate (Alfred Austin) should like Byron immolate himself on the altar of freedom ' !

The phonograph was one of the new toys of the age, and when I met Le Gallienne at lunch, he declaimed one of Watson's poems into the queer machine.

A curious portent was to hear a woman preacher from America discourse in Westminster Chapel as a regular minister. She preached a forcible sermon on the words ' Be strong '. Her advent was in connection with a Women's Congress held in 1899. In consequence of this Congress there were many eminent women in London, including Louise Michel, at whom I looked with wonder, and a very different famous woman, Miss Anthony of the U.S.A.

By autumn war had begun, and all the enthusiasm that seems to accompany any war, even one of this kind, was developed. Men enlisted, feeling sure that the headstrong and obstinate Krüger and his Boers would soon be defeated, and then came the terrible rebuff, culminating in the ' Black Week ', which no one who can recollect that time will forget. We were at Bath where my mother was taking a cure, and the place and time are indelibly marked in my memory. What hurt us most was 'the pity' expressed for us by foreigners, especially the French, for we had supposed ourselves invulnerable against a population undisciplined and untrained. We had I suppose been 'swaggering down the highway of the world' unconsciously, and we had to learn that much could be taught us by the homely Boer farmers. My cousin, Aylmer Haldane, was made prisoner at Pretoria, and his escape was a wonderful and exciting adventure.

The earlier part of the year 1899 had been bitterly cold and in consequence there was, in Scotland, much curling, the only game for which I really cared. We formed a club and were duly initiated into the secrets of the craft by solemn ceremonial, though I found myself too apt to forget the secret words and symbols. Still, it was satisfactory to be, for once, the member of a secret society as a woman, since Freemasonry was forbidden to my sex. Along with another lady, I played in the annual bonspiel at Carsebreck, my brother Willie being 'skip'. Ladies had never before taken part in the great contest, which, weather permitting, takes place annually between north and south Scotland. It is a most exciting scene and besides that very picturesque. The Highlanders wear their bonnets and come down in force, though usually to be beaten by the canny Lowlanders, more skilled in the game. Everyone who plays is armed with a 'besom' with which to 'soop' (sweep) and the broadest Scotch abounds, for the laird and the minister take part along with shepherds and ghillies and those whose trades are interfered with by the frost. Our northern rink happened to be 'drawn' against one from my brother's constituency in East Lothian, and its members were very concerned about the prospect of being beaten by ladies—which at first appeared likely. However, at the end they were, fortunately for themselves, 'up two', and went back happy.

The spring of 1899 in Bath had a pleasant side in spite of our anxieties, for my mother and I were joined by my brother John, who had been suffering from pleurisy in Oxford, but was now able to bicycle with me and explore the neighbourhood. Otherwise there were baths in which to swim and an excellent old library in which to read and a good bookshop. Old Lady Tweedmouth lived at Bath and went to an evangelical chapel, founded by Lady Huntingdon, in a bath chair, attended by her attractive American daughter-in-law, Mrs. Marjoribanks, who kept us all lively. My mother also had a bath chair and attendants, so that there was a small procession. The Harry Whites — delightful Americans—were also at Bath, as well as other friends. To me, each time I visited it, Bath seemed to carry with it much of its old attraction, and somehow its spirit had not greatly changed.

The gloomy war went on next year (1900), amidst depressing circumstances : it was seen that, as usual, the War Office was incompetent for its work and that there had been complete lack of foresight. The Liberal Imperialists under their leader, Lord Rosebery,

CURLING MATCH IN THE LIBERAL PARTY

ROSEBERY AND HARCOURT LOOKING ON, ASQUITH AND CAMPBELL BANNERMAN AS SKIPS

could not, it appeared to us, face the problem, of which my brother frequently spoke, of remodelling the Liberal party. Sir Edward Grey was constantly with the latter, discussing matters. The '80 Club, once so effective, was divided, and the proper lead was lacking. The upper classes who were supposed to represent the leaders in the war were being denounced as inefficient, despite their ' playing fields ' and training in ' leadership ', and there was a cry for their giving place to the newly educated democracy.

Richard however was appointed by Mr. Balfour to a committee on explosives, which brought him into contact with the War Office for the first time. It was the sort of thing that interested him immensely, and in the Literary Society in our little town, we arranged for him and his brother to lecture on explosives. It was an exciting lecture, for it was advertised as having ' practical demonstrations '. We went to the hall and found our worthy policeman stationed in front and the audience set well back from the platform. We did have minor explosions, such as might occur in a flour mill, Richard doing the talking, and John the (sometimes protesting) laboratory boy ; afterwards we duly burned a stick of cordite on the lawn at Cloan ; but some of the rest of the explosive powder was given by me to the butler to bury carefully, and he and a stable boy thought they would try it out, just to see what would happen. The result was that their faces were badly burned. The man indeed was nearly blinded.

N

My elder brother was extraordinarily busy with legal and political work at this time, though in autumn we had a spell of rest and peace. When in London he liked to have parties for me of guests of mixed politics, like George Wyndham and the Webbs. I was also at a party at the Prime Minister's (Mr. Balfour). I enjoyed it all, only I saw that my brother was working far too hard and getting quite insufficient sleep. I was busy with politics too and often met Lady Tweedmouth, my brother's great friend, who was so full of life—a life that was to be lived so pluckily to its tragic end. Her last political party I remember so well—she knew she was going to die, but few knew it and we saw her holding herself as bravely as ever. She loved her animals at Guisachan—her tame deer and her dogs and the squirrel that used to run up Richard's legs to his shoulders.

We all worked for the 1900 election, which again was disastrous to our party : Scotland for the first time returned more Unionists than Liberals. There was little chance in Perthshire for Mr. Charles Stuart Parker in a khaki election, and my brother's majority was only 373. Sir E. Grey came to help him, as well as others, and we canvassed as vigorously as possible.

Things had improved somewhat in South Africa, and my cousin Aylmer, later General Haldane, returned safely from his imprisonment in the school in Pretoria where he had spent nearly three weeks under the floor. He gave a racy account of it all to our people in Auchterarder—more especially to the Volunteers. In spring our mother was able to come to London and get about in a bath chair, and we had many dinner parties, one including Lord Rosebery, while we also saw something of Mr. Clemens (Mark Twain) and his wife. He delighted us. My brother John was busy with gas experiments, and Richard over the Federation of Australia and the Imperial Institute.

The unhappy differences in the Liberal party continued next year (1901). As to the war, it was clear that we had been caught napping and must change our ways. But all differences ceased for the time, when on January 22nd, Queen Victoria died. I can never forget the feelings that one had when the news came. It seemed as if a whole epoch had passed away and that a new era was about to begin. We had all lived through our lives never knowing another monarch or feeling that there could be another. And there never was another monarch with just the same personality and dignity, excellent as were the kings who succeeded her. Perhaps it was not possible that there could be such, for the new democracy had accepted Queen Victoria as a national institution, which, at her age and considering her life, could not be questioned. Now one felt that there would be a different type of sovereign to suit the different conditions, one more understanding of the modern view-point, though not one more devoted to the people over whom she ruled.

This event had followed sadly on our usual Christmas festivities, Christmas tree, etc.—I went up to London for the funeral. At 11 a.m. from Victoria

Station came the funeral procession, headed by the King—a word strange to us all who had lived nearly forty years in the world, and stranger still to those who had lived sixty. Then there was the German Emperor riding behind the coffin on the gun carriage, genuinely overcome by grief, and all the other royal mourners. I was with my brothers and little nephew in the House of Commons stand in the Mall. I returned with little Patrick, who was so soon to give his life for his country, after taking him to the lovely service in St. Paul's. It was indeed a lovely service, but he, poor lad, was bored, and in a loud whisper to me suggested that surely we might now go back to the underground railway!

This was a cold winter and there was plenty of curling. The roads were so blocked that one could hardly get through—certainly not till the snow-plough had pierced the drifts. I was greatly interested in my work as Manager of the Edinburgh Royal Infirmary. There was much detail work for a woman to do and only with great difficulty were two women elected to serve on the Board of Governors, which had for so long been a male preserve. There was no proper liaison between governors and nursing staff till women were appointed, and nurses' hours and pay were unsatisfactory. I took up the question of registration of nurses and other similar matters connected with nursing, and this became a great interest in life. Long after this, I was elected the Privy Council representative on the General Council of Nursing.

Florence Nightingale, as is well known, had brought about a high standard for nurses trained in her school, but it was a monastic one, and now nursing was becoming a profession into which women entered rather than a vocation. I remember a nurse getting into trouble because a man eminently respectable, had got into touch with her in the train and come to the matron to ask whether he might carry on his acquaintanceship. It was taken for granted that all the rest of a nurse's life must be subservient to her calling, and the younger nurses rebelled. The students liked to play pranks, one of which was to dress up one of their number as a nurse, and then watch for the matron going her rounds and proceed, at a suitable corner, to give the soi-disant nurse a smacking kiss ! Some of the older doctors used to tell me that they remembered the time when they had to meet the bodies of nurses lying prone on the ground, dead drunk, and the revulsion from these bad days was, I suppose, extreme in the other direction. I thoroughly enjoyed my work at the Infirmary, then the largest general hospital in the kingdom, and in many ways a model. In this work I made great friends with Walter Blaikie, who, in addition to his work on Scottish literature, was an enthusiast on sundials, one of which he had made for me. I came also a good deal into touch with Lord Knutsford over nursing and administrative questions in hospitals, on which he was an authority. Our expenses for the feeding of patients were less than at the London

Hospital, and he used to tease me by saying that the reason for this was that we fed our patients on porridge!

Besides hospital work, we were, as before, organizing various sorts of classes in Auchterarder—classes now undertaken by the County Authorities and Women's Institutes.

Later I went to Holland with two fellow-travellers, since I was writing the life of Descartes and wished to see his very numerous homes. Our first visit was to our friends Professor and Mme Tiele, who paid us a visit at Cloan when the Professor gave the Gifford lectures. He was Principal of the University of Leiden, and gave me much help in hunting for portraits of Descartes. Descartes' main place of abode proved to have been made a part of an asylum : indeed, it was the residence of the doctor in charge. We had difficulty in finding it, for people were surprised that a modern directory would be no good. We had to apply to various burgomasters and others, but were delighted in the end to discover the picturesque house practically intact. As Englishwomen, we were none too popular in Holland at the time, owing to our connection with the war against the Dutch in South Africa, and were advised to call ourselves Americans. However, on the whole, we got on very well, though as my younger friend had just lost a brother in the war, I dreaded what might be said to her about it. The professors to whom I had introductions were lavish in their hospitality (I never tasted such wonderful asparagus as they gave us), though, as the young friend said, they seemed to be deficient in sons and to have an enormous interest in hearing all about our belongings ! We greatly enjoyed the expedition, as the bulbs were in full flower. Friesland was quite unsophisticated, and as strangers, all the men took off their hats to us. This was embarrassing when we passed an immense funeral as we did not quite know how to respond.

The summer was pleasant, with riding for the children, shooting and walking for my brothers, and perfect weather for bathing. Mixed bathing was just beginning to be tolerated. My brother John and I had one of the cycling expeditions, visiting friends in the Highlands, that we both enjoyed, and he and I did experiments on air when at home. Richard's tricycle, known satirically as ' The Flying Fox ', lost its repute after it ran off and pitched him into a field, and he never took to bicycling. There are remains of a camp of some sort, Roman or Pictish, on the top of a hill at Cloan, and this Mr. (afterwards Lord) Abercromby set-to to dig. We all helped, but there were, unfortunately, no exciting results. The Buxtons, Greys and Horners were other pleasant visitors.

Though the South African War was supposed to be over, there were still concentration camps set up to house the women and children whose homes had been destroyed. The very large child-mortality in these camps was causing great concern to all right-minded people, and the Government sent a deputation to deal with the matter. John had taken great part in the agitation, and at his request, my brother Richard wrote to Lord Milner concerning it. Mr. Chamberlain, who was Colonial Secretary, resolved to despatch a large number of nurses to care for the sick in the camps and asked Miss Stevenson and me to select those who were to go from Scotland, for Scottish nurses were specially appreciated. This gave me a considerable amount of work, but it was justified, for the nurses sent proved most satisfactory and their letters were deeply interesting. The food question was naturally the vital one, especially for children, and by degrees the necessary milk, etc., was supplied to the 25,000 people occupying the camps. All this intensified the feeling between the various political sides, for by now people were sick of the war and clamouring for efficient government. There was lack of confidence, both in the Prime Minister, Mr. Balfour, and in the War Minister, Mr. Brodrick : recruiting was falling off and the income tax raised—all results to be expected from a war.

Educationally things were moving, if slowly. The London School of Economics, in which my brother Richard was interested and for which he collected much money, was working at the problem of getting the affairs of the nation placed on a business footing, and the newer Universities, like Birmingham, were doing the same. Mr. Carnegie had given benefactions to the Scottish Universities, providing facilities for research. But the political parties on the Liberal side were still rent in twain. It was matters educational that alone gave a ray of hope, especially as regards Liverpool University, which was going ahead.

In 1902 a great figure passed in Cecil Rhodes, who was, above all, a business man, with the power of impressing others. He asked the question of my brother, ' What have you *done* in your life ? ' And when he spoke of the Universities, in which he was so deeply interested, Rhodes said ' I think I could help you '. We all know what he did for university students. I never met him but Richard thought him a great man with a passion for action and high ideals of his own kind.

University education in London was indeed a real problem and my brother was successful in getting money for it, as well as for higher education of other sorts. Fortunately, at this time, partly owing to the influence of Rhodes and above all to the fortunes made in South Africa, it was possible to get large sums of money for such objects and rich men were ready to be generous.

This year there were preparations for the Coronation, and then came the news of the King's illness, with its terrible prognostications, for an operation for appendicitis was not the ordinary matter it now is, and the worst was expected, but happily not realized.

THE FIFTH DECADE
1902-1912

THE LIBERAL REVIVAL

THE year 1903 opened with considerable anxiety. There were many unemployed, of whom one used to see dreary processions in the streets. And one knew that money had to be raised to settle the South African claims, though, at the same time, the income tax was reduced so that the finances of the country did not appear to be at a very low ebb. The country had not yet taken to heart that it owed a collective responsibility for these unemployed men. There was plenty of personal charity and some State or municipal work, but the era of social responsibility, as we understand it now, had hardly developed.

On looking back it seems as if there ought to have been a break between one century and another ; but in the case of the twentieth century there was not much fundamental change until war broke out fourteen years later. At any rate the well-to-do classes and the Liberal politicians amongst whom we lived seemed hardly aware of how the world around them was changing. The latter were doubtless looking forward to the power that was actually going to be put into their hands in 1905, and to a certain degree planning for it. But meantime there was little prospect of any such development, since the party was divided and apparently unable to decide on any one course of action.

One realizes now the pity of it all, for the needs of the people of this land were so great. When one re-members that at the beginning of the new century one-sixth of the infants born in the poorer districts died under one year of age and that the housing of the people was a scandal, one wonders how we ac-cepted conditions so calmly. It was not that we did not care : it was that our leaders did not exercise their thinking powers or insist on matters being changed. The Labour Party was taken up with Trade Union affairs, the Liberal Party with its own discussions, and the Government had its own difficulties. Of philan-thropists there were plenty : I was personally inter-ested in the working of a Health Society in West-minster started in 1905, which made strenuous and successful efforts to deal with child welfare and maternal mortality by teaching the lessons of ante-natal and post-natal care that were so essential. This Society in its thirty-two years of existence has seen infant mortality in London decrease enormously, and has instructed mothers and fathers in their duties to their offspring. This was just a small example of what people were trying to do. But though it is true that this work, begun by volunteers as is so often the case in England, has been largely taken over by the State, the lag of past years is still pressing hardly upon us now.[1] It was not lack of knowledge that prevented the necessary steps being taken in the direction of child welfare, sanitation and housing. It was that the iniquity of allowing bad conditions to exist had not been brought home to the people of this land. One wonders now why we did not see that politicians should have concentrated their efforts on getting decent conditions of life for the poor as well as the rich.

As to education, though we may not be altogether satisfied with our teaching or with the opportunities for pursuing education in later life, it is at least a satisfaction to know that by 1929 90 per cent. of our London children were being educated and that only 5 per cent. of the parents were without school education. And yet more we rejoice that school education is now popular, and that the number of summonses for non-attendance has fallen fast. The members of school boards in old days remember the constant cases of truancy that had to be dealt with.

The Liberals were supporting Land Purchase for Ireland, but they never supported Mr. Brodrick's Army scheme which in connection with its ' Brodrick Cap ' became somewhat of an object of derision. Mr. Balfour was still holding out against Protection, though now that his work in South Africa was ended, Joseph Chamberlain promoted that policy strenuously

[1] At the time of my birth the number of children in London who died in the first year of their lives was 149 per thousand, and at the time at which this book ends it was 110. During the subsequent fifteen or twenty years it came to about half that amount. The general death-rate fell from 21·3 in 1862 to 13·8 in 1914.

Two little dogs in the Cabinet
  In the midst of stormy weather,
After raising a breeze about Fiscal Reform,
  Had tied their tails together.

They'd tied their tails with Protection Tape,
  And hoped that nobody knew;

But the wind of inquiry it blew so keen,
  That it cut their tape in two.
And one little dog rushed here & there
  Dumping speeches with might & main
The other sat still to scheme how he could
  Tie their tape together again.

With apologies to Messrs Bennett & D'Arcy Thompson.

BALFOUR AND CHAMBERLAIN

and by that means made himself the man of the hour. But the very fact that he supported this scheme, though it made him a man of importance in the political world, had the effect of bringing together the unfortunate Liberal party in their keen opposition to his policy. So now at last the Liberals were united, and prepared to find a good platform from which all could speak with freedom. For it was easy for us to deal with Free Trade at our meetings when foodstuffs were, according to Mr. Chamberlain, to be subject to taxation. Nothing could be more unpopular with those who remembered the ' bad old days ' when bread was dear and wages low, and I remember well how the old farm workers used to rise and describe the terrible time they went through in the ' Hungry Forties ', for there were men still living who remembered that time. It gave a real impressiveness to speeches that had often seemed dull and far removed from reality. It was also felt that a dissolution was approaching, since it was clear that Chamberlain was going to lead on his own lines, and there were people then within the Unionist party, like the Duke of Devonshire, who dissented from these lines.

All this domestic side made us women take a special interest in politics, and I had a good deal to do with the Women's Liberal Association of Scotland, serving as I did for a time on its governing body. In Perthshire we entertained our very attractive candidate, David Erskine of Linlathen. Sometimes, indeed, the meetings were disappointing, as when we had been sitting for an hour or more on infants' benches in one of those dimly lit schools, which always formed the locus of village meetings in those days when village halls were almost non-existent, the chairman called for a vote of thanks. The audience, excepting the speaker's party, was composed of young men straight from the plough and did not look good quarry for public speaking. But one long-bearded old blacksmith had leant forward, hand to ear, apparently drinking in every word. 'Would you, Mr. Macdonald, kindly move the vote of thanks?' said the chairman. 'What did ye say?' 'Would you please move the vote of thanks?' in a louder tone. 'Man,' was the unexpected reply, 'I didna hear a singell word the hale time!' But on the whole, the East Lothian meetings were more lively than those in Perthshire: there was usually a certain number of educated people present and that meant some opposition, which helped: possibly the minister or schoolmaster was there. And the 'hinds' were wonderfully intelligent. If we were near Whittinge-hame, we had at our women's meetings at least the ladies of the Balfour house-party from the big house, and the promise of an opposition meeting next night. The mining district was always enthusiastic, all, of course, being Liberal or Radical to a man. I have the pleasantest recollection of all these gatherings—of our nightly drive to three or four in an evening, losing our way in the dark and struggling to read road signs with the help of matches that continually went out, and when we returned, being given a sumptuous supper by our kind hosts, the Lawries.

In addition to political work, I had been elected by ballot as a member of the local school board, a position which I held for some years and indeed until the county took over the work, when I was elected to the County Education Committee. The parish school board was quite a good and conscientious body, but too restricted in its area and outlook, and unable to take a comprehensive view of what was educationally required. Each board was a law to itself.

As regards educational matters, there was also an Edinburgh committee, of which I was a member, which arranged for teachers to be sent to South Africa, where, at this time, they were welcomed. Later on it was different.

Then between 1903 and 1904, while my brother was giving his Gifford lectures, we were a good deal in St. Andrews. St. Andrews has the real university town flavour, unlike most of our Scottish university towns, and it was delightful to stay with Principal Donaldson and his wife in their official residence by the sea, and to meet many distinguished professors and other literary men. There were large audiences at the lectures, despite the fact that they were stiff matter. On going out of a concluding lecture, a lady was heard to reproach another lady who had not ventured to attend. ' But what was it about ? ' asked the latter, very naturally. ' I haven't the slightest idea,' said the first, ' but it was perfectly delightful ! ' The lec-

MRS. HALDANE IN HER EIGHTIETH YEAR, 1905

turer certainly had the gift of making obscure matters seem simple, whatever they really were, and the fact that he spoke freely, with only a few notes before him, made his lectures more interesting and attractive.

These lectures were given on the top of severe work, political and legal. Besides this, Richard always had on his mind the affairs of London University, whose progress seemed always to be blocked by the Government. He had hoped that Lord Rosebery might have helped in this, as in other matters, but though he made an excellent speech at this particular time, he seemed, as his followers said, to study political machinery more than political subjects, and absolutely declined to go into harness again however he was pressed.

By this time, motors were coming into use by private people, though horse buses and hansoms and growlers still held their own. Indeed we were afraid to go up steep hills in a motor-car in case it slipped back, and used to be ready to leap out at a moment's notice. I remember a discussion with an aunt, who lived in Hampstead, as to whether we might venture to ascend Fitzjohn's Avenue in safety ! In October, 1904, Lord Dalmeny, Lord Rosebery's son, drove Richard back to Dalmeny from Edinburgh at what I call in my diary ' an alarming rate of 40 miles an hour '. But this was unusual, and at home my mother kept to a victoria, which her son had specially built for her with rubber tyres, and a brougham for bad weather. I drove mostly in a dog-cart and often drove it tandem, sometimes to the alarm of the lieges. We had, how-

o

ever, a very nice mare called Tibbie who made a good leader and was very amenable. I also rode her sometimes. I think Richard got his first motor-car in 1905, but Mr. Balfour had his much earlier, as recorded by his biographer. Motor-cars were not cheap luxuries at first. Each seemed to require a man (as well as a boy to help him) to look after it. Also, a pit had to be made in the garage from which the internal workings could be examined, and they were perpetually requiring repairs.

In addition to transport, which was going to alter so radically, there were other differences of a social sort that were coming about. The food of the country was changing. Tinned food, hitherto disliked and suspected, came to be used as well as chilled meat, also formerly condemned. But above all, vegetables were being transported from afar in cold chambers, and this caused a change in the feeding of all classes. Apples and oranges became not just ' seasonable fruits ' but fruit procurable all through the year ; and other fruit, hitherto reserved for the rich since it was produced in hot-houses, became the stock of costers' barrows. Bananas, hardly seen in old days, were now a staple diet for children. Then machinery was producing quantities of things formerly the possession of wealthy people only, such as well-cut clothing for men, women and children, and all the furnishings which still were crammed into middle-class houses. They were machine-made but often of so-called ' modern art ' design : not too attractive.

We, too, were making alterations, for in 1904, Cloan was enlarged and altered by my brother, and electric light and heating were introduced. Hitherto, our lighting had been by oil lamps only : a pleasant light but a troublesome one. We were sure that we should suffer by the glare of electricity and that it would be terribly unbecoming. While this new process was going on my mother and I moved to a friend's house about two miles off. Our mother was not well at the time and eighty years old, so that her doctor discouraged her in every way in his power from moving, insisting that she should be content to live an invalid life. This only made her the more determined to carry out her schemes, especially as she loved building and making plans for it. Hence she was happy in hearing about it all and inspecting when she could, while I went to and fro to Edinburgh for my Royal Infirmary meetings and other interests. When we returned to Cloan, we had an enormous party from East Lothian as our guests, in addition to the ordinary ' Trips ', so-called, which formed a normal part of our summer plans. The trips were mostly composed of children, but frequently of other bodies of people from neighbouring towns, who were content with this simple form of entertainment. If wet, we had a barn converted into a hall which gave shelter, and I think everyone enjoyed their quiet pleasures.

In London one felt that matters political were becoming more and more critical ; and on the top of everything else came a huge legal case which concerned Scotland greatly and in which my brother was acting as counsel. The two great non-conforming Churches, the Free Church and the so-called United Presbyterian, had decided to unite, as the ' United Free Church' of Scotland. But there was a dissentient body in the first-named, which not only would not do this, but which declared the union illegal, and hence claimed to retain the very large funds of the Church. They became known later as the ' Wee Frees', most of whom were Highland.

The case had been carried to the House of Lords, and I listened to the arguments with the greatest interest, especially as my brother was leading for the union party. It seemed to me that a case which involved so much technical and historical knowledge should have been left to a Scottish Judiciary to decide, for it was almost impossible to make clear to English judges what were the real bearings of the questions in point, and I could not help marvelling how an Indian appeal, which so often also involved estimating technical points, usually gave satisfaction to the appellants, for their problems were surely even more remote and obscure. The arguments were profound and brought back to me the teaching of my childhood. When the question of Free Will and Predestination came to be discussed, one thought of the same puzzles that occurred to one then, and a good deal turned on the correct doctrinal interpretation of these mysteries. Could one consistently believe in both ? The Lord Chancellor (Halsbury) who was learned in church history, was evidently interested and understanding, but one could see that others, like Lord James of Hereford, were quite at sea. When this matter was put in the blunt fashion in which the man in the street would put it (possibly with some reason), my brother said that their lordships were regarding it in an 'anthropomorphic' manner. 'Anthropo—what, Mr. Haldane? Will you be good enough to use words we can understand.' We Scots knew so well what was meant and how it was not for our poor 'legal' (in the doctrinal sense) minds to try to interpret these deep things of faith!

It was a striking scene. Lady Frances Balfour sat watching all the time from the seat she usually occupied just opposite mine, and the Divines to whom it all meant so much were down below. The case was decided against the majority and they faced the situation with splendid courage. The Lord Chancellor had remarked at the opening of the appeal in August, that it might go on till he had given up the Great Seal to Mr. Haldane, who was now the counsel, and who might by then be sitting on the Woolsack. One wished for their sakes that it could have been so, as to them and to us the decision seemed unjust. But years were to elapse before that event occurred, and meantime, the Church that lost its millions retrieved its position. The change of government did not take place for a year and Richard was not Lord Chancellor for six or seven years after that.

If, however, the Liberal party had difficulties, the Conservative party had worse divisions, and as there was still unemployment and poverty, the Free Trade cry about the cheap loaf was effective. Ireland also was as usual a source of difficulty, as well as Chinese labour on the Rand. In India there was the dispute between Curzon and Kitchener. That was not all—there were other difficulties and Balfour resigned on December 4th, 1905.

The end of 1905 was thus eventful and made a difference in our future lives. The Government had been on the eve of a dissolution for long and its continuance in power after the summer seemed a mistake. The so-called Imperialists—Asquith, Grey and my brother particularly—had much intercourse here and at the Asquiths' temporary home in the Highlands. The whole story of what was done is told in my brother's autobiography and need not be repeated here, but at Cloan, my mother and I were in telegraphic communication with him over the matter. Campbell-Bannerman, fortified by his wife, took up a strong position after some deliberation, and would not go to the Lords leaving Asquith to lead in the Commons. Asquith became Chancellor of the Exchequer, and our mother, a woman of character like Lady C.-B., advised her son not to go in unless on satisfactory terms. C.-B. was bound to offer the Lord Chancellorship to Sir Robert Reid, and Richard did not wish to take the Home Secretaryship. I think he would have liked to have the Colonies since he felt that there was interesting work to be done there. But he had also a great interest in the War Office, for he had been a great deal in touch with War Office affairs over explosives and other things, and realized what a vast task lay before whoever took that office. As events turned out, there is reason to be thankful that he saw it to be his duty to undertake the administration of this office.

I am not going to deal with the work on which my brother was engaged as Minister for War, because that is told both in his autobiography and elsewhere. I am only going to say something of the repercussions that this new adventure had upon myself and my immediate surroundings, as related in my diary. As my brother was unmarried, it brought me much more into touch with political men and women, and I should like to say something more about this period. The great scheme of Army Reform engrossed my brother enormously, and when at Cloan, he and General Ellison and others were closeted together for hours, and many of our usual avocations had to be given up. In London he had Sir Edward Grey constantly with him after the terrible tragedy of Lady Grey's death through an accident in 1906, an event which almost overwhelmed him.

I was thus in London a good deal, for my brother had taken a beautiful house in Queen Anne's Gate —one of those perfect Queen Anne houses which makes its occupiers feel at home directly they enter it, so well proportioned are the rooms. It was suitably furnished with the effective help of Lady Horner, a woman of great taste and knowledge, but there was naturally a good deal to do in getting a household started, for latterly, when in London, we had lived in a ' service flat ' at Whitehall Court—that is to say, since we gave up taking a house in town.

I was naturally interested in going to the House of Commons and hearing the debates, especially those in which my brother was concerned. He worked so hard at drafting his Army Bill that he was able to introduce it in 1906, in a speech of three hours and twenty minutes. It was a little embarrassing to me to have the wives of the former War Ministers, Mrs. Brodrick and Mrs. Arnold Forster, in the Speaker's Gallery beside me. Mrs. Arnold Forster was quite delightful, but of course there were constant attacks on her husband's scheme in the course of the debate, and she was anxious about his health, since they had just returned from Jamaica where he had had fever. She herself had worked hard during the earthquake there, helping the surgeons with giving chloroform, etc. Her husband called on my mother, who was able to be in London that year, though rather frail, and while with her, he was taken ill. It was rather a surprise to my brother and me to come into the drawing-room one afternoon and find her doing her best to re-suscitate his opponent while he lay prone on the sofa ! Arnold Forster was one of many delightful antagonists.

In the War Office there was a great struggle to be gone through, and, as Richard used to say, ' to be a reformer one must have no nerves.' There were shrieks from fashionable society about what they called the disbanding of the militia, and influences were brought to bear in high places. But all went well in the end. A remarkable thing was that Campbell-Bannerman, with whom my brother had had very strained relations before the new Government came in, was helpful in his work. I met him at our much valued friends, the T. R. Buchanans, and though one felt he was a good Scot who knew his mind and took a sane and calm view of life, he struck me as disappointing when compared with the leaders I knew best. Though my hosts kindly put me by him, he would not talk of politics (very likely with wisdom), but did talk much of electric light as compared with gas in reference to his own arrangements at Belmont. He seemed to me to take little interest in the Education Bill negotia-tion which was concerning me, so that I was dis-appointed, perhaps unreasonably. Though both Scots, we were of different moulds. I always have the feeling that, probably from my own fault and early training, there is a fine type of Scot with which I cannot get into sympathy.

One great difficulty concerned the Scots Greys and where they were to be housed. There was not then the means of housing them at Redford, and it was settled to transfer them to York. Hence an indigna-tion meeting was called in Edinburgh, with the Lord Provost in the chair. He was supported by Lord Rosebery. The matter caused quite a stir amongst the perfervid Scots, who were to lose, even temporarily, their much admired regiment, and *Punch* had an amusing cartoon headed ' He's awa wi' my Horse and him a brither Scot '. I believe the original was bought by the Regiment : I have a first proof, signed by the two men concerned—Rosebery and Richard.

This year (1906), St. Andrews University bestowed on me an Honorary Degree of Doctor of Laws, perhaps on account of my *Life of Descartes*, which came out about then. Anyhow I had a delightful time at St. Andrews during the celebrations and met a number of distinguished people who were present receiving degrees. Amongst them was Professor Mahaffy of Dublin, whom I met later in Ireland, and Mr. Gennadius, the Greek minister in London, with whom we made friends and who had a marvellous library in the Legation which he loved to show to his visitors. The Oration was given by Lord Reay, and the subject was George Buchanan. I saw much of the Reays then and thereafter. He was a very distinguished scholar and a man of great dignity, and the dinner parties given by him and Lady Reay, to which they often asked me, were always delightful. He was Chancellor of St. Andrews University at this time, and Mr. Carnegie was Lord Rector. Mr. Carnegie kept the party, at the house of Principal Donaldson, in high good spirits, only he was then inclined to speak of religious matters in a way which somewhat shocked my mother, who was present. His views, I believe, were modified later on, and in any case he held my mother in the highest estimation and constantly spoke of her with great warmth and appreciation.

The establishment of the United Kingdom Trust by Mr. Andrew Carnegie was a matter of great satisfaction to us all. Mr. Carnegie set aside two million pounds for the purpose of doing what could be done for the ' elevation of the masses of the people ', but we trustees had a free hand, excepting that certain lines of operation were suggested, two of the main ones being to help in promoting the well-being of libraries and music. Our first meeting was on December 22nd, 1913. It was thought that the supply of organs for churches was more than sufficient, and that music could better be helped in various other ways—that is to say, by assisting musical societies and even young musical composers. We always felt proud of enabling Gustav Holst to produce his great cantata ' The Immortal Hour '. But the question of library provision was our main object at first, and we tried to find out what could be done to bring books within the range of country people. Mr. Carnegie had presented many library buildings for cities and towns, so that they were provided for.

The first task was to get a good report on the whole subject, and this was done (mainly just before the war) by Professor W. G. Adams, now Warden of All Souls. On this report a whole system of book distribution was ultimately established and was finally aided by the Education Act of 1918, which allowed the Rural Libraries to become County Libraries under county administration. The beginning of the work was comparatively humble, but gradually county after county came in, till England, Scotland and Wales were practically covered, and central libraries established as pools for the more expensive type of non-fiction books, which could be borrowed freely.

Long after this, I thoroughly enjoyed going round a Highland district in the librarian's van and seeing how all classes of a scattered community came out to get the books required. For a time I was chairman of the Library Committee of the Perthshire Education Authority, but that was much later on, when legislation made it possible to carry on a library policy.

The Irish library question was a difficult one, for the small libraries given by Mr. Carnegie were often used for any purpose but reading, and the so-called librarian sometimes took the simple plan of burning the books in order to escape from the trouble of keeping them. The bookcase was also sometimes nailed up and the room used for dances, as ' sure it's a little excitement they want'! But in Ireland also, the movement has gone forward with real success.

The Carnegie United Kingdom Trust has now operated for twenty-three years, and it has done work which has certainly made a difference to the lives of many of the less fortunate of our fellow-countrymen. The primary idea of its work has been to experiment, and no experimenter succeeds in all cases. Still, it has acted as a spear head which has made its way into new regions as regards social life, and it has found its justification in the fact that the country has observed its endeavours and very frequently after a time

LORD AND LADY ROBERTS AT CLOAN, 1906

—probably after some years of trial—made them its own. So it has been with libraries and adult education, so much neglected, especially in the north, and with many kinds of rural or urban social services.

In the case of much of its work grants from Government have gone along with the help it has given. But often its operations have been purely individual, assisted, of course, by other voluntary aid. In the early days of which I write principles were laid down which were afterwards followed with hardly any variation.

All who remember the old War Office in Pall Mall must regret its passing, though doubtless it was well that the great new buildings were there before the war, when they were soon filled to overflowing. Some of the beautiful mantelpieces were removed. The building of the new offices entailed the destruction of a certain elm tree once belonging to the garden of the Earl of Fife, whose arms still adorn the end of White-hall Court, close by : many will remember the tree, though when changes are once made I, personally, find it extraordinarily difficult to bring the old things back into remembrance.

I suppose that though we insufficiently realized it there was a new influence coming into politics, in the form of the Labour Party. The Trade Unions were asserting their rights, and the Taff Vale case was being debated. It was quite a new thing to have 51 Labour members in the House of Commons, and though the Liberal party did not wholly grasp the meaning of this new movement, it did seem that hereditary politicians were doomed, and that with this, dilettantism in politics might disappear. Even the attendants at the Ladies' Gallery were struck by the change to the 'New Ladies', though I am not quite sure that they thought them an improvement. A genuine effort was made to get closer to realities, which, had it continued, might have kept the advanced parties closer together. The House of Lords was the drawback to social reform, for it rejected bills as soon as they came up to it. However, the women's movement was advancing, we hardly appreciated how much, and the Women's Social and Political Union was formed.

I have often wondered whether, at this time, the Liberal party might not have made itself the great power that it ought to have been down to the present day. It was clear that a new outlook on the part of a large section of the people, to which Liberalism in the wide sense appeals, had arisen. The conventional and orthodox Liberal party never drew the more advanced party into its bosom. If it had done so, it would have been good for itself. It was little good having one or two moderate Labour people in the Government, if the spirit was not there. Perhaps it was impossible, for despite all we said on platforms, we were not ' of the people ', nor did we truly understand their needs. We were in great measure Whigs still and we enjoyed the pleasant atmosphere of Whig society and surroundings.

I had a good deal to do with the scheme for Army nursing, within the Territorial Army. The plan was clearly defined, and it was really an essential part of the scheme for Home Defence. But there were difficulties ahead, for there were other schemes in existence which had influential support and which feared being destroyed. It was indeed essential that Queen Alexandra's approval should be given to any new nursing scheme for the Army, and that was not too easy to secure. General Sir Alfred Keogh, the head of the Medical Service at the War Office, was full of enthusiasm, besides being most efficient, and he enlisted the medical men required and bespoke the requisite hospitals. Miss Sidney Browne, the matron-in-chief, became head of the Territorial Nursing Service and was a splendid organizer, and I did my best to help her. Somehow the Queen was dubious of the efforts made and sent for Lady Roberts to hear more about them. Lady Roberts came to Queen Anne's Gate, deeply concerned about it all, in March, 1907, and I went to stay with her and Lord Roberts at Englemere, Ascot, and met Lord Esher, who was influential in Court circles and very helpful. A modification was made with the view of retaining the old Nursing Reserve, but again the Queen was not satisfied. Finally, a committee was formed to consider the matter and its scheme was eventually adopted, but once more with difficulty, for H.M. did not agree to it at first, though at length her difficulties were resolved. The same sort of difficulties occurred later over uniforms, for H.M.

chose a khaki colour to which the sisters absolutely objected, for the very practical reason that they (rightly) thought it unbecoming. It was not for quite a long time, and by immense tact on the part of the Vice-President, that Her Majesty's consent was obtained for the very becoming grey Territorial uniform with its touches of red. The red cape of the First Line nurses was considered to be sacred to them, and as was always in those days the case in the Army, there was constant fear that the Territorials—the 'Terriers' as they were called—would usurp the rights of what many considered to be the real army. One could understand the feeling, for Territorial matrons and sisters, though they had definite duties and had a certain amount of army training as well as their civil qualifications, were not what was deemed all-time workers any more than the men. It was not until the war showed that these nurses and men could alike work for their country, with the same zeal as the regulars, that they gained a position of respect from old-fashioned people. It was grievous to us all that Lord Kitchener failed to use the organization, the value of which he did not appreciate in its fullness. The Territorial County Organizations were somehow confused with County Councils, at least that is how it appeared.

The building up of this scheme along with that of the Voluntary Aid Detachments, which formed part of the same scheme of medical aid in time of war, was a matter of immense interest to me and was one in which I could give a certain amount of help, especially

MANOEUVRES AT CLOAN, 1907

TERRITORIAL ARTILLERY CROSSING THE OCHILS, 1907

in the north. The whole scheme was somewhat complicated, and Sir Alfred Keogh devised a sort of diagram to explain it. Armed with this and other illustrations, in the way of maps, etc., I gave a good many lectures throughout the country, and helped to organize classes and demonstrations. We had several of these in Scotland, and they were carried on until the Great War broke out. One of the last which I attended was at Cloan, when my brother was present. The supposed hospital, which was equipped and ready for patients, was placed in our little hall, and the men's detachments had been training in Auchterarder. The pathetic thing was that a short time afterwards, the same men (as stretcher bearers in the Territorial Force) were actually doing the work on the battlefield that they were being trained to do at home, and this service was rendered by them even for individuals there present, while the little hall at Cloan was converted into a real auxiliary hospital for patients sent from Perth first line hospitals. In the sphere of nursing, all the Territorial nurses appeared to take their places in the terrains to which they were appointed, instantly and without a hitch. It was a remarkable instance of organization properly worked out, though we little thought it would be so speedily required.

I was glad, by means of the many discussions over the nursing service, to be able to make the acquaintance of Lord and Lady Roberts ; the latter was always called into counsel by the Queen when difficulties arose. Lord Roberts struck me, as he struck every-

P

body, as above all a high-minded man, whose actions were all directed by the highest motives, whether wholly practicable or not. He was immensely interested in Army reorganization and favourable to the new Territorial scheme, so far as it went, and thought Richard had done a great work ; but emphatic on the point that it did not go far enough and that compulsory service was requisite. He did not sufficiently consider the difficulties of a political sort that this would entail, even had a Conservative Government been in power, but felt that all efforts should be put forth to obtain it. He was most agreeable to me, and I was interested in his views on many subjects and especially on Gordon, whom he thought a fanatic, though a good man. I did not, however, gather that he really knew him personally.

In 1907 there were, at Cloan, great Army manoeuvres. About a thousand men and five hundred horse were encamped in the fields before the house, also guns, Territorial artillery. The regular soldiers were represented by the 18th Hussars, Seaforths and Scots Greys. It was very exciting to see them all and watch, so far as one could, their taking their guns or impedimenta over our Ochil range of hills. The Scottish regiments got local sympathy from people who took the matter very seriously, and when they were being pursued by the English, an old woman in a cottage refused to give information. ' Div ye think I wad gie' awa' my heeland laddies ? ' she said ! Prince Arthur of Connaught was there with the ' Greys ', and we had a houseful of other officers. Amongst those staying with us were Colonel Rimington, Sir Ian Hamilton, Colonel A'Court Repington, the famous correspondent of *The Times*, whose future fortunes were to be so strange and disappointing, and Douglas Haig, not then the famous man he afterwards became. He interested us as a typical Scot, sure of himself and if rather silent, decided.   General French often stayed with us, and was of quite a different type, more forthcoming, as an Irishman usually is, and entertaining in ordinary life.   Repington was full of keenness in his talk, and one felt had he had qualities of a personal sort that were lacking, he would have made a splendid and far-seeing soldier.   There were other prominent officers, whom we often saw, like General Jack Cowans, who was beloved by a multitude of my own sex, and who, despite his varied affections, was such a marvellous Q.M.G. or caterer for an army during the war. I don't think that there could have been a more entertaining talker, but he was a ' doer ' also, and deserves great praise and gratitude. We always liked him.

Thus we were plunged into an entirely different set of people from the serious philosophers and men of letters to whom we had been accustomed. For we had had many interesting friends, like Professor Pringle-Pattison of Edinburgh, Professor Herkless of St. Andrews, Professor Baillie of Aberdeen, and, above all, our much loved ' Professor ' par excellence, i.e. Professor Hume Brown, the Historiographer Royal of

Scotland, who had been our constant visitor since our childhood and who practically made his home with us in autumn. He had a way of quite kindly dissecting our visitors and defining their qualities. Possibly the soldiers presented some difficulties : many were apparently more susceptible and emotional in private life than the philosophers or the scientists brought by my brother John, but then they were possessed of powers of self-expression in certain directions that the others lacked, along with an unwonted knowledge of a world that was to him a sealed book. On the other hand, the interests of the men of learning were absolutely unknown to most of the soldiers, and even in scientific knowledge they were sadly lacking. We also had visits from distinguished German officers, who had been sent on a special mission and had to be entertained. Some of them were delightful ; one got into serious trouble of a social sort, but not, fortunately, at Cloan. I expect the visitors thought we were odd in our ways too. At manoeuvres they had some amusement. We had a very large St. Bernard dog, which had been christened Kaiser. He was young and playful, and while the General Officers were solemnly discussing the day's work on the lawn in front of the house, with their aides, he somehow got hold of the Orders of the Day and tore off with them in his mouth, pursued by all the valiant soldiers. Our dogs formed a great and important part of our lives. In the dogs' cemetery one is termed ' The Professor's Friend ', because, when dying of old age,

MR. HALDANE AND GEN. SIR IAN HAMILTON AND KAISER,
THE ST. BERNARD DOG, 1907

LORD HALDANE WITH V.A.D. NURSES AT CLOAN
DURING TERRITORIAL MANOEUVRES, 1913

he managed to creep up to Professor Hume Brown's room at the dawn. He heard him, opened the door and the dog who loved him lay down and died at his feet.

Perhaps my brother was happiest in addressing a committee established for the purpose of dealing with the ' Moral and Spiritual Welfare of the Soldiers '. He had clergy and ministers of all denominations, and men of no denomination, to speak to. ' If that's Hegel we should all be studying him,' said one member. ' No, it's Hegel grafted on to his father and grand-father,' said another Scot, a Highland minister, Dr. Mackay, beloved of all men. Some members wished to begin the proceedings with prayer : others objected. ' By all means let us begin with prayer,' Richard is reported to have said, ' but let it be silent prayer ! ' I don't think he could have got his Bill into shape with the Generals, who, though he liked them immensely, were none too easy to deal with, but for his enormous cigars, which seemed to melt the stoniest hearts.

The Rectorial Address, given in 1906, was a remarkable feat in the midst of all my brother's other work. It was given in a great hall and lasted for an hour and a quarter. Usually the audience on such occasions is far from attentive, being composed largely of students, often uproarious, but this time these last were absolutely silent ; and the great array of professors, with the Officers' Training Corps in uniform in front, was imposing. One of the most impressive-looking of the

professors was Professor Campbell Fraser—' the Prof'
he was called affectionately—with his beautiful face and
long white beard. He looked as if from a long way off at
his former pupil. Our mother was able to be present,
also the tutor of our childhood, Dr. Macdonald, who
had come home from India. At the luncheon which
followed, I sat next Mr. Balfour and we had as always a
delightful talk, for he had the unique and flattering
power of making his listener feel that it was she for
whose advice or opinions he had been all this time waiting. This time he told of the experience of the household at Whittingehame, where they had been made
prisoners, as a household of sixty inmates, during a
recent snowstorm. When our hosts at Murdostoun
Castle took me to church on Sunday, we were regaled
by a sermon on my brother's Rectorial Address, which
was taken as a suitable and improving topic.

I was deeply interested in the work of the Poor Law
Commission, before which I gave evidence as regards
Scottish poorhouses, the administration of which concerned me greatly. There was no qualified nursing
in the one I knew best, beyond the scanty and quite
inefficient attention given by fellow paupers, nor was
there skilled help in the case of confinements. I got
little sympathy from the Inspector, who believed that
the women who came in had their children with as
little trouble or pain as the lower animals; but after
much correspondence and complaint, a Departmental
committee was appointed, before which again I gave
evidence, both as to medical treatment and food. I

hope and believe that some good resulted from this agitation. I was shocked to find that a poor Swede, found at the foot of a small precipice by a lonely road in the hills, had been taken to the poorhouse and that it had not been noticed that he was suffering both from fracture and fever ; he had been treated and bathed as a common tramp. The man died (I was sent for, to see if I could understand what he said) and all I could do was to purchase for him a grave, so that he should not be buried as a common pauper.

Mrs. Webb did valiant service for poor law administration, but she was much criticized by some of her fellow commissioners for getting private evidence for her own satisfaction, for not attending the meetings when she did not think it worth her while to do so, and in general organizing her own activities. On the whole, she came out triumphantly, and the Minority Report, which was mainly hers, has been a sheet-anchor for the more advanced reformers. She wished pensions to be regarded as part of the whole system of Poor Law Reform, and to take out of the Poor Law sick, infirm, children, etc., and to institute receiving houses, along with proper means of allocating cases.

Though the recommendations of the Minority Report are not yet carried out, one is thankful to know that we are—after many years—progressing in the right direction. It is strange that reforms that seem self-evident take so long to mature in a civilized and fairly intelligent country. It is only of recent years that the sick poor have come to be treated in the same way as the richer sick patients, in that they have been given equally good nursing and attention. It grieved me at the time of which I write to see the old who had nothing against them excepting that they were old and poor, associated with the ne'er-do-wells, and along with them the little children who had been born into hopeless surroundings. What chance had any one of these children as far as living a decent life was concerned?

There were 'characters', of course, among my special friends, that is amongst the 'inmates' whom I knew best. There was a fine old fellow, the head of his clan, who had come into his present condition from a mis-spent manhood. He saw nothing before him but death, for he was very old. But death brought great compensations with it, for he was a chief among his fellows, and was to have a chieftain's funeral : his body was to be carried down the loch by boat to the family burial place, one to which no road came. This was material for endless talk and speculation till finally it all came true, and our old friend had in death the glory he missed in life.

Another was looking out on the green hills with apparent pleasure. 'Were you a shepherd?' I asked. ' No, I was not ; I was just seeing what could be seen. They ca' that poaching, but then I aye gave the gentlemen their bit sport afore I began ! '

I made friends with yet another very remarkable woman at this time, that is with Gertrude Bell. She had returned from ' digging ' for the time being, and had taken up warmly the Buddhist Shrine Society, with which I had much sympathy, having studied Buddhism somewhat when making my translation of Hegel's *History of Philosophy*. Chirol of *The Times* was another enthusiast with whom I talked of the Society. Gertrude Bell's vitality was marvellous and she seemed to imbue one with her enthusiasm. Her stepmother, Lady Bell, was also a great friend of mine, and her delightful dinner and evening parties in Sloane Street, which I constantly attended, seemed to me models of what parties should be. One met just the people one wanted to meet—all people of interest—and the atmosphere was one of complete friendliness and kindness. There were no refreshments in the evening, beyond the simplest, placed on a table in the back drawing room, and no one wanted more : nor was there a crowd—just a ' very small ' party, as the cards said, at each Wednesday gathering. Sir Hugh and Lady Bell seemed to make each of their guests feel that they were those they specially wished to see.

Another great friend with whom and her husband I constantly dined or stayed in the country, was Lady Burghclere. Winifred Burghclere was a daughter of the famous Lord Carnarvon of Victorian days, and inherited many of his qualities : she had a real historic gift, as her books show. But, in addition to being a woman of much and careful learning, she was a perfect hostess, entering into the special interests of her guests with such empressment that they became her own. I can hear her narrating all sorts of interesting things with her comments upon them and always asking 'don't you agree?', so that you should form part, and a sympathetic part, of her conversation or criticism.

I was fortunate in having many other friends, all of them with special interests of their own. Among the women there was Marie Belloc Lowndes, a friend since girlhood, for I knew her before her marriage as a girl teeming with interest in the world around her, and then as a married woman with delightful children; Ella Christie, the traveller in strange lands; Margaret Horn, the philanthropist, and many others. Amongst men, my constant correspondent and wise adviser was Bishop Burge, and then the sprightly and ever youthful Edmund Gosse, both of whom have gone from us. The then Dean of St. Paul's, Dr. Inge, and his attractive wife, we began to know at this time. Later the acquaintanceship developed into a deep friendship. This was also so with Frances Blackett.

The work for those who were in the forefront of politics seemed to me tremendous. I remember my brother being 15½ hours on end on the Front Bench, coming home at 6 p.m. and then, after taking a bath, proceeding with me to dine with the John Murrays (Mr. Murray, afterwards Sir John Murray, was his greatly esteemed publisher). He certainly had some difficulty in keeping awake during dinner, but hoped his hostess did not notice it. I looked into the House at 11 a.m. and it was a curious sight—everyone bedraggled and dissipated-looking, some in untidy evening dress.

A party at Cambridge in 1907, when I stayed with Professor and Mrs. Sorley, I greatly enjoyed. I had much talk with Dr. Ward, Master of Peterhouse, about Elizabeth Princess Palatine, who was Descartes' great friend and correspondent, and always interested me. Various persons received degrees including my brother, Lord Milner and C.-B., and it was amusing to listen through the peephole in the room of Mrs. Butler (the Master's wife) to the speeches taking place at the Feast which was held in Trinity College. Mrs. Sidgwick and many others were present. The whole surroundings seemed mediaeval.

After this my brother John and I made a very enjoyable visit to Essen, with my friend Ella Christie, while he was attending the meetings of a Royal Commission on Mines, which was taking evidence on the mining system in Germany. We visited various schools, twenty-six of the wonderful institutions run by the Krupps' works, and also studied the Elberfeld system and saw a new infirmary at Düsseldorf, which, efficient as it might be, shocked me by its methods ; for the patients, especially the mothers with their babies, seemed to me to be regimented rather than treated in our kindly English way. There were wonderful dinners to which we were invited, with long speeches between each course (and each course was served twice), and at last Mr. Smillie, the Scottish miner member, declared his intention of standing it all no longer, but going back to Scotland and to his porridge ! I learned a good deal about schools, of which I visited several, so the visit was useful. We were allowed to see nothing of the works at Essen itself.

In 1909 came the Finance Bill and all the consequent questions regarding the relations between the two Houses of Parliament. Super-taxes and the taxation of land value were held to be pieces of class legislation, and there came to be violent feeling and much anxiety in regard to the King's speech of 1910. It was a trying time for Mr. Asquith, but he remained sweet-tempered all through. One was sad to hear of Chamberlain's illness and Sir Courtney Ilbert told me how he could just touch the pen when he took the oath at the opening of Parliament. The last time I saw him was in a picture gallery, looking so frail.

The February of 1910 was an anxious month and Cabinet meetings were being held every day. The difficulty was to deal with the situation raised by the Lords' objections to the Finance Bill and the King's speech was devised with much care to meet the situation. ' Due guarantees that . . . ' etc., might mean reform of the Upper Chamber, Federal Government and indeed a very big policy, though the extremists wished simply for the veto.

I went to the opening of Parliament this year, in spite of the trouble of dressing for it, because one had the very mistaken idea that this might be the last function in its present form, since the tension between the two Houses was so great. I sat by Mrs. Randall Davidson, the much loved wife of the Archbishop—both she and her husband were true friends—and gazed at the gay scene. King Edward read his speech, I thought, as though he disliked it. It had been chopped and changed to meet the very difficult situation and was now ungrammatical and wonderfully vague. I was reading an account of the proceedings in the evening to my mother, who was lying down, when there came in the Prime Minister, Edward Grey and Richard, who had been dining at Grillon's. The P.M. talked to my mother of Mrs. Belloc Lowndes' last novel, which interested him, and of Archie Gordon, whose death was so tragic, and of his mother, Lady Aberdeen : ' Only religion makes her what she is.' And he seemed, in his wonderful way, to put all his troubles aside.

I heard the debate, in which he spoke admirably, setting forth his policy regarding the Veto and Finance and the Reform of the House of Lords. Balfour, with some justice, criticized the vagueness of the King's speech. Redmond spoke of the creation of peers, allowing that, if they went to the country, the Government would probably be defeated, so that the King would not be justified in assenting. There was rather a dramatic silence before the Labour party asked for adjournment. The next day, the debate was equally exciting. Barnes spoke for Labour, F. E. Smith was too brilliant and full of ' points ', O'Brien very anti-Redmond, Hilaire Belloc full of wit but irresponsible, Winston Churchill very good and statesmanlike, showing the difficulties in the way, which were so obvious.

I sat in the Speaker's Gallery, beside Lady Londonderry and Margot Asquith, and had tea with Mrs. Lowther, the Speaker's wife. The atmosphere was ' badly charged ', as it usually was, as few of the ladies kept their criticisms within their own hearts. I always remember with amusement C.-B.'s pawky answer to the question put to him in the House, as to why a Silence ' should be put conspicuously in the Ladies' Gallery '. ' There must be *some* mysterious reason,' was all he replied !

In March the Army estimates came on and got through with trouble. The situation was difficult, for there was an impasse, and no one was certain as to the line to be taken up by the Prime Minister, who, a Labour critic was supposed to have said, ' had a backbone made of tripe.'

Aviation in its earliest days came under the War Office, therefore I heard a good deal about it and its progress from about 1908. In August, 1910, I went with our friends Sir Robert and Lady King Stewart to the International Aviation meeting at Lanark, and we watched eagerly and anxiously for hours, hoping something would happen and that we should see these wonderful machines rise like birds from the ground. There were twenty-two competitors, of whom I believe eight or ten met their deaths flying in the following five or six years, including Mr. Dickson, whom we got to know a little, as he was staying at Drummond Castle and came to Cloan to dine. We expected most of Captain Cody, but he appeared simply to taxi round the Race Course as if his machine were too heavy to rise. I think the American, Drexel, finally flew for a time, but I did not see this. It would have seemed incredible to me, that in about five-and-twenty years I should be flying thousands of miles to Persia, in complete comfort and indeed luxury.

As to the nurses, things were going better, for the Queen was very helpful and she received the Territorial nurses who were to be given their badges, at Buckingham Palace. I stood beside Princess Victoria, who was much amused at Richard's mode of holding the cushions, which, covered with badges, were handed to him. When done with, he cast the one cushion from him, unceremoniously, in order to take up another. The Princess and he had often sat together on official occasions and she said 'We have had such pleasant drives and talks together at different functions'. He replied 'I am afraid, Ma'm, that these may be the last', for an election was looming.

I had at dinner a talk with Lord Althorp (better known as Bobby Spencer), when Lord Rosebery's speech, concerning what he called a revolutionary Budget, was discussed by different guests from different points of view. Lord Althorp himself could not make up his mind whether to strengthen or to weaken the House of Lords would answer best. He gave a most interesting account of the Phoenix Park murders, which his servant had actually seen when putting out his clothes. The body of Lord Frederick Cavendish was laid out, but Burke was so mutilated that his wounds had to be covered up before the body could be moved.

Lady Helen Munro Ferguson, who was at the dinner, was critical of the position taken up by Sir Edward Grey and Richard. They ought, she said, to have put down their feet firmly before and demanded reform of the House of Lords. To put the veto first, she said, was like cutting off the King's head and then asking people to crown him. As it was, the battle continued to rage between those (like Lloyd George) who demanded the creation of peers in the present Parliament, and those who said that in the event of a dissolution there should be an assurance that the nation's express wishes would be given effect to.

Though there was such difficulty over the matter, the Conservatives did not, Mr. Birrell said to me, want finance left on their hands, supposing the Budget to be rejected. He thought that the good temper of the Liberal Cabinet was wonderful, and that Lloyd George, in spite of the difficulties which arose, bore no resentment.

All difficulties, both regarding the Budget and the scheme for National Service, which was threatening to destroy the Territorial propaganda, were, however, brought to a temporary close by the King's death. I did not attend the funeral, being kept in Scotland, but later was impressed by the depth of mourning, especially the crape worn by Ministers' wives, when one thought crape was going out of fashion. Everyone seemed to outdo the other. One Minister's wife com-

plained that she received a snub for talking too cheer-
fully and for wearing pearl earrings. Luckily she
noticed that the Queen also wore them !

The conference called in the autumn of 1910 to
discuss the impasse regarding the House of Lords and
reform gave a momentary relief, though there was
not too much hope of success, and there was talk of a
National Government. However it was soon clear
that there was no possibility of agreement, and that
an election must be held. This took place in December, the second in a year. I spoke at six women's
meetings and many others (as my brother was laid up
till near the polling time), and they were well attended
considering the conditions. We went round the
polling stations on the day of the election.

The Prime Minister's family was living at Archer-
field in East Lothian, and there was a good deal of
intercourse with that lively household. One story
amused me. The local minister, when the P.M. said
he was going to lecture at Aberdeen on ' Style ', remarked, ' A difficult subject you have chosen, Mr.
Asquith, and a difficult audience to speak to ! ' He
esteemed his compatriots highly.

There were many Red Cross and nurses' meetings
this year and I was helping to complete a memoir of
my uncle, Sir John Burdon Sanderson, left incomplete
by his wife. Then there were celebrations at Hadding-
ton, when my brother was given the Freedom of the
Burgh, and various presentations on the 25th anniversary of his election as member for the county. This

Q

proved to be the end of his work there, for as was anticipated he went to the House of Lords almost immediately afterwards.

The Liberal Government, to which we Liberals had been looking forward so eagerly, had certainly a good deal to its credit even if it had not brought a new heaven on earth. There were old-age pensions, the feeding of necessitous children, medical inspection in schools, a new Workmen's Compensation Act and a new Housing Act, the Children's Act of 1908 and the Labour Exchange Act. But the picture of misery given in the Poor Law Report made most people feel that things had not gone half far enough : wages were still low, besides which, though there was a tentative Trade Board Act in 1909, sweating was still rampant and housing a disgrace. Education had not advanced very far and there were still half-timers between 12 and 14 years of age. There was no unemployment insurance or health insurance and the Poor Law system swept all sorts of people, sick, infirm, children, tramps, mentally defectives, into one category, until in 1929 a Conservative Government transformed Poor Law into Public Assistance. There was absence of ' planning ' in all the reforms : still they came, even if still inadequate, and brought about in what seemed the higgledy-piggledy fashion that we are accustomed to call British, though I dislike giving it such a name.

In May, 1911, I had an interesting time in London, since the Kaiser and his staff were there for the ceremony connected with the unveiling of the Queen Victoria Memorial before Buckingham Palace.   The ceremony was well carried through and the soldiers looked splendid, the Royal Family very cheerful.   The only drawback was that the new memorial, being white, made the Palace, as it then was, look extraordinarily dingy.   Someone said that the non-repair of the Palace represented the only continuity in policy between the old Government and the new !   The Queen and the Kaiser stood together and looked to be about the same height.   There were luncheon parties at my brother's house for the Kaiser and his staff.   He had with him General von Plessen, Graf zu Eulenburg, Admiral von Müller, etc.   When he lunched at Queen Anne's Gate, the Kaiser made himself extraordinarily agreeable, talking to the various members of the company suitably.   There were on the wall some German national pictures, given to my brother by the Kaiser, when he was visiting Germany, and Von Plessen called the latter's attention to them.   ' How long have they been up ? ' he asked at once.   He probably had much experience !   Von Plessen was fortunately able to assure him that they were there during his last visit, two years before.   He asked me about my visit to Essen and about those I had seen there, and talked in a friendly way, speaking of the excellence of the luncheon prepared by my brother's very good cook, Mrs. Pinnie, and noticed that I had got (indeed with some difficulty) cornflowers—the national emblem— for the table.   We did not say they came from France !

An amusing story was told me at a luncheon party, by Sir Frederick Pollock, of how the Crown Prince, looking at some new order of plant, was asked 'What is it?' 'Oh, some new Order bestowed by my Imperial Father on the Almighty!'

The question of Reform was now being debated in the House of Lords, over Lord Lansdowne's Bill—a 'machine Bill' Richard called it, i.e. a caucus Bill. I heard the debate but it sounded unreal. The Coronation put a temporary stop to politics, and the dispute which had been carried on in such a confused and almost muddled way ended in a sort of compromise, which at least worked. The Conservative peers voted with the Government, and the four hundred new peers of whom the newspaper *Reynolds* gave a list were at least not created. The P.M. said that up to three hundred they were excellent and would have been a credit! My brother was concerned with the scheme for a Court of the Empire which was enthusiastically received at the meeting of the Colonial Conference, though we all felt that great changes were impending as regards our relations with our Colonies.

Then there were strikes this year which gave cause for anxiety. The railwaymen's strike especially was serious and it seemed clear that war must be looked for in industry. The soldiers had been tactful, but the reserves were ready to be called up. Lloyd George had spoken straight to the men, citing the possibility of war and what might happen were no settlement come to. 'Don't ask me what I said,' as he put it, 'but give me champagne.' There was a real war scare, then Germany wished to know what assurances had been given to France.

The Coronation of King Edward in 1903 had been a quiet affair, since no one knew how serious might be the effect of a long service on one just recovered from a grave illness. Also the foreign delegates had gone back, and hence it was a more homely affair. Not only was the service shortened (there was no sermon), but I believe that the heavy crown, weighing over seven pounds, was only left on the royal head for a brief period. The chairs on which the faithful Commons sat were duly sold at a small price to those who had benefited from them—this seemed an admirable and economical plan, and has I believe been followed. Then we sat with the commoners, but by the time King George V was crowned in June 1911 my brother had been made a peer, and this time I had two invitations or commands to attend—one before and the other after my brother had been raised to the peerage. The end was that, not being a peeress, I was given a peculiar and excellent seat at the corner of the transept from which I could see everything in the ' theatre ' and also the Communion service later.

I was placed amongst the foreign envoys, who had the best positions in the Abbey. We had to be up at 6 a.m. and breakfasted at 7 o'clock, and then went to the House of Lords preceded by a mounted policeman, who cleared the way for us going and coming. Then we walked through the covered way to the Abbey about 8.30. The day was gusty and my veil kept blowing into the soldiers' faces. However, Dr. Gore, Bishop of Birmingham, walked with me in his robes and helped me to keep it within bounds. I cannot describe the strange and archaic ceremony and the beauty of the duchesses who held the gold canopy over the Queen. What struck us all most was the young Prince of Wales doing homage to his father, who then kissed him with affection. The boy had much bowing to do, for the ladies, including his sister, curtsied to him, and he was not apparently self-conscious, but in return bowed nicely and looked about to see that his train was tidy and his new Garter robes straight. The little Princess Mary and the younger boys sat in a row—the youngest, in a kilt, was rather restive, but they appeared to enjoy themselves. The Queen's trainbearers were dressed simply in white with white bows in their hair, and the ladies-in-waiting had gold brocade gowns. She herself looked magnificent. The peers did not all see very well, and my brother was asked by his physician to look after Lord Strathcona, who was ninety-two, and was very tired by the long ceremony. The Archbishop of York (Lang), not old Archbishop Temple, preached the sermon, which was on ' Service ' ; the Westminster boys did their huzzaing and Vivats, of course, splendidly : I thought that as impressive as anything, though I got much amusement from small incidents, such as the putting on of the coronets of the peers and peeresses and other idiosyncrasies of my immediate neighbours. Arranging their coronets was no easy task, and one or two peeresses succeeded in looking rather tipsy! The waiting time passed quickly for me, and I don't think I even ate the chocolate in my bag.

The service finished about two, but it was 3.30 before I could join my brother in the House of Lords for a much-needed luncheon in the Painted Chamber.

To me, as I say in my diary, it seemed strange that just while outside a violent controversy was going on and when the peers were being docked of their privileges by the Commons, the former alone should be accounted worthy of assisting in crowning the King of England. I don't suppose I should have believed that a coronation a quarter of a century later would in this respect differ not an iota. We are a conservative and aristocratic nation. The only difference—and it was a great one—was that the crowds were enormously greater in 1937 and the preparations made much more elaborate. Prices given for seats were thought large in 1911 but they did not equal those of the latter year.

In September I met Sir Arthur Nicolson (later Lord Carnock) at Raith, when staying there with his relatives, the Munro Fergusons, and had much talk with him. He struck me as distinctly anti-German, though he thought Germany must have room for expansion. She had come, he said, too late into the field, for all territory had already been taken up. He felt that the important matter was that France, Russia and England should hold together. Germany was always trying to point out to England that she should not hold to that effete country, France. The Kaiser he thought not very popular in Germany. He was so impressed by his reception here that he thought he had us in his pocket. Mr. Spender was, he thought, in Kühlmann's pocket—a libel indeed, able as Kühlmann was : he admired Jules Cambon greatly—more than his brother who was in London, since he thought him more vigorous. Kiderlen-Waechter he thought little of, and Germany generally was clumsy and untactful in her diplomacy, which was too true. Nicolson was extra-ordinarily Russophile I thought, and surprised me by telling me how attractive were the Russian prisons— so different from our cold and dreary ones ! He also told me of the morbid nature of the young Russians, and of how a father had asked his help in regard to a 14-year-old boy who had gone off from home just because of a reprimand, and feared that punishment might bring about suicide. He had no conception evidently of what was in store for that great land, but no one had or could have.

The year 1911 is also remarkable for a matter in which I took a good deal of interest, both because I had studied the German system when in Berlin and because of my connection with friendly societies, especially those for women. Mr. Lloyd George spoke to me a good deal about the insurance scheme and asked me to become a Commissioner for Scotland.

This office I could not accept, though it attracted me, for it would have taken too much of my time, being really a Civil Service appointment. Later on, I became a member of the Advisory Committee for Insurance in England. Lloyd George I found delightful to talk to, despite what seemed to me a haphazard mode of thought compared to the reasoned arguments that I was used to. I was able to press upon him—I thought with success—certain provisions in regard to maternity benefit, e.g. specially the right to call in a doctor as one of the claims on the maternity fund. My brother had to introduce the Insurance Bill in the House of Lords and I used to attend the debates there, but they seemed dead and uninteresting—as if a feather bed were weighing down upon speaker and audience alike. The by-elections were going none too well—people thought because of the unpopularity of compulsory insurance : anyhow it had been carried, with great zeal and under great difficulties, by Lloyd George, and he deserved credit for what he had done.

The sad thing to our minds at this time was that education was given a back place. There was not money for it : what my brother would have liked, would have been to be Chancellor of the Exchequer (as proposed by Grey in 1906), and be able to survey the finances of the country, allocating the money as circumstances demanded and giving system to the whole. Lloyd George was quite sympathetic about education, but he took things as they came, without making a real survey of requirements and working by it. Grey was centred on his own work as Foreign Minister, and education did not present itself to him as a paramount question in 1912.

There came my brother's visit to Berlin, so much discussed by all concerned. It was hoped that a good atmosphere might be created, such as Edward Grey might follow up, though the latter wished full responsibility to be given to Richard. All this is told elsewhere : we followed it with the deepest interest and anxiety.

As far as I was concerned, the year began the sittings of the Royal Commission on the Civil Service, of which I had been made a member. The first meetings coincided with the coal strike, and the Miners' Wages Bill was before Parliament. Our sittings commenced in March and the questions concerning women at once came up. Travelling from Scotland was none too easy. It took 15 hours to get home instead of 10. There was a great deal of distress in the Midlands. The collapse of negotiations, when it came, was a great blow, and Cabinets were held every other day. Edward Grey was very sympathetic with the miners, but their demands were rejected. Troops were sent to Wales, fortunately under a wise general, and no clash took place. The situation, in view of politics in Europe, was very anxious.

The Royal Commission on the Civil Service was of great interest to me and I formed real friendships with several of my fellow commissioners, such as Bishop

Burge, Sir Kenneth Muir Mackenzie, Sir Donald MacAlister (also a Scot) and others. It went on for three years, and even into the War time. I also served, as the only woman, on an Interdepartmental Committee on the out-door staff to be appointed under the Insurance Act, with Sir Francis Mowatt as its chairman. This brought me into touch with Mr. Stanley Leathes, Sir Robert Chalmers, Mr. Bradbury and many other interesting men, many of them in the Treasury. The most difficult question for me concerned the payment to be given to women, and as to this the Committee could not be brought to an agreement. Mr. Lloyd George, who addressed the Committee at its opening meeting, had gone a good way in equalizing pay for he had given equal pay to men and women in respect of the Insurance Commissioners, but of course a great deal was involved in the whole question, and the point has not as yet been decided in the Civil Service, or indeed elsewhere. Above all, we did not want a differentiation of work. To get the Insurance Act to work at all was extraordinarily difficult, and Sir Robert Morant, who had the task in hand and who was a very able man, was very despondent. An immense staff had been appointed and was working overtime. People had been laid hold of from every department, so that there was every advantage in so far as the personnel of the staff was experienced. But delay would have been a godsend, though, as usual, things worked out somehow in the end. The doctors were extremely hard to satisfy, and difficulties over the working of the medical service were not properly settled for a long time.

One of the duties of the members of the Royal Commission on the Civil Service was to visit the various public offices, and I selected the War Office, as I wished to see the manner in which the women clerks were housed, etc. I went with several other commissioners, including the Duke of Devonshire, one of our members, and we examined the books, methods of work, etc. We found the women clerks well housed in the new War Office, excepting that the windows were dimmed. I wondered if the fear was that they should see a soldier ! Conditions then were marvellously unlike those existing now, when women typists and secretaries are everywhere in public offices and no evil, such as was foretold, seems to ensue : the necessity for using them in war-time made all the difference. In those days, the women were comparatively few, and they were as far as possible ' segregated ', as it was called, so that they might be kept apart from the men. The views of our chairman at the time (Lord Macdonnell) were not advanced regarding the position of women, and my fellow woman commissioner (Mrs. Granville Streatfield) and I had hard work trying to support their claims as to pay, advancement, etc.

The whole women's movement was, however, going on apace and taking disagreeable forms so far as Ministers of the Crown were concerned, even those who were generally favourable to their cause. The Pethick-Lawrences and Mrs. Pankhurst were this year

(1912) sentenced to nine months' imprisonment for conspiracy. There were window-breaking raids, destruction of property, arson and the firing of pillar-boxes; and on the top of this a hunger strike on the part of the women prisoners at Aylesbury, which was followed by forcible feeding. This brought about a certain sympathy with the prisoners, especially as women of refinement were among them. Ministers could not walk out without being molested, whatever had been their view. At 10 Downing Street we had to make use of a back door and the same to a certain extent at Queen Anne's Gate, though on the other hand my brother had anonymous letters, sometimes in verse, proposing marriage as a solution of the impasse! He had queer experiences at meetings, and on one University occasion when some sort of medal or memento was to be presented to him, it was found that it had been laid hold of by women students. He was equal to the occasion and arranged that a jeweller's case should be solemnly presented, under the assurance that it would not be opened! I was never in the House of Commons when women chained themselves to the grille, but the police spoke of how they disliked the job of ejecting them. Adela Pankhurst called one day, in great distress about her mother, who was being forcibly fed. She was, however, liberated the next day.

I was often at meetings where there were nasty scenes ending with ejections, proceeding from one part of the hall to another. At a very big meeting in the Albert Hall at which Mr. Lloyd George spoke, he preserved admirable temper, despite constant interruptions. He evidently did not look forward to this meeting with pleasure for the hall was, he said, too big to get proper hold of the audience. Mrs. Snowden also spoke quite admirably, as she did in Perth at a meeting in the City Hall, over which I presided.

All this time the affairs of London University were giving my brother great trouble, especially questions regarding the site selected for the building. I feel certain that everyone must now feel relieved that the site on which it was finally built, and of which my brother approved, was at long last agreed upon. But the proceedings dragged on for an immensely long time and things was disappointing to those who could have got matters settled on advantageous terms much sooner. I was glad to be present at the ceremony of laying the foundation stone of the University by King George, seven years after my brother's death. I only wished he could have been there and seen the ideal for which he struggled, put into fact.

Sir Edward Grey lived at 28 Queen Anne's Gate when moving house to Sloane Gardens. He spoke to me of the romance of his early entry into political life, and of how later on, problems accumulate, whereas new Ministers *begin* with a clean slate. He said the great thing was not just to *talk* of the simple life but to *live* it, which I thought very wise. He amused me by saying,

when building a cottage, be sure not to make a lady's
maid's room, for that will be fatal ! These were
the days when women usually travelled with their
maids, even on the most informal country visits. We
talked of Wells, whom he thought an over-sexed writer,
for everything presented itself to him from that angle.
Grey's great discernment and simple views of life and
its duties were both attractive and unusual in a great
man of affairs, such as he was.

Later on he used to talk of middle age and contrasted
it with his young days when at Cloan. He said the best
gift he would ask for his boy, if he had one, would be a
love of fishing. He quoted Wordsworth and Dryden
in a way I envied. He felt that the Government was
breaking up and that the process of disintegration had
begun, and that a demand for an election would be
made before Home Rule could be granted. We had
a great deal of interesting discussion as to conditions
which never eventuated, such as the Unionists coming
in with a small majority, leaving the Irish and Labour
parties predominant. I dreaded an academic Liberal
party with no go in it, and I think he agreed. Education had not quite the interest for him that it had for
my brother. He told an amusing story, related by one
of his colleagues of another, ' Got 'ousemaid's knee
doing reverence on a cushion.'

Again we used to discuss how age should be met
and dealt with—we were about the same age—and
how, if we take up new interests and friends, we are
bound to give up others—that is, we must limit our

interests as well as our friends. His wife had done this, he said, and been miserable with those she did not care for and who did not care for her, as she believed. Probably, he thought, she would have felt keenly his immersion in politics. He instanced someone known to us both who had hundreds of friends, which is really impossible, and who distracted herself with supposed interests, and rang up those she knew to ask impossible questions, like the result of an election, thereby giving them unnecessary trouble for no real end.

On the 16th June, Richard handed to His Majesty the Great Seal and received it back from him, kneeling. Kneeling was always an effort and I am afraid he forgot to kiss hands ! He wired to Cloan and we put up the flag, and so it was intimated to our neighbours, who were delighted. Our mother, now aged eighty-seven, had not been enthusiastic about his being made a peer. Indeed she said when she heard the bells ring in the little town, ' They're tolling for Richard.' But this delighted her, for she had always hoped he might follow in the footsteps of her great-uncle, Lord Eldon, whom she remembered ; and she was the pivot round which all our actions and ambitions turned.

It was a great interest to the household when Richard came on Sunday, bringing the Great Seal with him. It has romantic associations, and there was great excitement among the young people when the ' Chaff-Wax ' came to Cloan and melted the sealing-wax on an outside fire, and someone was ennobled or some treaty was signed and sealed.

There was the usual King's Birthday dinner in June, and then my brother took leave of the Army, dressed in wig and gown of Chancellor. The Prime Minister spoke of his romantic career, being at the War Office and returning to his own profession as its head.

Queen Alexandra wrote to me about him and his wig. I had written a few words of sympathy on the death of the King of Denmark and she replied as follows :

> MARLBOROUGH HOUSE
> *June 17th*, 1912
>
> DEAR MISS HALDANE,
>
> I most gratefully accept your own, your Mother's and your Brother's kind sympathy in My great fresh losses and sorrows lately by the two tragic deaths following so close upon each other—Of my beloved eldest brother and my poor young nephew.
>
> They both were terrible shocks and blows to me, but God above helps me to bear all He lays upon me.
>
> I am so glad the Territorial nurses are prospering so well under your kind guidance. I well remember the day when I distributed the badges by the aid of your kind Brother.
>
> I am sorry he left the War Office but trust that he likes his new Office minus the wig which must be very hot !
>
> Yours sincerely,
> ALEXANDRA

The new German ambassador was Marschall von Bieberstein, and he took me in to dinner at Sir Alfred Turner's house. He was, like most of the distinguished

Germans whom I met, most deeply interested in his dinner, though he left those things, he declared, to his attractive wife. He was a little deaf and not young. We saw a good deal of him and his wife, of whom he spoke a great deal. Women led men always, he said, but he did not wish them to vote : he read the English papers but no German. His life after this was very short ; he seemed even then to be tired out.

There were many well-known literary men in London this year, owing to the Universities Conference and the 250th Anniversary of the establishment of the Royal Society. Amongst others I saw a good deal of M. Adam of Cartesian fame. He edited the great edition of Descartes' works, and thus was of special interest to me.

A dinner at the French Embassy was one specially to meet the President of the Chamber—M. Deschanel. He was interested in hearing details of political life and work, and was most complimentary to England, calling it the ' Ecole de politique ', saying that France had learned much from it. Though he spoke English, when he came to pour forth his praises of our land he broke into French.

The Archbishop of York (Dr. Lang), visited us at Cloan in autumn and amused us by his tales of Mr. Lynam's School at Oxford, chiefly composed, as it was, of the sons of Dons, whom he used to instruct in the Holy Scripture. A young boy's summary of his teaching was characteristic, ' The Bible has spiritually much truth, historically some, scientifically none.'

Amyddst yᵉ flowreſ I tell yᵉ houreſ. Tyme waneſ awaye aſ flowreſ decaye. Beyonde yᵉ tombe freſhe flowreſ bloome, ſoe Man ſhall ryſe above yᵉ ſkyeſ.

Stanley Houſe Chelſea 1914

TERRITORIAL NURSES

The Archbishop of Canterbury (Dr. Randall David-son) became, as I have said, a much-loved friend and wise adviser. He and his wife enjoyed walking on the hills as we did, and there were great opportunities in this way for talk. One who has held intimate relation-ship with kings and prime ministers acquires a fund of knowledge of this world as well as of spiritual things. And he took full advantage of his opportunities, and with the Scottish sense of humour that shone from beneath his bushy eyebrows he was able to make events that sounded tragic appear in a more homely and simple aspect. He was the one to whom all in diffi-culty naturally turned, and they never failed to get advice of a spiritual kind, as well as having the position put in its real relationship in so far as the world was concerned. His wife kept the torch of the spirit brightly burning, and spread around her a sense of love and devotion that made one feel that her life was set on things above and not on the trivialities of this earth.

On one occasion when my brother and the Arch-bishop had gone to walk through a rather precipitous ravine the paths suddenly ended owing to a landslip, and they found themselves for a time in a really anxious predicament, for there was nothing to lay hold of and the ground was unstable. Which helped the other it was difficult to ascertain, for both claimed to have done so, but on the whole the palm was given to the Archbishop. We all speculated on the sensation it would have made in the Press if the

Archbishop of Canterbury and the Lord Chancellor had been found lying together at the foot of a Scottish glen !

An interesting event to me was my brother's installation as Chancellor of the University of Bristol. There were many Quaker families present—Peases and Frys, and some kept their seats when Lord Roberts received his degree. All was done with great form and state and was more dignified than any such ceremonies that I had seen in the younger Universities. Then came the opening of the Law Courts. Lady Dorothy Nevill, who adored ceremonies, came with me to the previous service at the Abbey, where we sat in the Dean's pew. Through a thick fog, it all looked mysterious and impressive : there were just streaks of light coming through. The chatter in the nave before the service annoyed us, and an applicant for a ' post ' came up to me, just as I was leaving the Abbey. These applicants were numerous now my brother was Chancellor, and apparently they thought, if they had to do with clerical appointments, that I might make a good means of approach for livings ! In the Law Courts there was a curious first case—a man, cracked I fancy, who insisted that he should be heard by King and Chancellor.

Sir Kenneth Muir Mackenzie, who was permanent secretary to the Lord Chancellor, was a very great friend, and he always managed to throw an amusing light on all high occasions. As to the above, and Lady Dorothy's visit, I had evidently written to him, and he writes : 'Though I am not the verger (but the High Bailiff) of Westminster, you will be installed in the Dean's pew on Saturday at the Abbey, and see Richard as Pontifex Maximus from the best point of vantage. He, I fear, must reconcile himself to spiritual dignity and forget his prancing war-horse, the beating of drums and the flapping of flags.'

THE LAST TWO YEARS
BEFORE THE CRISIS
1912-1914

A DULL grey summer was succeeded in 1912 by pleasant harvest weather. The Belfast celebration on September 28th, which was Ulster Day, was carried out with rather ominous impressiveness, and one wondered what was in front of us. The Ministry, we then believed, might not have a long life to look forward to, but it had kept wonderfully together, and the Prime Minister had certainly shown marvellous business powers in handling it. When one looked back on old days, one felt that in this respect he excelled his great predecessor, Mr. Gladstone : he was indeed a true master in the House of Commons. Someone looking on at it amusingly described to me the scene : Grey and Haldane working in a dual capacity together, Lloyd George with his real democratic instincts but ready to make his actions paramount and his principles follow suit, Morley ' distilling like a scent-bottle nearly empty ' but with a quality all his own, and so on. All these criticisms might be unjust or inaccurate, but they pointed to a forceful Cabinet and one which was a formidable power in the country. Little did Ministers know what was before them.

What did concern them was the prospect of a conflict with the House of Lords and the necessity for making some preparation for the event. My brother had a scheme which sounded well and he worked it out in detail ; but every scheme failed, as we discovered later on, because the problem to be solved was not within the wit of man.

The Balkan war was another immediate anxiety. The Turks were always considered to be marvellous soldiers, but the Bulgarians seemed to be showing themselves yet better, and anyhow disturbance in that region was always an anxious affair.

In the autumn of 1912 there were various functions, interesting in themselves, for many bodies wished to do my brother honour. Besides that at Bristol, spoken of before, there was another smaller but very picturesque one when he received the Freedom of the old town of Dunbar, in his constituency, East Lothian. Then, in November, came the Freedom of the city of Edinburgh, where there was plenty of fun, especially as Lord Dunedin was receiving the same honour, so that there were two distinguished sons of Scotland to fête, both of whom were lawyers, though Lord Dunedin was considerably the senior. He spoke of how his old friend and fellow freeman might ' be found a very present help to the Corporation of Edinburgh in time of trouble ', slyly referring to a case in which decision had been given in their favour, and then he joked about how he or his successors would have the greatest difficulty in discovering my brother's domicile. It would, indeed, in his case only be discovered by his proceeding to marry, and then die and leave a badly provided-for widow behind him ! There was an opportunity also for Richard to refer to his noble friend, Lord Rosebery, sitting behind him, and remind him of their dissension over the Piershill Barracks and the temporary removal of the Scots Greys. The ceremony was held in the very beautiful hall of the Writers to the Signet, seldom seen by the general public.

But all this year there were two dominating interests and anxieties. The first was the fact that labour was establishing itself in a new form and that the working men were demanding a new place in the nation. Trade Unionism had grown to maturity and the new policy of ' direct action ' was coming into being, and sections of working men were developing into combinations, like the National Union of Railwaymen ; and now it was clear that there might be strikes which would cause general paralysis in the country. In addition to this dissension between capital and labour, there was the other question of women's suffrage. By 1912 the feeling had grown acute and intense excitement developed—an excitement which grew during the next two years.

It was indeed a time of militancy, such as had hardly been known before. Sir Edward Carson's declaration that ' We will never in any circumstance submit to Home Rule ', repeated word by word by 80,000 men in Belfast, was the first recent instance of law being taken into the hands of the individual who considered himself aggrieved.   The militant suffragists took up the same position : why should they be prosecuted any more than he ?   So the Pethick-Lawrences and Mrs. Pankhurst had gone to prison.   It was disagreeable for men to have women surrounding them and attacking them, verbally and physically.   The militants were no longer the elderly and unattractive, but, on the whole, young and good-looking, and an M.P. never knew under what circumstances he might meet, socially, the externally charming creatures.   Often enough evening parties were made the centre of attacks. The exhibition of pictures by Old Masters had to be closed, and, indeed, the British Museum also, when the attacks became general.   Sir Almroth Wright took up the matter by writing to the newspapers on what he called the ' sexually embittered ', and there was a most amusing reply by an anonymous writer (though her name was soon guessed at), agreeing with his strictures and stating that it was quite clear that the only cure was the radical one of exterminating this unwanted and objectionable section of the community.   ' Therefore let that be done and done at once ! '

In the earlier years the attacks were termed pinpricks, in the later they were dagger thrusts, and done by women, noble in themselves, who were persuaded that they were serving their country by doing this.   I remember the remarks made to me by the policeman stationed near the Ladies' Gallery in the House of Commons, ' I do dislike 'andling ladies,' and many felt like that, indignant, as they justly were, at the outrageous behaviour of the women. One often wonders whether the ' finished article ', the independent young woman of the present day, painted and powdered and so marvellously efficient, realizes what has been gone through with the object of giving her her independence. It all seems so obvious.

These were some of the many troubles at this time ; yet another was the progress of the Insurance Bill, which brought further threats to break the law. The mistresses of domestic servants objected to the Bill, but so did numerous servants themselves, many of whom had been tended carefully during their illnesses, without payment ; while the doctors, on their part, were pledged to refuse their services. Mr. Lloyd George showed great courage in persevering on his way, but the difficulty with the doctors was serious, and at one time it seemed to be insurmountable, since they objected strongly to the panel system. I came into touch with Mr. Lloyd George in some degree over these matters, especially as I was also in touch with Sir Donald MacAlister, President of the Medical Council, who was helpful and friendly. Nearly all one's friends, indeed, were concerned about the matter, and many of them angry. Lady Dorothy Nevill sent me an amusing doll, habited as Lloyd George, as a skit on his insurance plans. As I was in London every week for meetings of the Royal Commission on the Civil Service I heard much of the gossip concerning all these matters, which had their amusing side no doubt but whose repercussions were very serious.

I always enjoyed attending Courts, both because of their entertainment and because one met interesting people. My brother felt differently regarding them, because he had to attend in full dress, far from comfortable for one of his figure, carrying his Lord Chancellor's purse, which owing to the abundance of gold ornamentation was very heavy. Sir Edward Grey, who was responsible for the diplomatists, was still more depressed when the ' black days ' came round, for he had to attend every Court. Richard had two male attendants—' maids ', we called them— who went in a carriage behind ours, and helped with the carrying of the purse and arrangement of the attire. I was very lucky from not only having the entrée, but going in for presentation almost at the beginning of the Court, after the diplomatic corps.

Then, once presented, one sat down in the Royal Chamber and watched the further presentations with the rest of the Ministers' ladies. There were some very funny incidents : one of which concerned an elderly peer who trod on the train of the preceding lady. The ushers beckoned to him to get off, as the lady could not proceed. He thought the sign was to proceed, and the poor lady could not make her curtsey, or at least rise from it after she had made it ! Queen Alexandra had difficulty in keeping her countenance.

In the end of the year—in November—there was a snap division in the House of Commons on an unannounced amendment to the financial resolution of the Home Rule Bill, when the Government was defeated. Mr. Asquith was imperturbable and showed no intention of resigning, but when the necessary sequel took place—a rescission of the amendments two days later—there was a disturbance by the Opposition, and the Speaker had to adjourn the House. I came to London the day after this took place and heard all about the events and the consequent excitement as to what should be done and whether there should be a dissolution. The snap vote had been planned for some time and the Ministry did not seem to have taken due measures, but it was not taken too seriously. I had a chance of talking to the Prime Minister, who showed at his best in such occasions, for he understood the House perfectly and kept absolutely calm—as I write in my diary, he was ' cool as a cucumber '—and talked to me, not of the crisis, but mainly of the Royal Commission and its work. He was interested in hearing of how we spent the luncheon hour in the Abbey, and how Mr. Clynes, not then the well-known and appreciated figure he later on became, was so deeply interested on his first visit to the tombs of the kings that Mr. Graham Wallas, another member, and I could not persuade him to go back with us to resume our rather dull discussions.

With the beginning of the year 1913, there was great excitement over the Franchise and Registration

Bill, under which the whole suffrage question was to come up. This was an ingenious method of saving the face of the Government, that is to say, enfranchising women at the same time as clearing away various disqualifications from men. However, it was held by the Speaker that such a Bill, absorbing women's suffrage so to speak on the way, would be a different Bill, and it was ruled out. I went in and out during the debate, and as the Royal Commission met in the house formerly owned by Henry Labouchere, which became the Royal Commission House, just opposite the Houses of Parliament, I had a good view of the excited crowds. The tension was tremendous and a Cabinet Council was called, for which my brother had to return from Windsor, where he had been summoned.

Asquith once again was cool, and two of the prominent Ministers were seen at a cinema film of Big Game, so they were taking it quietly too : the cinema had now developed to something approaching its present excellence.

On Sunday night the supporters of the suffrage had an informal meeting at Mr. Lloyd George's house at 10 p.m. The next day Richard and Sir Edward Grey said they would resign if nothing were done, but Mr. Asquith was undisturbed, and it was resolved to withdraw the whole of the Franchise Bill and allow facilities to private members for a Bill next session, with a free vote. How matters would have gone had the Bill been pressed to a division it is difficult to say : Mr. McKenna told me that the suffrage portion would have been defeated. Anyhow, the feeling was bitter, and the militants were more rampant than ever, burning houses and railway stations and cutting telegraph and telephone wires. The alternative to the hunger-strike, followed as it was by forcible feeding, was release from prison, and that Mr. McKenna could not do. So he introduced a Bill giving him powers to liberate prisoners on licence while of good conduct. He was then enabled to get them back on further offence without trial, and yet escape the forcible feeding, when that would have otherwise been necessary. The 'Cat and Mouse' Bill was passed hastily, owing to fresh outbreaks of arson. Little good resulted, and a shocking incident occurred when a militant dashed in front of the horses at the Derby and was killed.

All these matters concerned me very much, as I had been a supporter of the suffrage all my life, though hating militancy. I had a good deal of talk over the matter with Sir Edward Grey, who was now living in Sloane Gardens, and he gave me useful advice. He had previously written to me to point out that if the amendment admitting women was carried, it would not entail resignation on the part of its opponents in the Ministry, while those for the franchise would resign if it were not carried. Mrs. Asquith and others were much concerned at his attitude.

Mr. Snowden was a member of the Royal Commission with whom I came a good deal into touch over the suffrage and education. He also came to Queen Anne's Gate in order to discuss education with my brother, and he assured him that Labour would help in the matter as did Mr. Massingham of the *Nation*. Others were interested, and so the beginning of an understanding with the Labour party on this subject was formed, which had developments later on, so far as my brother was concerned. As a matter of fact, he got little encouragement in this, to him, intensely engrossing matter, from the party to which he belonged.

I sometimes went to the House of Lords to listen to the debates, as I did on the occasion of one on the army in 1913. Lord Roberts was not at his best, and Lord Methuen spoke on the harm which he considered the National Service League had done. This debate, of course, excited the Lord Chancellor, and it was to me a queer sight to see this bewigged and berobed archaic figure, which, when bereft of its trappings, I knew so well, suddenly coming to life and showing itself to be not only living but excited, throwing about its arms in a way reminiscent of days gone by ! I also went to see the Royal Commission when Bills are assented to—one of the oddest sights surely in our ancient legislature, though not much odder than the reception of a new peer. One wonders what would be thought of it all by a foreigner who had been assured of our democratic form of government. A French lady, for whom I got a place, gazed at the Lord Chancellor and said, 'Est-ce qu'il est aussi Lor-Maire ? ' A Lord Mayor she thought of as having reached the acme of distinction.

In March of this year, 1913, the Royal Commission made its way to Ireland. I went there rather frequently as a member of the Carnegie United Kingdom Trust, since we had Ireland under our care as well as England and Scotland. At this time, though everyone was as I say at one another's throats, there seemed to be rather an interesting material and intellectual awakening going on. Of the latter, Sir Horace Plunkett and Mr. Russell (A. E.) were the principal exponents. I was invited to stay at the Vice-Regal Lodge and enjoyed my stay there, having an opportunity of examining the schemes set on foot by the Aberdeens for combating tuberculosis and other evils. Then the art in Dublin, the museums and Irish Academy, were all of the greatest interest. But the tragedy was that so many people, like the supporters of the Plunkett foundation and others doing equally good work, were at variance ; and then the narrow reactionary party sympathized with neither, but kept apart from anything approaching nationalism as if it were poison, even boycotting their country's representatives—the representatives of their King. No one could wonder at the result. One of the tragedies later on was the burning of the house of Sir Horace Plunkett, with all his papers and plans for his agricultural work for the land. Like so many others who were trying to do the same sort of work, we met for discussion in Sir Horace's beautiful home, and a charming place it was, a little way out of Dublin. Sir Horace was a fellow Carnegie trustee, so we met very

s

frequently. After the destruction of his Irish home he lived in England. I don't think he ever recovered from the blow.

At the opening of Parliament this year there was also a threatening of boycott on the part of the peeresses; indeed one always wonders how on such occasions they make up their minds to dress in evening attire on a cold morning in order to attend any function. Of course it was interesting to see the ceremony, especially since, as before mentioned, one thought that, with the prospective attack on the House of Lords, the function might in the future be anyhow devoid of its picturesque attractions. My brother was anxious to get a sentence into the King's speech, dealing with the prospect of national education. It was sadly truncated, whether by the Education Office or not I know not, but still it was there, though coming events made it of little import. At a dinner party the same evening, I was greatly interested in Lord Spencer's account of the papers in his possession, of which I hoped he would make use, though he insisted that as a politician and Whip he was forgotten. One of the company was upset by the loss of a diamond star, and Princess Lichnowsky, wife of the German ambassador, to whom everyone was devoted and who was a member of an interesting luncheon club of women to which I belonged, could not come owing to her alarm at a horse running off, when going to the opening of Parliament.

It was soon after this that my friend Lady Dorothy Nevill died, to my sorrow. I had lunched with her shortly before and met several interesting guests, including one who had seen a ghost in a German castle, and Mrs. Maxwell, who had been Miss Braddon. The guests being, like our hostess, mostly anti-feminist, were rejoiced over the county council elections in which, perhaps owing to militancy, nearly all the women candidates were defeated.

As my brother was rather frequently sitting in his judicial capacity on the Judicial Committee of the Privy Council, I occasionally went to listen. Few people realize that they can venture into these rather forbidding portals, just out of Whitehall in Downing Street, yet I always try to take or send my overseas friends to see where the cases that affect the Empire are being tried, and where they can see functioning one of the bonds that holds a great part of our Empire together. In addition to this, it is an interesting building, and the silver plate, dating back for hundreds of years, is itself worth seeing. One of the inkstands was, I believe, borrowed by Lord Curzon in order to give dignity to the Foreign Office table, which was thought by him to have a meagre appearance, but it was speedily recovered after his demission of office. The tribunal is simplicity itself, as the judges who deal with cases of portentous importance from the Indies, Australia, New Zealand and so on, are undecorated either with wigs or gowns. About this time the case of Sir Stuart Samuel was being dealt with. It had reference to a heavy purchase of silver made by the Indian Government through the firm of Samuel Montagu and Sons, and a member of the family was Under Secretary for India. It was, however, found that neither he nor Sir Stuart Samuel had any inside knowledge of the transaction. There was always a President of the Tribunal, and the day this case came up the President was Lord Morley, who talked to me afterwards and said how much he liked the position. My brother read the judgement and the others, Lord Halsbury, Lord Shaw and Lord Atkinson, agreed. It was an anxious time for Sir Stuart Samuel, though all went well in the end.

Soon after this, in June, came the really disagreeable Marconi case, but that is a matter of history. I went to hear the debate upon it, which was, of course, exciting to us all. The Ladies' Gallery was crowded. In my diary I say that I thought Sir Rufus Isaacs' speech rather too long, and that it would have been better to have left off after saying he had been indiscreet and unwise ; but Lloyd George's speech was very clever and he has the real magnetic gift of making people feel with him. My brother did his best as a conciliator, a useful office. The Ministers concerned spoke with due humility, and the expression of regret was accepted by the House by a not too large majority. The House is usually kindly on such occasions when dealt with frankly, as in the end it was. The Cabinet got a serious shake, however, for they had too easily decided that the matter would die down, and as the rumours were not dealt with by a select committee or otherwise, it looked as if the truth had to be dragged forth from them by force.

This was when I first met that wonderful Indian poet and mystic, Rabindranath Tagore, at Professor and Mrs. Prothero's hospitable table : Mrs., afterwards Lady, Prothero was a great friend, and her luncheon parties were always delightful. Tagore talked to me in a beautiful monotonous singing voice about his play *The Post Office* and impressed me by his calm outlook on the troubled world. I think he was more impressive talking than lecturing, though I heard both. Katherine, Lady Cromer, a delightful and interesting woman, was there and was also much impressed : another time when she was also present I made the acquaintance of Evelyn Underhill (Mrs. Stuart Moore), the very notable writer on mysticism, and Yeats. Lady Prothero was Irish, a sister of Professor Butcher and a woman of great distinction, who often had interesting Irish guests. Yeats told us stories of a new medium who seemed to be able to write in all sorts of languages totally unknown. His voice was audible and could tell one what to do in times of difficulty. Yeats talked of progress as being, as far as I understood, a series of starts—starts as I took it being states of emotion or contrition—from which you gradually fall back. Education too often, in his view, took away real knowledge. His face is a striking one and what he said interested me.

But as to mediums, I was put off by one we went to hear at General Sir Alfred Turner's house. He was supposed to be in touch with Sir John Rigby, the former occupant of the house on the Embankment in which we met, and an old friend of ours. Sir John duly appeared to us, but excepting that he was bearded like his prototype, there was nothing convincing, for all that he spoke to me about in reply to questions was what anyone could have known through the public prints, e.g. things dealing with my brother's public life. However, W. T. Stead, who was there, was immensely pleased because he got into communication with his dead son through the medium. He told us, to Stead's delight, how like life in heaven was to life here below. People apparently did the same things and lived in the same sort of way. That, to me, was depressing, though his view seemed to be shared by Sir Oliver Lodge, who stayed with us at Cloan in 1921 and discussed the matter with Archbishop Davidson, who was also a guest. One felt that one had had enough of the casual cigarette-smoking *milieu* on this earth.

We sometimes saw General Baden-Powell at Cloan. By this time he had set on foot his wonderful organization of Boy Scouts, soon to be followed by Girl Guides. The first picturesque organization captured the imagination of boys and was almost universally approved. The second had much criticism, but proved almost as useful in getting rid of the silliness bred in a certain type of girl by her surroundings. Sir Robert has a genius for making the life of the young cheerful and useful, and he himself had all sorts of dodges for doing this and was a clever draftsman. He drew amusing sketches of the Territorials, which I still have. It was a time when healthy life required developing, for so many of the younger people were rich and thoughtless, spending their nights in dancing the tango and frequenting clubs of a dubious kind.

What occupied me mostly after Easter, when the meetings of the Royal Commission began again, was the attempt to draft something of what I wanted especially in regard to the employment of women in the Civil Service. Their position was far from satisfactory, even in the Departments in which they had got a footing. I had a meeting with the women civil servants and much discussion with sympathizers like my fellow members, Mrs. Streatfeild and Mr. Snowden.

At Easter I had travelled northwards with Sir Edward Grey who seemed in good spirits about things generally, possibly in part because he was off to fish, leaving the Foreign Office with Lord Morley (who was delighted to have it), with the Prime Minister to refer to. He was, however, much concerned about Mrs. Pankhurst, who had starved for nine days. She was finally released. In June, 1913, he dined with us and was in great spirits after having issued his ultimatum to the Balkan envoys to sign or leave. They, of course, signed and he was being universally congratulated on the result of the Conference.

Next month, Poincaré visited London and a State Banquet and Ball were given in his honour, to which

I was invited with my brother. I had been specially interested in Poincaré as I had heard a great deal about him on the literary side. He pleased me by asking that I should be introduced to him as the translator of Descartes' works into English, and when we met he spoke of the difficulty of translating him. He was short and bourgeois in appearance, but with a quick alert expression, full of life, and impressed one as probably being good at organizing. I wish I had known his brother, the mathematician, of whom my friend M. Jean-Marie Carré spoke so enthusiastically. His death while still young was a great loss. Raymond Poincaré was not 'forthcoming' as one expected Frenchmen to be, but of course he was Alsatian, being born at Nancy or near it. Richard spoke to him of Renan, and I expect he and I had more points of contact than had the Prime Minister, who also had a good deal of conversation with him and did not find the talk easy. We know that he did not prove an easy man to deal with, later on, in the political sphere. Lord Esher and he did not apparently make much way together either, for the former said that he had shown him over Windsor Castle and he did not ask a single question till he came to Detaille's pictures! However, the French said that he would 'hold the helm' and see any Bill through, and that he certainly did.

In the early autumn of 1913 I went with my brother, and Sir Kenneth Muir Mackenzie, permanent secretary to the Lord Chancellor, to Montreal, where he

"The Territorial Manoeuvres have been a complete success." — Daily Press.

SKETCH OF A TERRITORIAL BY LORD BADEN-POWELL

August 1908

was to address the American Bar Association. It was an intensely interesting journey to me. We went and returned by the ill-fated *Lusitania*, so soon to go to the bottom. She was then the last thing in luxury, and we had a sort of 'maisonnette' to ourselves and could leave there what we did not want on shore. It was not then considered right for the Lord Chancellor to leave the Great Seal in Commission for more than a long week-end. Just as we were starting, Lord Strathcona, then aged 93, and his wife appeared, having suddenly decided to go for a week-end also. Both died a very short time after our return. We also had as a fellow traveller Mr. Justice Wendell Holmes, magnificent to look at and delightful to talk to. We went up the Hudson in Mr. Morgan's beautiful yacht and had a sumptuous dinner at Albany, only marred by one of the guests having her valuable jewellery stolen. Richard reviewed the young soldiers at West Point—such splendid lads in their antiquated uniforms —and then went by the luxurious but dusty train to Montreal. Here he delivered the speech, over which he had been cogitating for long, and had a wonderful reception. I had special entertainments ; there were banquets and thousands of handshakes. I had wisely armed myself with a quantity of heather from Cloan, and I found no gift more acceptable to the many Scottish Canadians. It was all delightful, but a rest to leave that overcharged atmosphere of hospitality and heat for the peaceful *Lusitania*.

This expedition was of much use physically to my

brother, and after a fortnight of quiet we had a number of visitors at Cloan, including the Prime Minister and his family. It struck me that just as Gladstone's head grew with age and (possibly) responsibility, so had Mr. Asquith's. He looked older, but was keen about everything. There was great talk, of course, about the suffrage, for his daughter Violet was violently 'anti'. She had had a tussle on the golf links, and said, perhaps truly, ' You can't be clawed without being against the clawers '. I had been helping with a meeting at Crieff, addressed by Mrs. Fawcett. The Prime Minister talked of the Royal Commission and of the United Kingdom Trust, of which Mr. Carnegie had just made me a trustee, of his son Cys and my nephew and niece, Jack and Naomi. We had much fun with a neighbour of whom Richard pretended to be jealous, and Mr. Asquith and he ragged like schoolboys. It was a cheerful time. This was our first visit from Elizabeth Asquith, then still a child, but as I say in my diary a marvellous one, so *rangée*. Her talk filled our other guest, Professor Hume Brown, with wonder. She was full of music and painting as she had just returned from Munich, and discussed them all as though, the Professor said, she were indeed Mme de Staël! Her friends she hit off as regards their foibles and virtues in well chosen phrases, and she quoted from Chateaubriand, to show that the love of one of them was herself! All this sounds marvellous, but unattractive, and the surprising thing was that, with all her uncanny insight, she was charming to everyone and full of humour. Lady Desborough came over from Drummond Castle with Lady Ancaster, and with the Buxtons, Mr. Runciman, etc. ; we had pleasant parties, and my mother, though now nearly ninety, received her visitors in her room and thoroughly enjoyed it all.

Irish affairs were still looming, and General French, when with us, was full of Ulster and how she should be treated. The Prime Minister and everyone else was pleased with a speech of Churchill's, but all the time we were wondering what Ulster would do and whether she would hold out against any offer of peace and prefer to use force. Bonar Law and Carson were in conclave, and to us, at that time, there seemed a certain absurdity in Carson's position, courageous as he was. He had undoubtedly been ready to give up much for what he believed to be a great cause.

When I went to 28 Queen Anne's Gate in the end of October, Mrs. Asquith was staying there with her daughter, the reason being that No. 10 Downing Street was in the hands of workmen for much needed improvements ; Mr. Asquith and his elder daughter were the guests of other friends a few doors off. Any house, however quiet, became lively with such lively guests as the two who were with us. The Prime Minister had, however, to go to Scotland for the unveiling of Campbell-Bannerman's statue at Stirling.

There were many things being discussed at this time, including the educational matters in which my brother was so interested, and the land policy, which my younger brother was discussing with Lloyd George. We all—the young Asquiths and I—went to hear Sidney Webb lecture, with Bernard Shaw in the chair, and had a talk with them afterwards. The attractive Lady Scott we sometimes met at dinner. The whole world had been thrilled and deeply moved by the news in the beginning of 1913 of her husband's tragic death, after his almost superhuman efforts made in the South Pole Expedition. It was just about a year before that we had heard of the sinking of the *Titanic* with 1635 persons on board, the great ship of 46,800 tons that had been glorified as the biggest liner in the world. The enquiry was held in a hall in Palace Street, near our house, and was presided over by Lord Mersey, who later became a great friend of mine during the years in which he was an invalid. I can never forget the horror of it all, when one saw the model of the ship in court and heard of what happened from survivors or others, and realized what it must have meant to the sufferers by the tragedy. Mr. Stead lost his life then, and somehow that sort of death seemed not inappropriate for that restless spirit, always warring with what he considered to be, and usually were, the forces of evil.

I think that there had not been time to use the wireless telegraphy, which was what wireless meant in those days. No one realized what it was going to signify in later years. For all those things were developing very fast. The cinematograph, as we understand it, was working, but there were no great cinematograph theatres then or elaborate programmes. Most of the shows were of crude melodrama, and the light was still jerky and most tiring to the eyes. ' Electric theatres ', so-called, were given up for the most part to the poorer people in towns.

Cars were now common, but they were not cheap, though there were now motor cabs and buses, the latter being mainly in London, and those living in the suburbs had still to find their way into and out of town by tube or railway. A wonderful innovation called the ' escalator ', destined to terrify many elderly ladies, was one of the amusements at a ' White City ' exhibition shortly before this time.

Naval estimates were soaring up, especially after the inconclusive results of the strenuous endeavour made by my brother in his visit to Germany to get an understanding between the two countries. Tirpitz, in Germany, was getting the upper hand and our country seemed to be drifting into a fatalistic acceptance of a struggle for superior force, and Churchill's estimates for the Navy were huge. But for most people the Irish question was over-riding all others. The feeling became intense, and when Lady Pirrie made an enquiry of Lady Londonderry in the Ladies' Gallery after the health of her daughter-in-law, Lady Castlereagh, who had had an operation, she was met by the assurance that her works (in Belfast) would be razed to the ground and she herself shot down, and a good deal more.

Lord Morley frequently lunched at Queen Anne's Gate, and often spoke of his wife and of how much she had suffered before her death. I asked him whether he could justify what he had said in his *Life of Gladstone*, that Oxford had been the mover in the reform of the Civil Service, for it was not what I had gathered in my experience on the Civil Service Commission. I wondered for instance whether he thought Jowett's influence had been in this direction. He justified his assertion by saying that anyhow reform emanated from Oxford men, like Gladstone, which personally I thought not too convincing. Another evening, when President Wilson's daughter and her husband, and Miss Page, daughter of the Ambassador, were present, he gave me his new book and we had a great discussion on whether the rising or younger generation had or had not less regard for contract and less sense of responsibility than the older. He maintained that it had less, instancing the want of respect for contracts in Trade Unions, etc. I said that I did not agree and that contracts had at all times been broken when occasion really demanded it. Morley professed to be greatly shocked at my subversive opinions and referred the whole question to my brother, who said that on the whole he thought that the younger generation had higher standards (and this was characteristic) just because it was better educated than the preceding. Of course, Lord Morley had Ulster much on his mind when he talked of disrespect for law. He talked, too, of law as administered in America, and of the rescinding of judgements : also of the quality of their judges, as well as of the Judiciary of Ireland, which he thought not what it ought to be.

Larkin's trial and sentence was the source of a good deal of trouble. He was an Irish striker who founded the Irish Transport Workers' Union, and with a man named Connolly began a regular campaign of ' direct action ' strikes, that is strikes without notice. In this case there was both a strike and a lock-out. Larkin's sentence was for using seditious language, and yet seditious language, people truly said, was being used in Ulster all the time. The Government gave in, but a big meeting in the Albert Hall decided to use militant methods with Ministers until Larkin was released. All these militancies were bad, and seemed an indication of a lawless spirit.

Indeed things were coming to a head in Ireland. Morley thought that an impasse had been arrived at. What was done for the North was anathema to the South, and whatever move was made seemed certain to spell disaster and create what Morley called ' Hell's Kitchen '. The only thing to be done seemed to be to go on and face the consequences. There was plenty of criticism of the Government for what it had done, and had not done, and Lloyd George suddenly burst forth regarding the reduction of armaments, as did the peace party with Hobhouse at its head. It was not certain what line Winston Churchill was going to take, and the social schemes in view were, it was thought, likely to require all the money available. But people often summed up the situation by saying ' the Government is rotten but it has the brains of the country and that counts '.

We had a large Christmas party at Cloan, the last Christmas before the war. One niece was just coming out, another younger one was writing poems. A German boy was staying with us to teach a sailor nephew to speak German. All the others were busy ; my brother John building a new laboratory at Oxford. One looked at the young ones dancing, German and English together, and never thought that in a few months they would, some of them, be fighting for their lives, trying to kill one another, and that all the matters that seemed so important to us would be as nought.

My elder brother left Cloan after Christmas but returned in the middle of January, after having made an important stay at Fallodon to discuss matters and hoping to get at some arrangement regarding Ireland. The Prime Minister had gone abroad. When I went to London in February, I found much worry about the Marconi case and about the question of Sir Rufus Isaacs' appointment as Chief Justice. I did not go to the opening of Parliament but did go to the debate in the House of Commons. Here Asquith was admirable. It seemed to me that his clear logical attitude was just what was wanted in discussing the Irish question. The mover on the Opposition side went straight for Ireland, and the seconder also. Both spoke well. I sat between Mrs. Redmond and Mrs. Asquith and

T

Mrs. Harcourt and Lady Dorothy Long were behind. Asquith began by denouncing his opponents, but became more conciliatory as he went on : indeed, he went so far as to say that he would discuss anything, even the separation of Ulster. I believe that the stalwarts of the Government thought he had gone too far and should not have shown his hand. Long spoke as one might expect, and Chamberlain was very bitter.

I did not hear Carson speak, but he also was bitter, though he said that the Nationalists must 'woo Ulster'. Sir Horace Plunkett wrote to *The Times*, and was, in the view of the P.M., doing his best, though the difficulties were great. But the Conservatives would not look at the time-limit plan that he suggested, and he blamed himself for not having realized the Ulster difficulty in 1904. I lunched with Mrs. J. R. Green, and found a large party of young Irishmen there, and also Mr. Biggar. She had been going through Ulster with him, addressing meetings and staying with priests. We had a long discussion : the idea of a convention was coming to the front, and the detachment of, say, four counties. Lloyd George is reported to have advocated any county having the right to vote itself out by plebiscite. The *News of the World* had a scheme, which it professed to be that of the Government, whereby there was a real separation of Ulster and the South, but Mrs. Green did not like the idea. 'There are two months still to settle the matter but a settlement of some sort must come,' as I wrote in my diary : one foresees the future so little.

There were various changes in political personnel. Masterman had been defeated, mainly by the Socialist vote, which was significant. Herbert Samuel was now at the Local Government Board, and Burns at the Board of Trade, a difficult department for him to deal with. Lord Buxton was going to South Africa and Lord Novar to Australia—both happy appointments. At one of our dinner parties we had the Bryces, Morley, Miss Godley and Miss Joan Balfour, etc. With Morley I had as usual a talk. He looked so frail : we discussed whether the sentiment of pity did more harm than good, and he spoke of his stepdaughter's work in a convent in Dublin. Lord Macdonnell, the chairman of our Royal Commission, was no favourite of his. I thought him prejudiced in his view, and got him to go so far as to say that, at any rate, he had done well in India. Lord Bryce was very well and full of energy, and interested in the great Loch Voil water scheme.

I describe in my diary a very odd dinner at 10 Downing Street. We were asked to come early—at 8 o'clock—and to enter by the garden because of suffrage demonstrations outside. Several men, including Laurence Housman, were arrested. The Prime Minister was kept in the House owing to a motion made by Mr. Falle requesting him to state his policy, and we went there after dinner, deserting the company, and heard Bonar Law and O'Brien.

The Prime Minister spoke very well, but the drift of his speech was to the effect that he would not make his statement till the financial business was over.

The House was very hot and there were many angry exclamations. Bonar Law spoke well but bitterly. He was singularly unimpressive in speech and manner, and reminded one of a mild middle-class Scot, not easily perturbed, and even when he called the conduct of his opponents ' abominable ', it did not sound at all abominable ! However, in print, as I say in my diary, it was perhaps more convincing. Carson looked on and never seemed even to show approval of his own people. ' One looks at his immovable face and wonders what may come and whether one can hope anything from him.'

In the morning I walked to the Foreign Office with Sir Edward Grey. He said he felt he had been at the Foreign Office too long. I replied that success had justified length of service in his case, and that success brought success, referring, of course, to the settlement of the Balkan affairs. He said that he was not at the end yet and some trivial thing might cause a fiasco. This was often the case, for people got careless about the minor things as time went on. I often thought of this interesting talk, later on, and after Serajevo. It seemed a small thing to outsiders, though it proved to be of such tragic importance. But Grey never grew careless of things, great or small.

We saw a great deal of Edmund Gosse, who was a great friend of mine as well as of my brother's. I met him at the Charnwoods, at dinner, at this time, and as usual he pretended to be an invalid, ' a faded flower ' as he put it. But this did not prevent him partaking of a very hearty dinner ! He talked of Lady Dorothy Nevill as one who really belonged to a century before her time, and of my brother's Creighton lectures, which he thought would have been good if the philosophy had been left out. Gosse never appreciated our love of philosophy, and was anxious we should leave alone that, to him, unsatisfactory region of knowledge. His desire that my brother should publish some of his judgements was realized : one at least has now appeared in an anthology and others have been quoted. Lord Moulton was another entertaining guest. He called Almroth Wright, whom he held in high esteem, the Bernard Shaw of the medical profession, which we thought an amusing summary of his character. My great friend Violet Markham, then anti-suffrage, was not in this matter too proud of her supporter, clever as he was.

But all this pleasant life was just on the surface, for negotiations and counter negotiations were going on regarding Ireland. By March, when I was in town over the drafting of a memorandum of dissent from the majority of Commissioners on the Civil Service upon the women's question, I found that serious developments had occurred in the Irish situation. The proposed separation of Ulster was full of difficulties, since it included counties politically nationalist and some nationalist minorities elsewhere. A scheme was, however, introduced by Mr. Asquith, which was swept aside by the report that officers at the Curragh were resigning their commissions rather than risk having to march against Ulster. This followed a vote of censure on Mr. Asquith spoken to by Sir Edward Carson on March 19th, when he and other Unionists walked ostentatiously out of the House.

In spite of all these difficulties the Prime Minister, whom we met at the Sheffields', was apparently undisturbed and seemed to be mainly interested in a book by the librarian of the House of Commons on Homer. He spoke of returning to The Wharf, the Asquiths' country house, next day if fine, and he was certainly able, in a remarkable way, to detach himself from his preoccupation. Venetia Stanley, Lord Sheffield's daughter, was at dinner, and she always entertained him. I believe he spoke well on the vote of censure, but Carson was a sort of prophet amongst the others of his party, and uttered with such fervour that he carried people with him. Winston Churchill had got his gunboats ready and one could not but feel that he was enjoying the situation.

For a week, things were alarming, and most of the officers of the Cavalry Brigade at the Curragh, with the Brigadier-General (Gough) himself, intimated that they preferred dismissal to obeying orders for service in Ulster. But there were explanations given at the War Office and they returned to duty. Further misunderstandings followed, and the officers apparently thought that the coercion of Ulster was to begin. Then came difference of opinion within the party itself. General Gough had received a document from the War Office, signed by Colonel Seely, Minister for War, General French, Chief of the General Staff, and Sir J. S. Ewart, Adjutant-General, which after a couple of short paragraphs stating the duty of troops in keeping civil order and so on, went on to say that ' the Government has no intention whatever of using this right in order to crush political opposition to the policy or principles of the Home Rule Bill.' This paragraph caused an outcry from Nationalists, Liberals and Labour members as being a sheer surrender to the Army, and it appeared that Colonel Seely had had to leave during the discussion for an audience of the King, and the discussion being over when he returned, on his own responsibility, though with the assent of Lord Morley, added the intimation about the Government's intentions. The Prime Minister stated that all the three signatories to the document had tendered their resignations but that these had not been accepted.

When I reached London in March, I thus found a regular turmoil going on over what Lord Morley called the 'peccant paragraph'. Morley signed the paragraph with some verbal amendments only. The nation seemed to go on fire over the matter, and Colonel Seely resigned : his resignation was not at first accepted, though it had finally to be so. The whole cry was like that of ' Parliament versus Army '. At a dinner party, there were a number of soldiers and much talk. Winston Churchill had made a fiery speech, which fanned the flames, as had Lloyd George's ; only he, as frequently

happened with him, became voiceless and was laid up.
When with us, Mr. Churchill was full of his speech :
he had been, it was held, unwise in ordering the fleet
to Lamlash, though some said it was only two small
cruisers.

My brother did his best with General French, who was
an old friend, and went with him to Downing Street
before the Cabinet, but the Prime Minister made no
way with him. There was an infinity of gossip and
confusion of counsel. On Sunday, 29th March, General French, General Ewart and Colonel Seely called
at Queen Anne's Gate with urgent messages. Richard
was with them in his study for two hours or more,
trying to draft a letter from General French to the
Prime Minister that might help matters. They
made some progress. Lord Morley came at one
o'clock and he and I sat in the drawing-room, waiting
for results, for an hour. Then the others came down
and read the letter to Morley, who approved. Mr.
Bonham-Carter [1] was also there, and after that he went
to The Wharf to see the Prime Minister, who, I gathered,
was doubtful. Lord Morley and I had a bet of a shilling
on whether the letter would be successful and avoid the
resignation of the Generals. I thought I should win, but
I lost in as much as the whole excitement ended in a
dramatic scene when the Prime Minister announced in
the House that Colonel Seely, General French and
General Ewart persisted in their resignation and that
he was going to take over the War Office.

[1] Mr. Asquith's Private Secretary.

This was what seemed the end of the fracas, but the real end came later and I claimed and still have my shilling.

I heard first Lord Morley's explanation in the House of Lords and then my brother's speech, and finally the bitter speeches of Churchill and Bonar Law in the House of Commons. The feeling was tremendous, and as I came away from the House of Commons Ladies' Gallery, a notable Conservative hostess said, very audibly, of Churchill, ' Wretch, I'd like to kill him.' After Asquith made his announcement about the resignation he abruptly left the House, since automatically he vacated his seat.

We often talked of this remarkable man—my brother's friend since young manhood and whom he knew as few did—of how he had been a favourite of Jowett's and then a faithful follower of Gladstone. There were no ' rabbit holes ' with him, Richard said, as there had been with others, and he was always ready to meet difficulties very ably, when required. He was an excellent Home Secretary. He really bargained with C.-B. about having Grey and himself in the Government, and C.-B. knew his worth and recognized him as his successor. Without either initiative or magnetism, he had a wonderful power of getting up a subject and excellent powers of expression. Indeed he was the best example one could have of the value of a classical education. In the House of Commons his manner was inimitable, but he was not so good in guiding his Cabinet. He let things slide along and did not take pains to know the things he ought to know. Everyone was encouraged to set forth freely their opinions, but even if he disagreed, he was able to sum matters up in such a way that everyone was satisfied, although they might not be very clear as to what was decided.

Unfortunately, though at first there was a feeling of moderation and the promise of settlement, things in Ireland were hardening. The Prime Minister was off to Scotland, for he had a contest in view. One was sorry for Colonel Seely, who made a good speech in defence of Morley and took his place at once on the back benches without sulking. ' I've lost myself but saved the Army,' as he is said to have put it.

In the middle of May I was again in London, for the Royal Commission and for the Banquet and Gala Performance in honour of the King and Queen of Denmark. At the Banquet I sat between Bonar Law and Lloyd George, who took me in. The former was curiously Scottish and silent, or at least quiet, for we had a good deal of talk. I found that he positively disliked music, like Dean Inge, and wished on Monday, which was the night of the Gala Opera, that he was a Republican ! He also confessed to having no idea of art, which few people do. He was a funny contrast to my neighbour on the other side, for Mr. Lloyd George is full of music like most Welshmen and was even humming to himself while the band played. He and I discussed what music we should like at our respective funerals. He said he would like Handel's

Largo, which indeed was then being played by the band. I said I should like Chopin's Funeral March but pointed out that unfortunately I should be the one to enjoy the Largo, he the Funeral March ! Then we talked of education. I said to Mr. Bonar Law that I trusted he would carry on the good work that had been begun in this direction, but found him very tepid on the subject. He thought education an unimportant matter compared with the development of character. Character he believed alone tells in the end. We had a good deal of amusing talk, and I told them that I felt honoured in being placed as a buffer between the two. And I was glad to tell Mr. Lloyd George that, to my personal knowledge, he was emptying the workhouses.

I enjoyed the Banquet, despite the long stand after dinner whilst the Royalties shook hands with different guests. The Gala Performance was on the other hand dull, and the paper roses which decorated the Opera House ugly. Still one had interesting talks with the Ministers placed near us two. Sir Edward Grey talked to me about diplomatic appointments, which we were discussing at the Royal Commission, and I told him our impressions. He thought diplomatists should not be too clever, e.g. Sir A. Hardinge, who was very clever, was not as good as De Bunsen, who was very tactful and not so clever. He agreed with our views on bringing the Foreign Office and Diplomatic Service together. Then we got on to birds and the nesting box at my mother's window at Cloan.

One matter that was being very much discussed at this time had to do with the responsibility placed on the new Department of Health for the health of young children. The head of the Medical Department of the Board of Education, Sir George Newman, and that of the Local Government Board, Sir George Newsholme, had very different points of views, as had their political chiefs. I had a talk over some memoranda that I had made with Mr. Herbert Samuel and Mr. Selby-Bigge. The difficulty was to decide on whether at a certain age the care of the health of the child should pass from one department to the other. The Local Government Board (as it then was) wished to have the care of health right on from birth to school, and I rather think this would have been better than the division actually made between infancy and school age.

On the 20th anniversary of the Asquith wedding we went to Downing Street, taking our 'pewter' presents. Somehow it was all depressing, though I don't know why, excepting that there were so many anxieties outside. Lady Dickson-Poynder gave an excellent farce—an interview with her coiffeuse in Paris, and there was also mimicry of a Hyde Park meeting.

A strange thing, as it turned out later, was that at the Royal Commission we had evidence given by Sir Roger Casement of tragic memory. He impressed us as a hot Irishman, of striking appearance, who had lost his health in his good work for the Congo and South America, and we did not wonder at it or at his taking an extreme line about government work in distant places. He had seen horrible abuses and had difficulty in making himself believed. After he had given evidence he lunched with us and we had a private talk. It was soon after this that he became, to all appearances, a traitor to his country, but one wished that his death had not been the ignominious one it was, for he had done fine work in his time.

After that I attended a Carnegie Trust meeting at Dunfermline and met Sir Horace Plunkett, who was very despondent about reaching any sort of settlement in Ireland, despite all his efforts. Things seemed to be going thoroughly badly. There were various attempts being made by our people. Redmond was dissatisfied with what the Government had done, but the Nationalist Volunteers were getting ready, and a crash, we felt, might come at any time.

There was also a sense that in society things were far from satisfactory. We were at one or two large dinner parties, when the talk was all about the tragic tale of a young man's death from leaping off a steamer in the Thames on returning from a pleasure party. The story shocked all who heard it. It seemed to betoken a measure of carelessness in respect of the manner of living of the so-called upper classes, which was especially upsetting at a time of great anxiety. For things were getting worse in Ireland : there was the feeling of a nightmare. Peers, elderly Dons and great soldiers like Lord Roberts signed the 'British Covenant', declaring that any action to counter a Bill they disliked was justified ; and though Sir Edward Carson made

some efforts at getting an understanding, all seemed
vain. Militant suffragism was rampant : beautiful and
famous pictures were destroyed and a case of porcelain
in the British Museum smashed. In April there was
gun-running in Ulster and the coast guard was destroyed. Rifles and cartridges were bought from Germany, and this was enough to make her think civil war
was imminent. When at the end of May the Home
Rule Bill received its third reading, Sir Edward Carson went to Belfast ' to make arrangements for the
final scene '.

The last effort for conciliation was made by King
George who invited the political leaders to a Conference
on Ulster at the Palace. The leaders on both sides
attended, but no one was surprised when it broke up
quickly. On July 24th Mr. Asquith announced in the
Commons that the Conference had been unable to
come to any agreement on principle or detail, and two
days later the Nationalist Volunteers pulled off a
great gun-running near Howth. Some people were
shot by the regular troops and every one was in a state
of highest tension. No wonder foreign nations
thought we were on the eve of a civil war.

In my diary of July 25th, I write that the Conference was ended and that crowds were cheering the
various parties to it. The Irish Guards cheered Redmond. In the midst of all this a garden party, on July
23rd, had been arranged at Downing Street. The
Prime Minister was there, holding his small son
Anthony by the hand. He looked so well, despite

his anxieties and efforts, that I said he seemed to flourish on conferences, at which he made a wry face. One met many friends and acquaintances, including Sir R. Morant and Benckendorff and the very depressed Sir George Murray, but no one seemed to think of anything but Ireland. At dinner, we had Lord Morley and Sir Edward Grey to meet Ballin, who said he was anxious to have an opportunity for talk. Ballin was not very expansive to me, and a friend who was with me made an attempt to talk of the possibility of war and was speedily told that this was a subject not to be discussed. There was much general conversation. Lord Morley and I talked of how we had spent the day. I detailed a fairly busy day, or what I thought such, and asked him what he had done. ' I,' he replied tersely, ' thought ! ' ' And what did you read ? ' he asked. I said only newspapers. ' That doesn't count,' he answered. He began to read at 5 a.m., but I was not to envy him for that, for he was tired at noon. Then he talked of his friend Chamberlain, who had lately died, and of his widow. Her stepson Austen had told him that to be with Mrs. Chamberlain was to be constantly uplifted.

·   ·   ·   ·   ·   ·   ·   ·   ·   ·

It was after this, on Friday the 24th July, that ' Bron ' (Lord Lucas) came in to tea at Queen Anne's Gate and told me of the Palace Conference, and how they had never got near the great questions, but just talked round them. The extremists urged one another to remain firm, though, I was told, Captain Craig had said to Dillon, ' We have sat together in the House for so many years and have never spoken. Let us shake hands.'

We were talking of these things when my brother came in from the Cabinet meeting. We felt that all interest was centred on the Irish question, and he expressed much disappointment at the failure of the Conference. But then he told us that the Serbian question had come up, over, of course, the assassination of the Grand Duke at Serajevo, and the Austrian Ultimatum to Serbia might end in a European war. He was, I thought, tired and pessimistic, for such a tragedy was surely unthinkable. I cannot forget the scene in the Queen Anne drawing-room, with ' Bron ', so handsome and adored by his friends, sitting at tea : and suddenly having a vision of what might be in front of one. Poor ' Bron ' was to lose his life with the rest. He had lost a foot and could not fight as an ordinary soldier, so his death came in the air.

And now I quote from my Diary :

' It was after that that as everyone knows the situation developed at lightning speed. Serbia, with Russia at her back, refused to submit. Germany declared war against Russia and after some delay France and Germany were at war—the war so much dreaded for years. The position of England was critical. Should she side with France according to the Entente ? The greatest efforts for peace were made by England. Her offer of a conference was refused. King George appealed but was told it was too late.

' Sir Edward Grey was staying at Queen Anne's Gate with my brother and the two went through a time of mental strain amounting to torture. Both strained for peace. To Richard it was a personal sorrow of the greatest magnitude to come to war with a power like Germany. He was engaged on a very big and arduous case (*The Olympic* v. *The Hawke*) and terribly overwrought with this and the Cabinet on his mind. The country seemed divided and ten of the Cabinet were against war and ready to resign. Then came the advance on Belgium, a friendly Power, whose rights we were bound as one of her guarantors to respect. To E. G.'s mind this settled matters. He went on Sunday, 2nd August, to Downing Street with Richard and Lord Crewe who had been dining at 28 Queen Anne's Gate. There he found the party assembled. They waited about an hour. Then E. G. wrote to the French Ambassador a note to say he would hear from him after the Cabinet next day—a personal note, but one which indicated his views. He would, of course, have resigned and so would Richard had the Cabinet gone against them. He read the note to the others, and the Prime Minister agreed to sending it. He told me afterwards that he woke at 4 a.m., and thought how he had given it to the messenger in the dark, and that as the German Embassy was nearest he might have misread the address and taken it there. He could sleep no more at the thought. He had said would M. Cambon call at 1.30, and in the morning he telephoned to ask whether M. Cambon was coming to

u

lunch ? And had he got his note ? The reply was—
yes, he would come to lunch but at what hour ? Sir
Edward's fears were redoubled and he asked ' was a
letter received ? ' Casually they replied, yes, a note
came—immensely to his relief.

' The Cabinet was at one excepting Morley and
Burns. Morley was fine but would never have carried
on. He was timid and old and always asking whether
there had been Cabinet sanction and similar questions.
Burns was quite consistent all through and immovable.
Personally I wonder at his resigning. I remember
how keen he was about soldiers' marches and conditions in the old days.

' I had gone to the north but returned on August 6th
for a Territorial Nurses' meeting and was only $2\frac{1}{2}$ hours
late, while the return journey took 18 hours instead of 10.
London was very strange—like a garrison town. There
were crowds round the War Office where we met,
hoping, I suppose, to see Kitchener. It was reported
that no women were to be admitted but I was warmly
greeted as usual by the officials and police. Our
meeting was rather informal but we got things settled
with Miss Sidney Browne the matron-in-chief, and
the Hospitals were mobilized. Sir Edward looked
older as if he had come through an agonizing time but
he spoke to me most gratefully of having been with
Richard all the time and of the help it had been to him.
Neither had been very well. They could not sleep
and the weight of responsibility weighed them down.
To Richard it is a personal sorrow. He was asked by

the Prime Minister to take over the War Office for
him and this he did temporarily. He would indeed
have given up the Chancellorship in order to help
but that did not seem wise, and he himself advised the
Prime Minister to get Kitchener, assuring Kitchener
that he wished this and the latter asked him to help him
as he did not know the new organization. Some of the
Generals were very sad that their former head was
not to be there, but he believed that it required a
soldier to override soldiers' decisions and also K.'s
appointment would carry great weight in the country.'

One hardly dares to think of that time—the tread of
the men marching along Birdcage Walk in front of the
windows comes back to one, their tramp, tramp,
keeping time to their song ' It's a long, long way to
Tipperary '—knowing how few would probably return,
unless they returned maimed and crippled. The
diary goes on, but here it must stop, for we have truly
reached another century. One thinks of our own
losses, of the nine names in the Gleneagles Private
Chapel—nephews and cousins—but infinitely more
of the millions of men who never returned to their
parents or homes and who left the world a poorer
place to live in.

When one looks back sixty or seventy years it is hard to estimate the changes that have occurred in that time. An eminent writer has said that the two dominating forces in later Victorian England (in which one must include the brief Edwardian period) were first the institution of the Family, and secondly the belief in Representative Government. I think he is right in so far as these were important influences, but I should be inclined to say that it was the development of the democratic spirit, that is the Spirit of Liberty, that was the predominant influence. The others were surely subordinate to this. It is, of course, a spirit which has still far to go before it is really developed in any true sense, and the meaning of liberty as distinguished from licence has to be determined. The family was only the forceful body that it was because it was an essential stage through which society had to pass. It was magnified so as to represent not just the means necessary for bearing and bringing up children, but also that for keeping together the complicated thing called the Home, which is clearly essential for the carrying on of an orderly decent life. In the earlier days of which I write, however, there was much more in it than this, for the family had taken a place in communal life which was not just protective and helpful, but really stood in the way of free development and liberty. All who lived in those times know what I mean, though the evil, if evil it were, was much more accentuated in some cases than others. In all classes—rich and poor alike—there was a sense of repression which was concealed very frequently by an overwhelming love that prevented its existence being realized, much less considered. In childhood there was the desire, so natural for the parent, to speak *for* the child : words were almost taken out of his mouth on the plea that he must be taught to express himself aright. Learning by rote was preferred to learning to think ; doing for him, to letting him do for himself. How far these things must be done for a child is the business of a wise educator to determine, but certainly the changes in method are very marked. It could not be good that even a child should be made to feel that his smallest actions were not his but his parents'.

It thus seems to me that it was not so much that the family was being magnified, as that the sense of liberty, which surely should be present in embryo even in the earliest days, was not being made an essential in a life which should be a life of freedom. It is true that, as is constantly being said, freedom and liberty cannot be had without restraint. But the restraint should be from within and not from without as something foreign and external, otherwise there is conflict, or else an unwilling submission to fate.

The problem is no easy one now that it is realized to be a problem : before it was so, bringing up children was an easier business. Obedience in old days was the first duty, and obedience to parents and submission to them was paramount. This had its good side, for it produced an orderly family life, while conflicting interests are apt to bring about a disorderly one. No doubt the difficulties of freedom were greater in former times, when families were large and means often small. Conformity seemed essential and many are thankful for the discipline it brought with it.

The worst of it was that usually a breaking-point came when, as it appeared, suddenly the desire for self-expression and guidance caused the individual to set asunder his trammels. In olden days this may never have happened, but in those which I describe, when people were living in an atmosphere of so-called progress, it was constantly the case and caused much heart-burning of an unnecessary sort.

The self-respect of race was, I think, unusually vivid in the family of which I have been writing— more so than in many, as I have pointed out before. But it results from a tradition to be found in all classes of the community. This self-respect is one which one hopes may never be lost in whatever changes come to pass. It differs from the false pride that brings many families to nought.

And happy family life, such as that described, is no doubt helped by happy surroundings and no lack of the ordinary amenities of life.   But it is made happier by struggle, and if there is not struggle for temporal existence there is probably intellectual and moral struggle.   Were it not for that it would seem a poor thing, hardly worth living.

One of the greatest mistakes is to regard the atmosphere of later Victorianism as other than one of extreme keenness and liveliness.   It was far from being the dead period the moderns are apt to think it.   Not only had it a literature and art of its own—writers of the best order and an art which, whether or not of the highest sort, is coming to its own—and an awakening to music of a quite original kind, but it had that which affected our immediate surroundings most : a fresh awakening to the philosophy of life.   And this movement was led by some of our foremost philosophers. The difference between the new movement and what we call the modernism of the twentieth century was that we seemed to have a firmer anchor by which to fix our craft, and were almost unreasonably certain that we were safely established by its help.   The modern, on the other hand, is uncertain and usually cynical about his beliefs.   Perhaps that very certainty made us trying members of an old-fashioned household.

The loss of religious belief in the present day has, of course, been one of the most upsetting of the influences that have determined the change in the normal course of life.   It is supposed by many to have dated from the Great War, but no doubt it began even earlier. In our day, belief was still fundamentally present even when the truth of its exterior form was disallowed. The young who broke with the past were always ready to show that they had something equally good and true, something which could guide them through life with even more precision, something not fundamentally inconsistent with what had gone before. Now that seems lacking and cynicism often takes its place. To me this appears as tragic and leading to great unhappiness.

If all these new influences have affected men, they affected the other half of humanity much more. Representative Government, which was the boast of the nineteenth century, did not, in the earlier or middle part of the century, really exist, for only one half of the community was represented and for a good part of the period only selected men—selected for their wealth— were placed on the electoral roll. It is true that the principle of representation was accepted, and that men really believed in the old shibboleth ' Government for the people and by the people '. But it was after all just a popular cry, as were many other similar cries which decorated political life, and perhaps especially liberalism. There was doubtless a great deal in them, but they were so muffled and stultified by conventions that there was little encroachment on the old established and aristocratic standards. For life in England was still thoroughly aristocratic, or at least thoroughly undemocratic. The industrial revolution had indeed passed, taking with it the simplicity of rural life, and leaving a heritage of hideous towns ; and later Victorianism realized this and was genuinely trying to get things right and make life tolerable for the workers. That task was what really pierced the hearts of all of us younger people. We felt that things were wrong. We set to to make things better, by starting innumerable societies for the welfare of the poor—the urban poor especially—and establishing quantities of institutions, hospitals and homes, for this end. It made us miserable to go from the homes of the poor to our own happy surroundings, and we felt we could help so little, even were we to go and live amongst the poor. We seemed to want something much more radical than this, for we knew that even in living with them we were not of them, and that they knew this too.

The period was, doubtless, one of an attempted amelioration of conditions, not only by means of personal work but also by the application of scientific inventions, which gave better conditions, better light and more heat as well as improved food and clothing. The improvement in housing itself was in towns a task not properly undertaken because of its vastness, but sanitation went on apace, as well as education. For the first time, these objects were sought as desirable in themselves, for we had forced ourselves away from the old idea that they were only adjuncts to religious life, so-called. The older generation had in our childhood said, ' make men good through religious influences and other things will follow '—a doctrine which had much truth but was operated in an entirely one-sided fashion.

Thus we attacked life in a spirit of hope, even if we made many mistakes and found most of our hopes dashed to the ground later on. For women, it was a period of struggle, but not of hopeless struggle, for they set certain definite ends before them—ends that meant so much less than they believed—and a great many of these were realized. They started on this period bound hand and foot, for they did not even possess their own property or have the right to guide their own lives or to direct those of their children. That their influence was great was due to other factors and above all, to their own characters. Bit by bit they got what they wanted, the right to own, the right to act and finally the right to vote. In Scotland women had a certain standing in a democratic Church in which they could exercise their democratic rights, but until local government arose, there was nothing to mark most women as responsible citizens. The greatest advance came from the seventies onwards, as new local bodies arose, on which women could not only vote but serve in their own persons. The die, indeed, was cast when the first great Education Act of 1870 was passed, an Act of overwhelming importance, for it was the beginning of local government generally : it was more important in my mind than the extension of the parliamentary franchise which was, indeed, implied in it. After that, the professions were gradually opened to women, and though it took an immense time for them to enter these professions in numbers or to summon up courage to stand for popular election numerously, the social change in their position was enormous. They took themselves (and were taken by others) seriously, and carried into fact what a few brave spirits had advocated, by reforming in the first place the occupations hitherto restricted to their own sex—those of nursing and teaching—followed by others—and taking on new duties of a civic sort, which had the effect of hurrying on dilatory legislation. Gradually, Mrs. Grundy was partially displaced and problems of morality and sex relations were boldly spoken of, and many of them eventually tackled. Convention is always hard to dispel, but harder in the case of a sex which has been for numberless generations absolutely subject to it. Possibly, in the end, the sex problem took too predominant a place.

The nineteenth century cannot be said to have concluded until the first decade of the next century had passed. In most European countries, revolutions had at some time in their history made changes, such as those from aristocracy to democracy, but they came suddenly. This country has been free of sudden upsets and has hence lived on, preserving certain ancient forms for which its people have a sort of love from old association. The war came as its awakening to the fact that we were living in conditions which were indefensible and could not continue indefinitely. Great changes have followed, and greater changes seem likely to

come.   Pre-war days, which at the time seemed
often enough full of agitation and anxiety, appear like
a peaceful time of quiet as we look back on them.
They were really a time of fermentation and it is for
History to say what has been brought forth.

INDEX

Abercromby, Lord, 199
Aberdeen, Lady, 103, 124, 154
Abraham, Miss, 137
Acland, Mr. Arthur, 144, 157
Adam, Prof., 258
Adams, W. G., 219
Adult Education, 119
Ainger, Canon, 189
Alexandra, Queen, 223-24, 239, 257, 268
Allenby, Lord, 62
Althorp, Lord, 239
Amos, Mrs., 139
Anderson, Dr. Garrett, 56
Arch, Joseph, 82 seq., 125
Army Manoeuvres, 226 seq.
Arthur, Prince, 226
Ashton Dilke, Mrs., 139
Asquith, Elizabeth, 283
Asquith, H. H., 100, 106, 124, 131, 148, 153, 167, 173, 214, 241, 263, 269, 284, 294-97, 302
Asquith, Margot, 238, 284, 289
Asquith, Violet, 283
Austin, Alfred, 190
Aviation Meeting, 238

Baden-Powell, General, 278
Baird, Dorothea, 171
Balfour, Arthur, 140, 207, 210, 230
Balfour, Lady Frances, 213
Balkan War, 264
Ballin, Herr, 303
Barouche, 39

Bath, 130
Bell, Gertrude, 233
Bell, Graham, 169
Bell, Lady, 233
Belloc, Hilaire, 237
Berlin, 177
Bernhardt, Sarah, 71
Besant, Mrs., 139
Besant, Walter, 130
Bicycling, 96, 145 seq., 184
Bieberstein, Marschall von, 257
Biggar, J., 290
Birrell, Mr. and Mrs., 144, 240
Blaikie, Walter, 197
Blue Ribbon Movement, 66
Bonar Law, Mr., 292, 298
Booth, Charles, 115, 136
Booth, General, 136
Bradley, F. H., 107
Bright, John, 4, 12, 105
Bristol, 261
Brodrick, St. John, 204
Brown, Prof. Hume, 227-28, 283
Browne, Miss Sidney, 223, 306
Brunton, Mrs Lauder, 163
Bryce, Lord, 291
Buchanan, T. R., 217
Bunyan, John, 28
Burdon-Sanderson, Sir John, 176, 241
Burge, Bishop, 234
Burghclere, Winifred (Lady Burghclere), 233
Burns, John, 125, 129, 306
Buxton, Lord, 291

Caird, Principal, 158
California, 178
Calvinism, 64, 65
Cambon, Jules, 305
Campbell, Mrs. Patrick, 171
Campbell-Bannerman, Sir H., 181, 186, 188, 214, 217, 238
Caprivi, 177
Carlisle, Lady, 124
Carlyle, Thomas, 104, 165
Carnegie, Andrew, 101, 102, 116 seq., 154, 200
Carnegie United Kingdom Trust, 220
Carnelly, Prof., 99
Carson, Sir E., 265, 284
Casement, Roger, 300
Cavendish, Lord F., 239
Chalmers, Dr., 115
Chalmers, Sir Robert, 251
Chamberlain, Joseph, 148, 161, 181, 204, 206, 236, 290
Chamberlain, Mrs., 303
Châtillon, Mme de, 70
Child Mortality, 203 seq.
Children's Books, 27
Christie, Ella, 234, 235
Church Case, 212 seq.
Churchill, Lord Randolph, 157
Churchill, Winston, 237, 288, 294
Clemens (Mark Twain), 195
Clubs, Women's, 189
Clynes, J. R., 269
Cody, Captain, 239
Combe, Mr., Phrenologist, 99
Concentration Camps, 199
Cons, Miss, 139
Cowans, General Jack, 227
Crewe, Lord, 305
Crockett, S. R., 189
Cromer, Katherine, Lady, 277
Cunninghame, Sir Henry, 156

Cunninghame Graham, 125, 137
Curling, 191
Currie, Sir D., 153
Curzon, Lord, 189, 190, 275
Cust, H., 140

Dalmeny, Lord, 209
Davey, Sir H., 101, 153
Davidson, Archbishop, 260 seq., 278
Davidson, Mrs. Randall, 236
Davies, M. Llewellyn, 141
Davitt, Michael, 155
De Bunsen, Sir Maurice, 299
Descartes, R., 198
Deschanel, M., 258
Devonshire, Duke of, 206
Dicey, Prof., 105
Dickens, Charles, 19, 27, 87
Dickson-Poynder, Lady (Lady Islington), 300
Dillon, John, 152, 161
Disraeli, B., 77, 84, 156
Donaldson, Principal, 208
D'Oyly Carte, 92
Dress, Victorian, 98
Dreyfus Case, 186
Drummond, Henry, 127
Du Bois-Reymond, 177
Dunedin, Lord, 264

Economics, School of, 200
Edinburgh Royal Infirmary, 196
Education, 209
Education Act, 50, 57, 314
Edward VII., King, 237, 245
Edward VIII., King, 246
Eldon, Lord, 256
Electric Lighting, 92, 103, 211
Eliot, George, 116
Erskine, David, 206
Esher, Lord, 280
Essen, 235

Eugénie, Empress, 72
Ewart, General, 295
Examinations, 20
Experiments on Air, 142

Fabians, 110, 115
Farm Workers, 29
Fenians, 3
Ferguson, Betsey, 1, 14, 86, 187
Ferrier, Prof., 175
Fisheries Exhibition, 109
Food, Changes in, 210
Forster, Arnold, 216
Franchise Bill, 269
Franco-Prussian War, 11
Fraser, Prof. Campbell, 230
French, General, 227, 284, 296
Friendly Society, 127

Gaboriau, 105
Games, 29 seq.
Gaskell, Mrs., 105
Geddes, Prof., 112, 118
Gennadius, Mr., 218
George V., King, 245, 302, 304
Gifford Lectures, 208
Gladstone, Mrs., 154
Gladstone, W. E., 11, 78, 105, 108-09, 148, 150 seq., 172, 181
Goschen, Mr., 135, 137, 152
Gosse, Edmund, 234, 292
Gough, General, 294-95
Gould, F. C., 171
Green, Mrs., J. R., 138, 290
Green, T. H., 107
Greenaway, Kate, 142
Grey, Edward, 187, 194, 254 seq., 268, 270, 279, 292, 299, 305 seq.
Grey, Lady, 123, 132 seq., 139
Gully, Speaker, 186

Haig, Douglas, General, 227
Haldane, Aylmer, Gen. Sir, 191, 194

Haldane, Mrs., 143, 211
Haldane, J. S. (Prof.), 130, 142 seq., 193, 199, 235
Haldane, Patrick, 196
Haldane, R. B. (Viscount Haldane), 173, 182, 193, 199, 229, 256, 289, 296 seq., 304 seq.
Haldane, W. S. (Sir William), 143, 178
Halsbury, Lord, 212
Hamilton, General, 227
Harberton, Lady, 139
Harcourt, Sir William, 103, 172
Hardie, Keir, 172
Hardinge, Sir A., 299
Health Society, 203
Healy, Tim, 163
Hegel, 107, 120, 175, 229
Hill, Miranda, 56, 115
Hill, Octavia, 112 seq.
Hobhouse, Lord, 128
Hogg, Quintin, 128
Holland, 198
Holmes, Mr. Justice Wendell, 282
Holst, Gustav, 219
Home Reading Union, 118
Home Rule Bill, 125
Horn, Margaret, 234
Horner, Lady, 215
Hospitals, 95
Housing of Working Classes, 144
Housman, Laurence, 291

Ilbert, Sir Courtney, 236
Inge, Dean, 234
Insurance Bill, 249, 251
Isaacs, Sir Rufus, 276, 289

Jacque, Rev. George, 44 seq., 165
James, Lord, 152, 213

Jameson, Dr., 180
Jex Blake, Miss, 55
Jubilee, Diamond, 185
Judicial Committee, 275

Kaiser, The, 242
Keogh, Sir Alfred, 223
Kiderlen Waechter, 248
Kitchener, Sir H., 186, 224
Knutsford, Lord, 197
Krüger, 181
Kühlmann, 248

Lang, Archbishop, 246, 258
Langtry, Mrs., 74
Lansdowne, Lord, 244
Larkin, 288
Leathes, Stanley, 251
Le Gallienne, 190
Liberalism, 12, 50, 57, 77, 202
    seq., 222, 242
Libraries, Public, 116, 219, 220
Lichnowsky, Princess, 274
Lindsay, Sir Coutts, 92
Lloyd George, D., 168, 177,
    244, 248, 263, 267, 276
Lodge, Sir Oliver, 278
Londonderry, Lady, 286
Lowndes, Marie Belloc, 234,
    237
Lowther, Mrs., 238
Lucas, Lord, 303-04
Ludwig, 177
Lusitania, The, 282

MacAlister, Sir D., 251, 267
McCarthy, Justin, 160
Macdonnell, Lord, 252, 291
McKenna, Reginald, 270
Maclaren, Mrs. Eva and
    Mrs. Charles, 139
Mahaffy, Prof., 218
Manning, Cardinal, 125, 129
Markham, Violet, 293
Mary, Queen, 246

Massingham, H. W., 190, 272
Maurice, F. D., 112
Meiklejohn, Miss, 189
Meredith, George, 163 seq.
Mersey, Lord, 285
Methuen, Lord, 272
Mill, John Stuart, 12, 58, 104
Milner, Alfred, 183, 200
Montreal, Visit to, 280
Moody and Sankey, 8
Morant, Sir Robert, 251
Morley, John, 104-05, 106,
    134, 157-58, 187, 263,
    276, 287 seq., 295 seq., 303
Motor Cars, 210
Moulton, Lord, 293
Mowatt, Sir F., 251
Muir Mackenzie, Sir K., 251,
    261, 280
Munro-Ferguson, Edith, 150
Munro-Ferguson, Lady Helen
    (Lady Novar), 189, 240
Munro-Ferguson, Ronald(Lord
    Novar), 183, 247
Murray, Sir George, 303
Murray, Sir John, 234

Nairne, Lady, 40
Nevill, Lady D., 167 seq., 261,
    267, 274
Nicolson, Sir Arthur (Lord
    Carnock), 247-48
Novikoff, Madame, 141
Nursing Profession, 196

Oliphant, Mrs., 40 seq.
Omnibuses, 37, 87

Page, Miss, 287
Pall Mall Gazette, 140
Pankhurst, Adela, 253
Pankhurst, Mrs., 252, 266, 279
Paris, 60, 69, 72, 92
Parker, Charles S., 67, 194
Parnell, C., 110, 159 seq.

Paul, Herbert and Mrs., 102, 160

Penrhyn Quarrymen, 185

Pethick-Lawrence, Mr., 252, 266

Pirrie, Lady, 286

Plunkett, Sir Horace, 273-74, 290, 300

Poincaré, R., 279

Pollock, Sir F., 244

Poor Law, 230-31

Pope Leo XIII., 188

Potter, Beatrice (Mrs. Webb), 172

Pringle-Pattison, Prof., 227

Prothero, Lady, 277

Puseyism, 13

Railway Race, 128

Railway Travel, 85

Raleigh, Sir T., 157 *seq.*

Reay, Lord, 218

Red Cross, 100

Repington, Colonel, 227

Rhodes, Cecil, 201

Rimington, Colonel, 227

Roberts, Lady, 223, 225

Roberts, Lord, 225, 301

Rosebery, Lady, 127, 150

Rosebery, Lord, 128, 150 *seq.*, 172, 174, 181 *seq.*, 192, 209, 265

Royal Commission on Civil Service, 250

Ruskin, John, 94, 114

Russell, A. E., 273

Russell, Charles, 155

St. Andrews, 208

Salisbury, Lord, 109

Samuel, Herbert, 291, 300

Samuel, Sir S., 275

Sandhurst, Lady, 138

Sandwich, Lord, 32

School Boards, 51 *seq.*

Scots Greys, 217

Scott, Lady, 285

Seely, Colonel, 295 *seq.*

Selby-Bigge, Sir A., 300

Shaw, G. B., 110

Simson, Frances, 120

Smillie, R., 235

Snowden, Mrs. (Lady Snowden), 254

Snowden, Philip (Lord Snowden), 271

Sorley, Prof., 235

Souls, The, 140, 171

South African War, 190 *seq.*

Spencer, Lord, 274

Spender, J. A., 171

Spurgeon, C. H., 104, 125

Stannard, Mrs., 139

Stead, W. T., 278

Stephen, J. K., 101

Stevenson, Misses, 54 *seq.*, 200

Stewart, Sir R. King, 238

Strathcona, Lord, 282

Streatfield, Mrs., 252, 279

Sturges, Mrs., 164

Tagore, R., 277

Tea-shops, 32

Telephone, 169

Tennant, Margot, 172

Territorial Army, 223

Tiele, Prof., and Mrs., 198

Tillett, Ben, 129

Tirpitz, 286

Toynbee, Arnold, 107-08

Trade Unions, 5, 137, 221, 265

Turner, Sir A., 278

Tweedmouth, Dow.-Lady, 192

Tweedmouth, Lady, 194

Underhill, Evelyn, 277

University of London, 209, 254

V.A.D.s, 100, 224, 225

Verne, Jules, 28

Victoria, Queen, 185, 195 *seq.*
Virchow, 177
Von Plessen, General, 243

Wagner, 60
Wallas, Graham, 171
Ward, Mrs. Humphry, 126, 177
Ward, Prof., 235
War Office, 214 *seq.*, 252
Weavers, 29
Webb, Mrs., 135, 136, 172

Webb, Sidney, 106, 135, 194, 285
West, Sir A., 158
White, Hale, 107
White, Harry, 192
Wordsworth, 105
Wright, Sir Almroth, 266, 293
Wyndham, George, 194

Yeats, 277

Zu Eulenberg, Graf, 243

PRINTED IN GREAT BRITAIN BY ROBERT MACLEHOSE AND CO. LTD.
THE UNIVERSITY PRESS, GLASGOW